The Institute of British Geographers
Special Publications Series

22   Population and Disaster

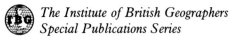 The Institute of British Geographers
Special Publications Series

EDITOR:
Dr N. J. Thrift
University of Bristol

For a complete list see p. 293

Population and Disaster

Edited by
John I. Clarke
Peter Curson
S. L. Kayastha
and
Prithvish Nag

Basil Blackwell
in association with
International Geographical Union
Commission on Population Geography

First published 1989

Basil Blackwell Ltd
108 Cowley Road, Oxford, OX4 1JF, UK

Basil Blackwell Inc.
3 Cambridge Center,
Cambridge, Massachusetts 02142, USA

British Library Cataloguing in Publication Data

Population and disaster. — (The Institute of British Geographers special
publications series; 22). 1. Population.   Effects of disasters I. Clarke, John I.
(John Innes), *1929–* II. Series 304.6′2
ISBN 0–631–16682–3

Library of Congress Cataloging in Publication Data

Typeset in 11 on 13pt Plantin
by Vera-Reyes Inc., Philippines
Printed in Great Britain by
Butler & Tanner Ltd, Frome and London

Contents

Preface

Disasters are always news. Few readers can escape from the clash of their impact. Before the growth of the world economy and the universalization of news, knowledge of disasters was more circumscribed. Now we are besieged with a catalogue of catastrophes, large and small: earthquakes in Armenia; famine in the Sahel; floods in Bangladesh; hurricanes in southern England; ferry sinkings at Zeebrugge and in the Philippines; fighting in Afghanistan and the flight of millions of refugees; rail, road and air crashes . . . the list is endless. The impacts of these events are variable in volume, time and space. Some cause a little loss of life; others kill millions. Some are momentary; others spread out over years. Some are located within a few hundred square metres; others cover several countries. No part of the world, no period, no population, indeed no person is exempt from disasters, but until the improvement of communications enlarged our daily knowledge of world events we were unaware of the full impact of the unexpected upon populations. Our experience of disasters was more personal and more localized, less statistical and less demographic.

In recent decades much attention has been given to the role of hazards, disasters, crises and catastrophes upon human history and the relationships between humans and their environment, but the literature on demography and population studies is far from replete with references to such phenomena. More attention has been focused upon mortality crises in the past than on the more varied effects of disasters. Although demographers are keenly aware of the inherent unpredictability of human behaviour, their projections are largely based upon assumptions related to recent behaviour and they pay little heed to random, unexpected events. Disasters are, of course, only one set of such events, but they may have all manner of direct and indirect effects upon population characteristics and dynamics. Their overall demographic significance, however, must not be exaggerated, as it is usually more local than general. Nevertheless, it is often sufficiently important to change the tide of demographic change.

One great advantage of an international commission is that it brings together people from all manner of countries, creeds and political orientations to look collaboratively at specific topics in an objective, scientific manner. The International Geographical Union Commission on Population Geography has long been involved in producing books and special numbers of journals on a wide variety of topics for which an international perspective is valuable. The topic of this volume, 'the impact of disasters upon population', was first suggested by Professor S. L. Kayastha many years ago as a possible theme for an international symposium. In fact, this proved impossible, and consequently the International Geographical Union Commission on Population Geography, through its newsletter, called upon authors from numerous countries to contribute articles to a study. Hence this volume which brings together contributions from 22 authors and 13 different countries.

The volume highlights the wide range of disasters from those with a strong physical causation, sometimes referred to as 'natural hazards', to those which have mainly human causes. It also reveals the great variation in scale of impact, from the small localized event to the major cataclysm. It is hoped that it gives greater perspective on these fascinating phenomena.

The editors are grateful to members of staff of the University of Durham Department of Geography for their work on the typescript and illustrations, in particular Mrs Joan Dresser and Mr Arthur Corner and his cartographic staff.

John I. Clarke
Durham
January 1988

1

Introduction

Peter Curson

Peter Curson

DISASTERS AND SOCIETIES

Disasters are all-pervading phenomena in human affairs. They loom large in the history of human events and profoundly influence all they touch. The threats of death, disease, injury and destruction that flow from these tragic confrontations with nature, technology or human error serve to remind us continually that we are mortal and, despite the apparent security of late-twentieth-century life, still vulnerable to the vagaries of the biological, physical and man-made environment. In addition, disasters like all catastrophic events reveal something about ourselves that under normal circumstances might remain hidden, in particular how we behave and react when faced with events beyond our comprehension and control. Disasters have the ability to strip away much of the veneer of human life to reveal the basic patterns of human activity and behaviour. Further, in the words of Quarantelli and Dynes (1973:5), disasters '. . . stimulate the imagination and provide a backdrop for speculation on the significance of man'.

Disasters have always been a common feature of human societies. Epidemics, famines, wars and floods would spasmodically devastate a population leaving behind their indelible marks on demographic and social structures. Major disasters were seen to play an essential role in the 'boom and bust' model for explaining fluctuations in population growth in the past (Watkins and Menkin, 1985:647).

Malthus clearly appreciated the role of disasters in maintaining a balance between population and resources. His message is clear and frank:

'Famine seems to be the last, the most dreadful resource of nature. The power of population is so superior to the power in the earth to produce subsistence for man, that premature death in some shape or other visits the human race. The vices of mankind are active and able ministers of depopulation. They are the precursors in the great army of destruction; and often finish the dreadful work themselves. But should they fail in this war of extermination, sickly seasons, epidemics, pestilence, and plague advance in terrific array, and sweep off thousands and ten thousands. Should success be still incomplete, gigantic inevitable famine stalks in the rear, and with one mighty blow, levels the population with the food of the world'. (Malthus [1798] 1967:49)

Crisis mortality was also seen as a basic component of the demographic and epidemiological transition theories. In the former, the entire transition is precipitated by a decline in mortality rates accompanied by lengthening life expectancy. In part, this decline in mortality is brought about by a greatly reduced incidence of disaster-related mortality, particularly from famines and epidemics. Disaster mortality also forms an integral part of the epidemiological transition theory, which focuses on the complex changes in patterns of health and disease and their demographic, socio-economic and eco-biological determinants and consequences as societies undergo modernization (Omran, 1983: 305). Societies are postulated to pass through three stages, each accompanied by a series of epidemiological, social and economic transformations. During the first phase of this transition (Age of Pestilence and Famine), the health picture is dominated by high and fluctuating mortality brought about by the high prevalence of endemic diseases and malnutrition, exaggerated by frequent explosive outbursts of infectious disease, famine and war. Under such conditions, fertility levels are high and population growth largely stationary or cyclic. In the second transitional phase (Age of Receding Pandemics), disaster mortality declines as pandemics recede and famines become less frequent. Thirdly, with further improvements in public health, living and working conditions and major advances in science and technology, societies enter the final stage of the transition where intrusions of crisis mortality are replaced by degenerative and man-made diseases.

The concept and definition of disaster have tended to change over time. Prior to the first few decades of the twentieth century, epidemics floods and famine were considered to be natural disasters and largely unavoidable 'acts of God'. In the past 50 years, however, not only has a much wider range of disasters come to be considered but also ideas concerning cause and effect have changed and such events have come to be seen as amenable to human intervention. In addition, emphasis has shifted away from the view of disasters as simply physical phenomena to one which sees them more as social issues based on demographic and socio-economic vulnerability.

Disasters involve the interaction of a disaster agent and a vulnerable population (UNDRO, 1986:12) and occur at the interface of extreme geophysical, meteorological, biological, and social phenomena and human vulnerability. The 'act of God', the independent operation of incomprehensible and uncontrollable forces, is no longer seen as the dominating element of a disaster situation. Disasters are always more prevalent where human populations occupy vulnerable positions. The increasing vulnerability to disasters of many of the world's poor is one of the major problems facing the world today. People remain the essential reference point for all disasters. It is their vulnerability, misfortune and behaviour that are of central concern. Although disasters result from the interaction of natural and social systems the two cannot be considered as causative (Burton et al., 1978:19). Natural and social environments are inherently neither malevolent nor benevolent but largely neutral to their human populations. Primarily it is people who by the nature of their philosophies, attitudes and behaviour modify or transform this environmental neutrality into either a useful resource or a potentially disastrous scenario. Thus all disasters are population-oriented, for arguably without people there can be no disaster. Disasters are about human populations, how their lives and activities are imperilled or changed, how they react to crisis, the attitudes they hold, the adjustments they make and how they confront the everyday problems of risk and vulnerability.

INCREASING FREQUENCY OF DISASTERS

Most of the reviews of the world disaster situation indicate that there has been an increase in the frequency of large-scale disasters and that the most striking increases have occurred in developing countries. This has occurred largely because of an increase in the vulnerability of the populations at risk. Vulnerability to disaster is related not only to poverty and economic resources but also to population growth, urbanization and changes in human behaviour. In developing countries, while conditions are often marginal in rural areas, it is the cities which have attracted much recent attention. Today possibly as many as 270 million people live in urban areas under conditions of absolute deprivation and poverty. In many cities the fastest growing sector is the slum and squatter settlement population. Every day more people are being exposed to hazardous and life-threatening circumstances, be they from infectious diseases, industrial accidents, earthquakes or flooding. In the past 20 years throughout the developing world there has been a rapid increase in the numbers exposed to the risk of disaster. The factors responsible for this increasing vulnerability are four-fold. In the first place, there has been rapid population growth in recent decades, related in part to increasing levels of rural–urban migration. In the second, there has been the inability of governments to meet the most basic housing and public health requirements for the bulk of urban dwellers, in many cases forcing people to occupy high-risk sites or to be at high risk from infectious disease. Thirdly, many transnational companies have been directing products either no longer tolerated or more rigorously controlled in industrialized countries to the markets of the developing world, as well as exporting polluting industries to avoid the cost of meeting the more stringent controls and standards of developed countries. Finally, the rapid expansion in motor vehicles and manufacturing industry and the indiscriminate use of pharmaceuticals, pesticides and insecticides has created an environment marked by high levels of pollution and heavy-metal contamination and a high prevalence of industrial and occupational diseases.

Today the prevalence of infectious and occupational diseases in the disadvantaged areas of a developing city is between three and ten times that prevailing in the city as a whole. Food energy intake in only one half to two-thirds the city average, the incidence of malnutrition three times greater and access to health-care facilities between two and ten times worse (Basta, 1977). Physically, housing is flimsy and makeshift and many people are forced to occupy the most hazardous physical sites such as ravines, river flood plains, swamps, hillsides, gullies and areas close to noxious industries.

In the industrialized world, advanced technology, public health, welfare and living conditions act to a large extent as a safety net providing sophisticated monitoring, prediction and avoidance services in the case of most disasters. This has led to a lowering of mortality rates in disasters (although to no equivalent trend in costs or damage). Despite this, disasters still remain of considerable significance in many countries. In the USA, for example, between 1941 and 1980 there were 392 tornadoes, floods and hurricanes causing more than 9,000 deaths as well as 1,506 fires and explosions resulting in 13,398 deaths. During the same period there were 38 disasters causing 100 or more deaths. Hurricane Audrey in 1957 caused 395 deaths while a series of tornadoes which ripped through 11 southern and mid-western states in 1974 caused 307 deaths as well as eight in the Canadian city of Windsor (Metropolitan Life, 1982:3–5). More significantly, the threat of epidemics of infectious disease remains current throughout the industrialized world, particularly among disadvantaged and ethnic minority groups. Most of these threats arise from long-established infections like influenza and the sexually-transmitted diseases as well as from the emergence of more lethal infections like legionnaires' disease and AIDS. In some cases morbidity and mortality from such infections can be substantial, as for example during the 1957–8 Asian 'flu pandemic which caused 70 million cases of influenza in the USA or the Hong Kong 'flu pandemic of 1968–9 which produced a mortality in excess of 27,000 in the USA. Changes in behaviour in industrialized countries can also have wide-ranging implications for disasters. The widely publicized middle-class fears of complications arising from whooping cough vaccinations in the UK in 1977–8 produced the greatest epidemic of that disease seen since the 1950s. Finally, there is disturbing evidence of parental indifference to immunization and child care emerging in a number of industrialized countries, which has considerable implications for epidemics of childhood infections.

Any general review of the number and impact of disasters over the last few decades is hampered by the fact that the published surveys employ a very conservative definition of a 'disaster'. Most surveys (e.g. Dworkin 1974; Thompson, 1982) exclude consideration of wars, epidemics, famines and industrial/nuclear disasters from their lists. Consequently, their tables of loss of life by disaster type and the relative frequency of particular forms of disaster are overly dominated by geophysical events such as cyclones, hurri-

Table 1.1   Human losses in disaster events, 1947–1981

	Total loss of life	Number of disaster events
Epidemics	45,000,000[a]	> 400[a]
Famines	40,000,000[a]	50[a]
Wars	9,677,500[b]	42[b]
Cyclones/hurricanes/typhoons	500,808	211
Earthquakes	426,998	161
Floods	196,168	343
Thunderstorms/gales	21,140	36
Volcanic eruptions	9,457	18
Tsunamis	8,568	10
Tornadoes	8,215	40
Other	36,653	243
Total	95,885,502	

[a] Rounded estimate.
[b] 1947–74.
Major sources: Thompson (1982); Bouthoul and Carrère (1976); WHO (1970–81);
Nash (1976); U.S. Department of Health, (MMWR) (1970–81); Garb and Eng (1969).

canes and earthquakes. Of the total disasters considered by Thompson, for example, floods were found to be the most common, followed by cyclones/hurricanes and earthquakes. Together these three types of disaster accounted for 67 per cent of the 1062 disasters recorded. In addition, they accounted for 93 per cent of the total loss of life in disasters between 1947 and 1982. The most recent review of disaster frequency and mortality in the 1970–81 period (UNDRO, 1986) would still seem to ignore some disasters like famine and wars, as well to underestimate severely the impact of epidemics of infectious disease, for 70 per cent of all disaster deaths are recorded there as being produced by earthquakes and windstorms; floods are cited as the most frequent type of disaster, followed by windstorms. Table 1.1 represents an attempt to provide a more comprehensive assessment of human losses from disaster events in the period 1947–81. The figures for epidemics and famines represent very conservative estimates based on a wide variety of sources. It is immediately apparent from these figures that compared to the ravages of epidemics, famines and wars all other types of disaster pale into insignificance. Epidemics and famines together accounted for a staggering 85 million deaths, or more than 88 per cent of all disaster loss of life, and when wars are added the figure increases to 94 million, or almost 99 per cent. Included in these figures is the Chinese famine of 1958–61 which caused possibly as many as 29.5 million deaths (many presumably from infectious disease) making it one of the greatest disasters of all time.

Even in the 1970s and 1980s disasters have continued to take a heavy toll of human life and cause much physical destruction and human suffering. The earthquake in Peru in 1970, for example, caused 67,000 deaths and more than 170,000 casualties, and the Guatemalan earthquake six years later was responsible for more than 24,000 deaths and 100,000 casualties. In 1987 a forest fire raging out of control in the northern Chinese province of Heilongjiang claimed more than 200 lives, destroyed over 50,000 homes and ravaged 700,000 ha of forest worth about 400 million yuan. Currently, AIDS threatens to become one of the greatest biological disasters of the twentieth century, particularly in Africa, and the tragedies of Bhopal and Chernobyl indicate that man-made disasters are often as devastating as any inspired by nature.

DEFINITIONS OF DISASTER

It is difficult to define disasters with any precision. Some authors include biological events such as epidemics of infectious disease, while others concentrate on geophysical and meteorological events. Few would seem to include wars, industrial and nuclear accidents or social and political decisions in their definition. Consequently, the term 'disaster' continues to be used in a wide variety of ways, reflecting in part the particular requirements of the moment and in part the lack of agreement on what criteria should be used to differentiate disasters from other less dramatic occurrences. Any discussion of what constitutes a disaster invariably entails an arbitrary decision. Making a simple division between disaster and non-disaster periods must imply producing a historical pattern whose characteristics depend upon the criteria that are utilized in defining disaster (Wrigley and Schofield, 1981:332).

Demographers have tended to accept a fairly simple definition of what constitutes a demographic crisis or disaster. An excess of deaths (or illness) over normal expectations in a restricted time–space framework is usually enough to denote a population

crisis. For demographers the crucial variables in this equation are
(1) the size of the population affected; (2) the actual excess mortality
rate; and (3) the duration of the crisis (Hollingsworth, 1979).
Implicit in their reasoning is that mortality must exceed some
normal level by a certain factor of magnitude. In contrast to demographers, geographers and other social scientists working within the
natural hazards framework have tended to define disasters more in
environmental and behavioural terms, placing emphasis on such
things as the nature of the disaster event itself, the level of physical
damage caused, the degree of disruption to the structural arrangements of the society and the amount of collective stress engendered.
To Sjoberg (1962:357), for example, a disaster is a '. . . severe,
relatively sudden, and frequently unexpected disruption of normal
structural arrangements within a social system, or subsystem,
resulting from a force, "natural" or "social", "internal" to a system
or "external" to it, over which the system has no firm control';
whereas to Heathcote (1979:3), disasters are 'extreme geophysical
events greatly exceeding normal human expectations in terms of
magnitude or frequency and causing significant material damage to
man and his works'.

Most definitions of disaster, whether demographic or geographic,
stress temporal and spatial characteristics, that is they describe a
relatively sudden event concentrated in time and space. This would
not necessarily preclude consideration of slow-onset disasters such
as AIDS or widespread events such as famines or droughts, providing a flexible definition of time and space were allowed. It would also
seem that disasters have an unexpected/unforeseen nature which
exceeds the community's normal expectation. Above all, disasters
are high-magnitude events in physical and demographic terms
compared to some normal period of human experience. Finally,
disasters have considerable environmental, social and psychological
effects and place unforeseen pressures on existing facilities and
societal structures.

Unfortunately, much research concerning natural hazards/disas-
ters leaves unanswered a series of crucial questions. At what point,
for example, does a geophysical, biological or societal event become
a disaster as distinct from some less dramatic occurrence? Must
extensive physical and demographic damage occur, and if so, how
much? Is loss of life, illness or injury the essential variable or can
psycho-social factors such as fear, hysteria and panic also be taken

as yardsticks? In some cases it may not necessarily be the actual impact of the disaster agent as measured in terms of deaths and injuries that is important so much as the public perception of and reaction to the agent involved. Thus a handful of plague or AIDS cases in a large city may be regarded as a disaster simply because of the fear and hysteria engendered by the disease itself. Probably different types of disaster generate different degrees of psychological shock. The short, sharp impact of an earthquake may engender less stress than the prolonged effects of a pandemic like AIDS.

The question of exactly how to define a disaster is one on which there seems little general agreement; consequently, the term 'disaster' lacks quantitative precision. Further, if a major criterion in that definition is the demographic magnitude of the event or its effects, just how many deaths, cases of disease and injuries, and how much physical, social and economic damage must be caused before an extreme event becomes a disaster? On this point demographers are perhaps more explicit than those studying natural hazards. Wrigley and Schofield (1981:649-50), in identifying local demographic crises in English parishes between 1541 and 1871, rely on a close analysis of the monthly frequency of deaths. Any single monthly total that was 3.36 standard errors above the forecast trend value for that month was classified as a month of crisis mortality.

Attempts by analysts of natural hazards to define some criteria for distinguishing disasters have been largely unsatisfactory. Hewitt and Burton (1975:28) for example, produce a series of criteria based on the degree of property damage or economic loss (to more than 20 families or losses exceeding US$50,000), the degree of strain on essential public services and/or the manpower involvement required to handle the event, and a mortality of ten or more or a morbidity of 50 or more. Only one of these criteria needs to be satisfied for the event to be classified as a disaster (or 'natural hazard' in the author's terminology). Baird et al. (1975:14) increase these levels to at least US$1 million damage and/or at least 100 deaths and 100 injuries. There are, however, many difficulties in applying such schemes cross-culturally or to small-scale societies or sub-groups. It might seem more useful to follow a demographic approach and relate the number of deaths, illnesses, and injuries and the degree of physical and social damage to some normal period or expectation, as well as to the social, demographic and geographic population at risk. This does, however, raise an important issue. If the normal experience/expectation is a major measles epidemic or flood every year and if the population involved has incorporated such an event into their everyday scheme of living as a normal occurrence, can any such individual event logically be called a disaster? There is a tendency among many working on natural hazards to label as disastrous any event in the third world which meets a series of abstract criteria based on western experience. Again, how does one quantify fear and hysteria? In the case of AIDS, for example, the magnitude of cases and deaths is largely negligible compared to the socio-psychological effects.

Many definitions of disasters place emphasis on the nature of the actual onset – a relatively sudden and unexpected event. Yet given the fact that many disasters are neither sudden in onset nor totally unexpected, this would seem a less than ideal criterion. Many disasters are in effect slow-onset events, be they slow viral diseases like Kuru or AIDS, or famines or droughts. This raises the question: at what point does a famine, drought or outbreak of a disease like AIDS become a disaster? In the case of AIDS, was it when the homosexual community became affected, when the disease spread to blood transfusion recipients, when young children were affected, when the disease spread to heterosexuals or when the disease was reported to be widespread in Africa? Bound up with this is the equally important question: disaster for whom? Undoubtedly one person's misfortune may be another's gain. What is catastrophic for one particular group may be viewed trivial, unimportant, or even beneficial by another. Perhaps it is the differential nature of disasters that makes them so tragic. The poor, the disadvantaged and the marginal generally suffer most, whether the disaster is an epidemic, famine, earthquake, flood or war. Moreover, some disasters are more visible than others, and some are largely invisible to the wider community because of the particular status and/or location of the group affected. The tribulations of a group such as those of Skid Row in an American city or a squatter settlement in a developing country may pass relatively unnoticed.

Clearly we must be fully cognisant of the various components of a disaster – physical, demographic, epidemiological, social, economic and political. To obtain a satisfactory definition some measure of magnitude must be employed. This must be related to the population at risk and to some index of the normal demographic experience of that population. The definition must also do justice to the various elements that stem from disasters such as the physical effects of immediate impact, demographic effects (both short- and long-term), psychological effects, social disruption, economic effects, political effects, etc. It must also do justice to some of the less easily measurable elements of disasters such as stress, fear, hysteria and panic.

THE IMPACT OF DISASTERS

Mortality

Despite the fact that mortality is seen as one of the major demographic impacts of disasters and as an integral part of many definitions, it is very difficult to find reliable estimates of the magnitude of particular disasters before the modern period. Possibly the greatest disasters of all time in terms of mortality have been epidemics of infectious disease such as plague, typhus, cholera, smallpox and influenza. Periodic outbursts of such diseases have exacted a fearful toll of human life, had a profound effect on the course of human history and at times threatened the viability of whole societies. The sheer magnitude of mortality from epidemic disasters is staggering to behold and makes mortality from most other forms of disaster seem trivial by comparison. The plague epidemic which spread from Egypt in 541 and which in less than five years had reached most of the civilized world caused millions of deaths and was responsible for a major demographic decline in the Mediterranean area (Biraben and Le Goff, 1975) while in the fourteenth century the Black Death is reputed to have killed more than 50 million people – about 25 million out of a total population of 90–100 million in Europe alone. In 1349 many west European cities lost between two-thirds and four-fifths of their total population; at Givry, a prosperous Burgundian village of 1,200–1,500 people, there were 615 deaths in the space of 14 weeks compared to an average of 30 deaths a year in the previous decade (Tuchman, 1979:95). In Mexico, the introduction of smallpox at the beginning of the sixteenth century resulted in the deaths of more than 3 million people; millions more followed when the disease spread to Brazil in 1560. Possibly as many as 30 million died during the cholera outbreaks between 1826 and 1875 as well as millions in the first great influenza pandemic of 1889–91. The greatest epidemic disasters of modern times remain the bubonic plague pandemic of 1896–1930 and the influenza pandemic of 1918–19. The former was responsible for approximately 12–14 million deaths; the influenza pandemic affected more than a billion people and caused the deaths of possibly 24 million.

It is at the regional and local level, or in small self-contained societies, that epidemics have had perhaps their most devastating effects. The measles epidemic in Fiji in 1875, for example, killed 40,000 of the island's total population of 130,000–150,000. A malaria epidemic (perhaps in conjunction with influenza or typhus) in 1830–3 on the lower Columbia river in the USA killed between 75 and 90 per cent of the Indian population below The Dalles (Gibson, 1982–3), and the High Plains smallpox outbreak in 1837–8 killed tens of thousands of Indians and completely altered the balance of power among the Indian tribes in the upper west area (Dollar, 1977;15). In roughly the same period, smallpox devastated the indigenous population of the north-west American coast from Prince William to Puget Sound; among some groups mortality was as high as 75 per cent (Gibson, 1982-3:72).

Famines, like epidemics, predominate among world disasters and have caused premature deaths for at least 6,000 years, being a frequent but largely unexpected occurrence throughout the inhabited world with wide-ranging demographic, social and economic effects. China, for example, is reported to have had 1828 famines in one or other part of the country between 198 BC and AD 1911, or 91 famines for every 100 years (Cépède and Lengellé, 1953). The 1333–7 Chinese famine is said to have caused 6 million deaths while the famine which broke out in north China in 1877–8 affected almost 70 million people and caused the deaths of between 9 and 13 million. Generally, the nineteenth century was a time of devastating famines, particularly in China and India. In India there were at least 20 major famines during this period with a total mortality in excess of 43 million. In China four famines alone in the nineteenth century caused nearly 45 million deaths. Famine was also a very frequent occurrence in Europe's demographic pattern before the nineteenth century. Western Europe experienced 450 major famines between 1000 and 1855 (Southard, 1948) and there were more than 150 famines in eastern Europe between 1500 and 1700 (Dando, 1980:79). Russia in particular seems to have suffered unduly from famine, having experienced at least 100 hunger years and 121 famines between 971 and 1974, or one year of hardship in every five (Dando, 1980:85). France and England did not fare much better, particularly in the period between AD 501 and 1500 when they suffered 170 famines between them. In some cases crude death rates could reach 500 or more per thousand compared to more normal rates of 50–80. In the 1921 famine in Russia, for example, the crude death rate has been estimated at 600 per thousand (Sorokin, 1942), while two-thirds of the population of Italy are said to have died in the famine of 1376, equivalent to a crude death rate of 667 per thousand (Watkins and Menkin, 1985:651). More recently, the Chinese famine of 1958–61 is estimated to have caused almost 30 million premature deaths, including 12.2 million under the age of ten (Ashton et al., 1984).

One aspect of the mortality–disaster relationship is the differential impact upon particular sub-groups in the population. Disasters have always tended to be socially selective and a great crisis had the effect of weeding out many of the most vulnerable in a population, in both an economic and a physiological sense (Wrigley, 1969:68). It is significant that disasters have the effect of underscoring the mortality rates of the social and demographic groups which normally exhibit the highest rates. The Matlab and Bangladesh study showed a substantial increase in the infant mortality rate at the peak of the 1974–5 famine (Chen and Chowdhury, 1977), and during the West Bengal famine of 1943–4 infant mortality rates in many of the towns of West Bengal were between two and six times higher than the average rate of the previous three years (India, Public Health, 1947). There seems little doubt that the impact of any disaster falls disproportionately heavily upon the shoulders of the most disadvantaged and vulnerable groups. During the 1943–4 West Bengal famine, for example, refugees fleeing from the Japanese occupation of Burma and landless agricultural labourers exhibited death rates between five and ten times greater than those of the urban poor (Sen, 1982). Plague particularly affected the poorer parishes of European towns and cities, and even as late as 1920–1, when bubonic plague broke out in Paris the disease was concentrated among the itinerant rag-picker population in the north of the city.

The upper and middle classes have been less affected by mortality crises partly because their mobility allowed them ample opportunity to move out of affected areas at the first sign of disaster and partly because they were cushioned against such events by virtue of greater personal resources and better living conditions. In respect of epidemics of infectious disease, rural peasants were also less affected than urban artisans, workers, or merchants. If they were affected it usually represented an index of their interaction with infected towns and cities. Famines, by contrast, did occur among the rural peasantry and landless agricultural labourers as well as the urban poor.

Demographically, although the evidence is conflicting, it would seem that the very young and the old suffer the highest mortality rates during times of disaster, as for example during the eighteenth-century epidemics of plague in Russia (Kahan, 1979:258). Schofield (1977:113–18), in his study of mortality crisis in seventeenth-century Colyton, highlights the infant age group as having experienced the highest mortality. Chen and Chowdhury (1977:46) also found infants, young children and the elderly to be most at risk from disasters in the Matlab *thana* of Bangladesh during the crisis years of 1971–2 and 1974–5, while a study of the Guatemalan earthquake of 1976 revealed the most vulnerable groups in terms of mortality to be children aged five to nine and people aged over 60 years (Glass et al. 1977:639–40).

Some disasters are widespread, such as the famine of 1313–17 which affected all of Europe and most of European Russia, the plague of 1348–9 or the influenza pandemics of 1889–91 and 1918–19. Most, however, are regional or local crises affecting small, geographically discrete populations. For example, Wrigley and Schofield (1981:649-50) have documented 5470 local mortality crises in 404 English parishes between 1541 and 1871, and in the provinces most affected by the 1920–2 famine in China one-third of all counties were unaffected (Bergere, 1973). The geographical distribution of the incidence of local mortality crises in Europe strongly suggests that such patterns reflected regional and local variations in climate, demography and economy. Also, crises were linked to particular characteristics of individual communities such as size, remoteness and external communications. With respect to weather and farming economy Wrigley (1969:76) writes:

> men in preindustrial economies were very much at the mercy of the elements. One farmer's meat might be another's poison. A year of light spring and summer rainfall with long warm spells

might bring a bumper harvest to wheat growers on clay lands . . . while bringing very thin crops to those farming the chalks and sands . . . Weather was perennially important. All were vulnerable, but some were more vulnerable than others.

Fertility

During disasters such as famine, wars and epidemics, declines in fertility would seem to be the rule. There is ample evidence of a decline in conceptions during times of high grain prices in Europe and Asia, during times of war and epidemics in Europe and during famine in Africa and Bangladesh.

Work in Bangladesh indicates a close relationship between a decline in fertility and major food shortages. A number of factors seem to be involved in this relationship, including a decrease in fecundity related to psychological stress stemming from the disaster, a lower frequency of intercourse in part related to the separation of spouses due to temporary migration, an increase in voluntary birth control and a postponement of marriage. In the case of the Chinese famine of 1958–61 these factors produced a shortfall of 33 million births from the figure which might have been expected on the basis of the fertility experience of preceding years. The relationship between famine and temporary sterility has been studied since the 1940s when Meuvret first postulated that for any drastic increase in the death rate there was usually an accompanying adjustment in fertility rates. Historically most periods of major famine seem to have been accompanied by a drastic drop in conceptions. Goubert's (1960) classic study of mortality crises in seventeenth-century Beauvaisis reveals how crucial the price of wheat was to the demographic regime of small communities and how during times of crisis the number of deaths on the one hand and marriages and conceptions on the other tend to move inversely to one another. The period 1936–47 is particularly rich in studies of famine amenorrhoea particularly in the cities of Western Europe. During the Dutch famine of 1944–5, for example, more than half of all fertile women in Dutch cities were struck by temporary amenorrhoea and the number of conceptions as measured by births nine months later fell to one-third of its normal level (Le Roy Ladurie, 1975:164). Epidemic disease too could significantly affect fertility levels, not only because of a postponement of marriage and concep-

tions during times of crisis but also because of the long-term effects
of disease. The effects of disease on fertility can be vividly seen
today in a broad zone of central Africa extending from Gabon
through the Cameroons and the Congo to the southern Sudan.
Throughout this area levels of infertility are of the order of 20–40
per cent, high enough to cause severe social and economic problems.

The effects of wars on fertility are also well documented. During
the First World War the French birth rate fell from 17.9 per
thousand in 1914 to only 9.5 per thousand three years later at the
height of hostilities. During the same period the German and
Austrian birth rates fell by 48 and 42 per cent respectively (Urlanis,
1971:255). For particular cities the decline could be even more
spectacular. Berlin's birth rate, for example, fell from 17.2 per
thousand in 1941 to only 7.6 per thousand five years later (War,
1948:297).

Migration

Migration from an area afflicted by a major disaster to an unaffected
area would seem to be one of the most common responses to disaster and an important survival strategy. Historically, flight has always
been a significant human response to great catastrophes and it is
only in recent years that such a response has been labelled a
'disaster-myth' (UNDRO, 1986:13–16). Disaster-impelled population movements are exceptional migrations in that they lie outside
the pattern of population movements tied to normal life-cycle/life-
style considerations. Such movements are sudden, violent, chaotic,
largely involuntary and essentially tragic. The history of Europe
and Asia is full of references to large-scale permanent and temporary movements of people initiated by major disaster. The partition
of India in 1947, for example, produced one of the greatest refugee
migrations of recent times while the Bangladesh civil war, cyclone
and famine in 1971 saw an estimated ten million people flee across
the border into India in less than eight months.

In European history major famine has always precipitated population movement. The series of agricultural crises in Denmark and
Sweden in the fifteenth century, for example, led to a major drift of
population to the towns and by the end of the century to large-scale
emigration. In some cases such population movements and the

waves of people wandering desolate across the land formed a contributory factor in helping the spread of disease, and may also have been a factor in political unrest such as the Hussite risings. In France during the eighteenth century a number of severe famines produced as many as a million rootless emigres (Hugo, 1984:23). The great Irish famine of 1846–51 initiated a massive outflow of population to England and to the USA. In the five years following the famine probably in excess of a million Irish emigrated, one-eight of the total population. The Indian famine of 1876–8 engendered large-scale emigration from Madras in the form of plantation labour to Ceylon. By mid-1877 more than 200,000 had made the journey (Lardinois, 1982:385). In more recent times there is clear evidence that famine-induced migration continues to play an important part in the population dynamics of many African and Asian societies. As late as 1982 a series of crop failures in the northern provinces of Wello and Tigray in Ethiopia initiated a major refugee movement south towards Addis Ababa. Within six months there were more than 40,000 refugees camped in the town of Korem. Two years later drought and famine are said to have displaced more than 200,000 in Chad (MacKenzie, 1984). In China, disasters have always encouraged major population relocations. During the famine in north China in 1920–2 there was extensive migration away from the affected areas to the extent that whole villages were abandoned (Watkins and Menkin, 1985:652).

In European history, epidemics generally seem to have provoked panic and migration not only among the poor but also among the better-off sections of the town populations who frequently fled the cities to the countryside. During the Black Death of 1348–9 flight was the chief recourse of both rich and poor – the rich to their country palaces, the poor to wander aimlessly among the towns and countryside. The plague epidemic in Provence in 1720–2 which claimed more than 105,000 lives, 39,334 in Marseilles alone, provides a good example. In 1720, before protective cordons could be put in place 10,000 of Marseilles' inhabitants are said to have fled the town (Biraben, 1968). In some cases impending epidemic disaster produced a form of compulsory migration, as, for example, in Pistoia in 1630 when all 'foreigners, mountebanks and Jews' were expelled from the city for fear of their spreading plague (Cipolla, 1981:53). During the 1832 cholera epidemic in York a large number of the upper-middle-class population fled the city

(Durey, 1974:25). The outbreak of bubonic plague in Oporto in 1899 produced scenes of incredible panic and hysteria among the local population and despite various attempts to seal off the town it is estimated that at least 30,000 of the city's inhabitants attempted to flee, mobbing railway stations and river craft of all types in the process (Low, 1902:65).

APPROACHES

There is a basic contrast in approach between those who study historical disasters and those who focus on contemporary hazards and disasters. The former, for the most part historians or demographers, have tended to concentrate on the demographic impact of disasters, particularly subsistence crises, wars and epidemics of infectious disease, on population and on social and economic structures. Often working at the local or parish level using nominal sources of demographic data they have largely been concerned with how best to identify population crises in the past, the periodicity of such events, the charting of the temporal and geographical extent of such crises and the assessment of their impact on demographic, social, economic and political structures. Much of this work has been concerned with questions of measurement, such as how to develop a demographic approach to measuring the intensity of a demographic crisis. Most work, however, has pursued the goal of evaluating the social and demographic impact of population disasters as well as tracing linkages with other demographic variables and reconstructing the political, social and economic environment within which disasters occur. Few attempts have been made to reconstruct attitudes and behaviour or to see such disasters as emotional or psycho-social events.

The study of twentieth-century disasters, and in particular of how people perceive and react to environmental or technological crisis, has been of fundamental importance to the discipline of geography for some time. Much of the work subsumed under the heading of 'natural hazards' has been dominated by geographers ever since Gilbert White's (1945) pioneering study of human adjustments to floods almost 50 years ago. Subsequent work in the 1950s and early 1960s adopted a behaviourist approach in studying human response to disasters based largely on Simon's (1957) theories of decision-making. Kates (1962) was a major exponent of this approach in his flood-plain management studies, and in his attempt to understand the way in which people perceive the risks and opportunities inherent in their everyday situation and how such things shape their attitudes and the decisions, particularly in respect of resource management. Initially concentrating on floods, this work was eventually extended to consider coastal storms, earthquakes, droughts, tsunamis, frosts and coastal erosion. Most studies undertook: (a) to assess the extent of human settlement in potentially hazardous areas; (b) to identify the range of human adjustments to extreme events; (c) to document the way in which people perceive and react to disasters; (d) to monitor the various adjustments and choices people make to minimize or reduce the magnitude of disaster impacts; and (e) to estimate the impact of official policies and actions upon the lives of disaster victims (see White, 1974:4). In order to shed light on these issues, geographers directed their attention to three key questions. First, why do people, even when apprised of the consequences of a disaster continue to occupy hazardous social and spatial locations? Second, what information do people actually possess about the disaster-proneness of particular locations or situations, and how do they process this information? Finally, how do people reach decisions relating to disasters? On what evidence do they base such decisions, what choices do they canvass and were they fully aware of the consequences of particular lines of action?

To some extent this book draws on both these approaches, but in doing so it adopts a much more catholic approach to the study of disasters, considering not only such geophysical events as earthquakes, volcanic eruptions, floods and drought but also famine, epidemics and a series of disasters stemming from human intervention and human error, such as war, industrial and nuclear accidents and political interventions. Traditionally, geophysical, biological and meteorological disasters have been considered separately from disasters like epidemics, wars and technological catastrophes: yet there are physical, social and demographic considerations common to all these forms of disaster, and consequently they should all be considered as part of an integrated process. The papers included here focus upon the diversity of disasters, natural and human, and their demographic impacts. They examine disasters in virtually every region of the world and cover a wide range of scales and temporal frames from the local to the world level and from the short term to the long term, in order to assess the significance of disasters upon population growth, distribution and characteristics.

Most studies of disasters have also tended to concentrate on examples drawn from rural or industrializing countries, and indeed the present work largely continues this tradition. Few would question the increasing importance in such societies today, particularly with increasing levels of marginality and vulnerability among their inhabitants. Nevertheless, this approach does reflect a certain imbalance in looking at disasters. We do not underestimate the role of disasters in the industrializing world, yet we also feel that more attention should be directed to such events in industrialized countries. One message to emerge from these papers is that disasters remain a significant problem in all societies, whether industrializing or industrialized, capitalist or socialist. This collection is also unashamedly multi-disciplinary in approach. For this we make no apologies, as we firmly believe that the study of disasters needs to be approached on such a basis.

REFERENCES

Ashton, B., Hill, K., Piazza, A. and Zeitz, R. (1984) Famine in China 1958–61, *Population and Development Review*, 10, 4:613–45.

Baird, A. et al. (1975) *Towards an Explanation and Reduction of Disaster Proneness*, University of Bradford Occasional Paper 11, Bradford.

Basta, S. S. (1977) Nutrition and Health in Low Income Urban Areas of the Third World, *Ecology of Food and Nutrition*, 6:113–24.

Bergere, M. C. (1973) Une Crise de Subsistence en Chine (1920–1922), *Annales: Economies, Sociétés, Civilisations*, 28, 6:1361–1402.

Biraben, J-N. (1968) Certain Demographic Characteristics of the Plague Epidemics in France, 1720–22, *Daedalus*, 97,2:536–45.

Biraben, J-N. and Le Goff, J. (1975) The Plague in the Early Middle Ages, in Forster, R. and Ranum, O. (eds), *Biology of Man in History*, Johns Hopkins University Press, Baltimore:48–80.

Bongaarts, J. and Cain, M. (1981) *Demographic Responses to Famine*, Center for Policy Studies Working Paper 77, The Population Council, New York.

Bouthoul, G. and Carrère, R. (1976) *Le Défi de la Guerre*, Presses Universitaires de France, Paris.

Burton, I., Kates, R. W. and White, G. G. (1978) *The Environment as Hazard*, Oxford University Press, New York.

Cépède, M. and Lengellé, M. (1953) *Economie Alimentaire du Globe*, Librairie des Medicis, Paris.

Chen, L. C. and Chowdhury, A. K. M. A. (1977) The Dynamics of Contemporary Famine, in *Proceedings of the International Population Conference*, Mexico, 1977, vol. 1, IUSSP, Liège.

Cipolla, C. (1981) *Fighting Plague in Seventeenth Century Italy*, University of Wisconsin Press, Madison.

Dando, W. A. (1980) *The Geography of Famine*, Edward Arnold, London.

Dollar, C. D. (1977) The High Plains Smallpox Epidemic of 1837–38, *The Western Historical Quarterly*, 8, January:15–38.

Durey, M. (1974) *The First Spasmodic Cholera Epidemic in York, 1832*, University of York/St Anthony's Press, York.

Dworkin, J. (1974) *Global Trends in Natural Disasters*, Natural Hazards Research Working Paper 26, University of Colorado, Boulder.

Garb, S. and Eng, E. (1969) *Disaster Handbook*, Springer, New York.

Gibson, J. R. (1982–3) Smallpox on the Northwest Coast, 1835–1838, *B.C. Studies*, 56, Winter:61–81.

Glass, R. et al. (1977) Earthquake Injuries Related to Housing in a Guatemalan Village, *Science*, 197:638–43.

Goubert, P. (1960) *Beauvaisis et le Beauvaisis de 1600 à 1730*, 2 vols, Ecole Pratique des Hautes Etudes, Paris.

Heathcote, R. L. (1979) The Threat from Natural Hazards in Australia, in Heathcote, R. L. and Thom, B. G. (eds), *Natural Hazards in Australia*, Australian Academy of Sciences, Canberra:3–10.

Hewitt, K. W. and Burton, I. (1975) *The Hazards of a Place: A Regional Ecology of Damaging Events*, University of Toronto Press, Toronto.

Hollingsworth, T. H. (1979) A Preliminary Suggestion for the Measurement of Mortality Crises, in Charbonneau, H. and Larose, A. (eds), *The Great Mortalities: Methodological Studies of Demographic Crises in the Past*, Ordina, Liège:21–8.

Hugo, G. J. (1984) The Demographic Impact of Famine: A Review, in Currey B. and Hugo, G. (eds), *Famine As a Geographical Phenomenon*, D. Reidel, Dordrecht:7–31.

India, Public Health (1947) *Annual Report of Public Health Commissioner with the Government of India for the period 1940–1944*, Government Press, Delhi.

Kahan, A. (1979) Social Aspects of the Plague Epidemics in Eighteenth Century Russia, *Economic Development and Cultural Change*, 27, 2:255–66.

Kates, R. W. (1962) *Hazard and Choice Perception in Flood Plain Management*, University of Chicago, Dept of Geography Research Papers 78, Chicago.

Lamb, H. H. (1982) *Climate, History and the Modern World*, Methuen, London.

Lardinois, R. (1982) Une Conjoncture de Crise Démographique en Inde du Sud au XIXᵉ Siècle. La famine de 1876–1878, *Population*, 2:371–404.

Le Roy Ladurie, E. (1975) Famine Amenorrhoea, in Forster, R. and Ranum, O. (eds), *Biology of Man in History*, Johns Hopkins University Press, Baltimore:163–78.

Low, R. B. (1902) *Reports and Papers on Bubonic Plague*, HMSO, London.

MacKenzie, B. (1984) Ethiopia: Countdown to Disaster, *New Scientist*, 1 November:3.

Malthus, T. R. [1798] (1967) *Population – The First Essay*, University of Michigan, Ann Arbor.

Metropolitan Life (1982) Catastrophic Accidents – A 40 Year Review, *Statistical Bulletin*, 63, 2:3–5.

Nash, J. R. (1976) *Darkest Hours: A Narrative Encyclopedia of World-Wide Disasters*, Nelson-Hall, Chicago.

Omran, A. R. (1983) The Epidemiologic Transition Theory: A Preliminary Update, *Journal of Tropical Pediatrics*, 29:305–16.

Quarantelli, E. L. and Dynes, R. R. (1973) When Disaster Strikes, *New Society*, 4 January:5–8.

Schofield, R. (1977) An Anatomy of an Epidemic: Colyton, November 1645 to November 1646, in *The Plague Reconsidered*, Local Population Studies, Derbyshire:95-126.

Sen, A. (1982) *Poverty and Famine*, Clarendon Press, Oxford.

Simon, H. A. (1957) *Models of Man: Social and Rational*, Wiley, New York.

Sjoberg, G. (1962) Disasters and Social Change, in Baker, C. W. and Chapman, W. (eds), *Man and Society in Disaster*, Basic Books, New York:356–84.

Sorokin, P. A. (1942) *Man and Society in Calamity*, Dutton & Co, New York.

Southard, F. (1948) Famine, *Encyclopedia of Social Sciences*, vol. VI:85–7.

Thompson, S. A. (1982) *Trends and Developments in Global Natural Disasters 1947 to 1981*, Naural Hazard Research Working Paper 45, University of Colorado, Boulder.

Tuchman, B. W. (1979) *A Distant Mirror: The Calamitous 14th Century*, Penguin, Middlesex.

UNDRO (United Nations Disaster Relief Organization) (1986) *Disaster Prevention and Mitigation: Social and Sociological Aspects*, vol. 12, United Nations, New York.

United States, Dept of Health and Human Services, (1970–81) *Morbidity and Mortality Weekly (MMWR)*, Center for Disease Control, Atlanta.

Urlanis, B. (1971) *Wars and Population*, Progressive, Moscow.

War, (1948) The Demography of War: Germany, *Population Index*, 14, 4:291–308.

Watkins, S. C. and Menkin, J. (1985) Famines in Historical Perspective, *Population and Development Review*, 11, 4:647–75.

White, G. (1945) *Human Adjustment to Floods: A Geographical Approach to the Flood Problem in the United States*, University of Chicago, Dept of Geography Research Paper 29, Chicago.

White, G. (1974) *Natural Hazards*, Oxford University Press, London.

WHO (World Health Organisation) (1970–81), *Weekly Epidemiological Record*, United Nations, Geneva.

Wrigley, E. A. (1969) *Population and History*, Weidenfeld & Nicolson, London.

Wrigley, E. A. and Schofield, R. S. (1981) *The Population History of England 1541-1871*, Edward Arnold, London.

2

The Impact of Natural Disasters on the Population of Japan

Takeshi Mizutani and Takamasa Nakano

THE JAPANESE POPULATION

In the eighteenth century Japan's population was in the 30 millions, and at the beginning of the twentieth century only 44 million; by 1985 it had reached 121 million. However, the natural rate of increase was by then slowing down, and during 1975–85 it was only 0.8 per cent annually. Because the birth rate is decreasing, it is anticipated that the population will reach a maximum of 140 million in the 2020s. Densities are of course high. The urban population in 1985 accounted for 55 per cent of the total population, although urban areas take up only 3 per cent of the land surface. While the average overall population density was 324 persons per sq km, in the plains it exceeded 1,000, because mountainous regions occupy roughly three-quarters of the country.

THE CURRENT SITUATION WITH RESPECT TO NATURAL DISASTERS

Japan is an island arch which belongs to the monsoon region, and is frequently subjected in all seasons to heavy rains and strong winds caused by typhoons, fronts and depressions. The average annual precipitation is 1,700 mm, two or three times the amount received in other areas of the same latitude. Japan is also situated in the circum-Pacific seismic zone, and suffers from severe seismic and volcanic activities. About 10 per cent of the world's earthquakes occur in and around the Japanese islands, especially in the outer zone of the island arc. Japan's active volcanoes make up one-tenth of the world's total. As a result of these geographical characteristics, Japan is afflicted with severe and frequent natural disasters of various kinds, including typhoons, windstorms, river floodings, landslides, debris flows, earthquakes, tsunamis, volcanic eruptions and snow avalanches, all of which have a significant impact on social and economic life.

The annual average number of deaths from natural disasters during the period of 1965–84 was approximately 300, and that of houses destroyed about 6,000. Annual property damage is estimated at roughly $5 billion, about 0.5 per cent of GNP. The greater part of the damage is caused by so-called storms and floods due to typhoons, fronts and depressions. The annual average number of occurrences of storm and flood disasters is about 60, of which disasters due to heavy rain number 30 and strong wind disasters, including snowstorms, about 20. Typhoon disasters occur less often, but cause about half of the total damage.

In recent years landslides and debris flows induced by heavy rain are becoming major causes of disasters. About two-thirds of total disaster-related deaths are caused by such mass wasting phenomena. Many of the casualties are aged people who are unwilling to relocate and evacuate, as well as the physically weak. Deaths caused by epidemic disease and famine occurring after natural disasters are rarely experienced nowadays.

The percentage of total deaths caused by natural disasters is very small, only 0.00025 per cent, and therefore has little impact on the overall death rate. In contrast, the death rate for traffic accidents is about 0.01 per cent, which is the highest of all the percentages for accidents and disasters in Japan, just as it is in many other countries. The yearly fluctuation in the death rate for natural disasters is very high, as shown in figure 2.1, and this rate is expected to amount to more than that for traffic accidents once a catastrophic disaster occurs. The most significant natural disaster in Japan is the earthquake. A strong earthquake hitting Tokyo now would be expected to produce the worst disaster in the world.

Although casualties from natural disasters are at present very small in relation to the country's population size, this is not a result of the shifting of population from hazard-prone areas. On the

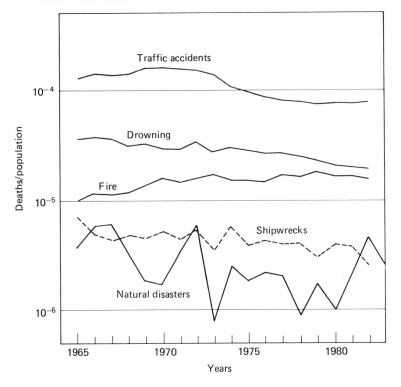

Figure 2.1   Yearly change in the death rate in Japan for accidents and disasters

contrary, the potential for loss of life has continuously increased with the progress of urbanization. Nearly 40 per cent of Japan's population is concentrated in the three largest megalopolises – Tokyo, Osaka and Nagoya – most of which are highly vulnerable to earthquakes and storm surges which claim a lot of casualties

THE IMPACT OF PAST DISASTERS

According to the records of past disasters, the number of deaths caused directly by any short-lived phenomenon such as an individual earthquake, tsunami, flood or storm surge has been in the tens of thousands at most. On the other hand, food shortages from poor harvests asssociated with unusual climatic conditions claimed many more lives in ancient times. In the northern part of Japan, especially in the Tohoku districts, poor harvests caused by unusually cool summers have occurred very often; these districts are directly struck by a cold north-easterly wind when high atmospheric pressure on the Sea of Okhotsk is strong and when the sea-water temperature is low in summer. In such cases, when food has not been provided for the areas suffering from poor harvest, famine has resulted (see chapter 19).

In the eighteenth century and the first half of the nineteenth century, when Japan was still organized in the feudal manner, severe famines occurred many times. Of these, the famine which lasted for several years starting in 1783 was the most disastrous. It was initiated by the eruption in 1783 of the Asama volcano, one of the most active volcanoes in Japan. A great volume of volcanic ash was blown up in the stratosphere and remained there for a long time; as a result, solar radiation on the earth surface decreased and a cool summer resulted. The number of deaths directly caused by the eruption was about 1,000, but the number of deaths resulting from the famine which followed is estimated to be roughly one million, then about 3 per cent of Japan's population. The death rate for the Tohoku districts, where the famine was most severe, is supposed to have been 20 per cent or more.

According to the censuses conducted by the feudal government, Japan's population decreased by 1,120,000 in the period 1780–92, and by 995,000 in the period 1732–50 (see figure 2.2). The main cause of the population decline was severe famines and the following epidemic diseases. Consequently, Japan's population remained in the 30 millions for more than 100 years starting from the middle of the eighteenth century. This was an unusual period in the trend of Japan's population. It is supposed that the severe famines caused large-scale drifting of population, mainly to Edo (now Tokyo), though free choice of residence did not exist in the feudal age. Thus, the famines in the eighteenth and the nineteenth centuries had the largest impact on the population; they were not simple natural disasters but for the most part were man-made calamities.

The largest natural disaster in the twentieth century was the Kanto earthquake of 1923. The number of deaths was about 105,000 and the number of collapsed and burnt houses 702,000. Those who were killed or injured and whose houses were destroyed amounted to 3,405,000: about 6 per cent of Japan's population. The main cause of human life loss and damage to houses was fire. In

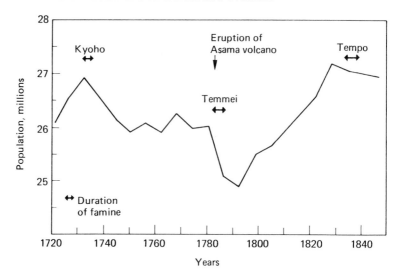

Figure 2.2 Impact of the three largest famines in the Edo period on the population of Japan

Tokyo, fire broke out at more than 130 places immediately after the earthquake, and two-thirds of the built-up area of the city was completely destroyed by fire. Total deaths in Tokyo were 69,000, over 3 per cent of the population of 2,265,000; but the total number of sufferers from the earthquake was 1,700,000. After the disaster, there was an exodus from devastated areas, and approximately 600,000 of the sufferers were still outside the city area by 15 November, two-and-a-half months after the earthquake. The population of Tokyo Prefecture at 1 October 1923, a month after the earthquake, showed a decrease of 124,800 persons (3.1 per cent) against that of the previous year. In 1924 and 1925 the population increased at a rate twice as large as that before 1923. It was four years later when the increase rate returned to the normal level (see figure 2.3). In 1945, when the Second World War ended, Tokyo's population decreased by about one-half that of the previous year.

The damage from the 1923 earthquake was more severe in Yokohama City, which was closer to the epicentre. The death toll here was 26,000, a death rate of 5.3 per cent, but 93 per cent of the inhabitants suffered from the earthquake damage. The Kanto earthquake was without doubt the largest natural disaster in Japanese history in terms of impact on the society, the economy and the population.

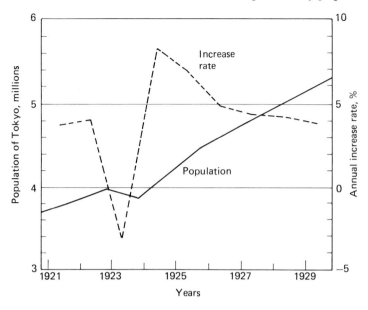

Figure 2.3 Impact of the Kanto earthquake of 1923 on the population of Tokyo prefecture

Tsunamis, generated mainly by earthquakes under the sea bed, have caused a large number of casualties. Among the many tsunami disasters recorded in history, the damage caused by the Meiji Sanriku tsunami of 1896 was the worst, with a death toll amounting to 27,000. Damage was most severe on the Sanriku coast region, in the Tohoku districts, where a drowned-valley, ria-type coast is characteristic. In narrow V-shaped, bays the wave height exceeded 30 m, and many hamlets on the coastal lowlands were annihilated. The death rate for four counties located on the Sanriku coast, with a total population of 104,000, reached 20 per cent.

While the regional impact of the Meiji Sanriku tsunami on the population was the greatest, in 1933 the Sanriku coast was again attacked by a severe tsunami with a 30 m wave height. Although the number of houses destroyed was almost as large as in the 1896 tsunami, the number of deaths was not so large by virtue of emergency evacuation. Nevertheless, human life loss amounted to 3,000. After this disaster, about 8,000 households were relocated from coastal lowlands to higher places.

The worst natural disaster since the Second World War was the Isewan typhoon disaster of 1959, in which 5,000 people were killed.

It was caused by a high storm surge in the Ise Bay coastal area where the city of Nagoya, with a population of 1,500,000, is situated. Since the delta at the head of the bay was below sea level, as a result of land subsidence, the 4 m high storm surge invaded far inland, about 15 km from the sea coast, and inundated the delta for more than a month. In the towns and villages located on the coast of the delta, a high death rate resulted from the direct attack of the storm surge; the death rate of Kisozaki village with a population of 3,000 was 11 per cent, and that of the town of Nagashima, with a population of 8,500 was 4.5 per cent. In the coastal area of Nagoya, about 1,500 persons were killed by timber drifting in from lumber yards.

After the Isewan typhoon, loss of life from natural hazards fell steeply to an annual rate of about 300. Nevertheless, in recent decades disasters due to landslides and debris flows generated by heavy rain have had a great social impact on local communities. In order to mitigate landslide damage, the relocation of houses built beneath steep high slopes has been promoted by government subsidy. In the period from 1972 to 1984, 12,544 households were granted subsidies for relocation. In 1972, subsidization for group relocation from the areas vulnerable to all kinds of natural hazards was institutionalized. From then until 1987 1,387 households in 26 towns and villages moved to safe areas. In 1972, the eastern part of the Amakusa island in Kyushu was seriously damaged by landslide and debris flow, and 14 per cent of houses were destroyed, but after the disaster 750 households were relocated in groups.

The group relocations carried out so far fall into two types: preventive relocation and rehabilitation relocation. Needless to say, preventive relocation is the more desirable to pre-empt damage. Preventive relocation was carried out by all the residents in a small, remote and isolated hamlet where an influential leader resided and the hazard awareness of the residents was raised by past hazard experiences. A new residence was chosen in a more convenient location far from the former one. Rehabilitation relocation has been carried out in severely damaged urban districts mainly by the households whose houses were in need of reconstruction. Groups have been motivated to relocate not only by the hope of avoiding future danger, but also by the expectations associated with beginning life in a new environment.

THE PREDICTED IMPACT OF FUTURE DISASTERS

The worst threat of natural disaster in Japan comes from the earthquake, especially when it strikes major urban areas like Tokyo. Major earthquakes with a magnitude of more than 8.0 on the Richter scale have occurred repeatedly in the outer zone of the Japanese island arc, with Tokyo experiencing violent tremors at 50–100-year intervals. Such earthquakes usually cause various secondary events and result in compound disasters over broad areas. Because most of Japanese houses are made of wood, fire is the most destructive secondary event. It is estimated that about 677,000 wooden houses will be burnt or collapse if Tokyo is hit by an earthquake with an intensity similar to that of the 1923 Kanto earthquake. If such an event were to occur, the resulting death rate for Tokyo is predicted to be about 3 per cent (250,000 persons), extrapolating from past instances of disaster in urban areas. In modern cities, however, new kinds of danger factors must be considered. These include the presence of poisonous gases, petroleum tanks, crowds, congested traffic, high-speed transportation, etc. Therefore, there is a strong possibility that the number of casualties will be much greater than that which has been predicted from past disaster instances. In any case, a forthcoming earthquake disaster in the Tokyo region will undoubtedly have the most powerful impact on the population.

Storm surge generated by a strong typhoon sometimes causes a great number of casualties. The worst storm surge disaster occurred on the coast of Ariake Bay in 1828, when some 10,000 lives were lost. Because most typhoons attack Japan from the south or the south-west, high storm surge occurs in the bays which open southward onto the Pacific coast. Major urban areas such as Tokyo, Osaka and Nagoya are situated at the heads of such bays. The ground height of these areas is below sea level as a result of land subsidence induced by withdrawal of ground water, which makes them more vulnerable to storm surge. If one of these big cities were hit by a storm surge with a tide level similar to that of the Isewan typhoon of 1959, thousands of deaths would be expected to result. Prediction of storm surge, however, can be carried out fairly precisely, and therefore loss of human life can be prevented by dissemination of warnings and by emergency evacuation.

The energy of a large-scale volcanic eruption is far greater than that of either an earthquake or typhoon. Though it would be very rare, a gigantic eruption occurring near an urban area would result in a catastrophic disaster. In southern Kyushu, thick pyroclastic flow deposits effused from Aira caldera about 22,000 years ago were distributed widely. The flow rose across mountains 700 m high and reached as far as 100 km from the crater. In Japan there are many large calderas which effused a large amount of pyroclastics in the Holocene epoch. If such a gigantic pyroclastic flow were to occur in southern Kyushu now, millions of lives might be lost just by the direct effect of the flow.

FACTORS AFFECTING HUMAN CASUALTIES

Human casualties are greatly affected by various kinds of factors which influence people's behaviour, mentality and general state of preparedness against hazards. Such factors are locality (regionality of natural and social characteristics), time (human behaviour at the time of impact), period (secular change in socio-economic factors), type of natural event directly causing damages, hazard experience and so on. The quantitative effects of these factors on the scale of casualties can be estimated from the damage data from past instances of disaster.

The degree of human life loss due to typhoons clearly differs with the time of the typhoon hitting the shore when major damage is caused. The measure here is the ratio of fatalities to the power of the typhoon, which is represented by a power function of the central atmospheric pressure and the radius of the typhoon circle. The loss of life in incidents occurring between 10 p.m. and 2 a.m. is about ten times as large as in those during the daytime and early evening. The death rate due to storm surge is represented by an exponential function of mean submerged depth. Time affects human behaviour and the perception of residents. It is obvious that the recognition of danger, the dissemination of warnings, the execution of evacuation and the various other kinds of activities against hazards are easier in the daytime than late at night. In the early evening, before 10 p.m., when most people are still out of bed, evacuation can be executed fairly easily even when it is dark outdoors.

Geographical location also affects the degree of human life loss. In south-western Japan, which is frequently struck by typhoons, the degree of human life loss is fairly low even when the typhoons strike hard at midnight. Many hazard incidents show that recent hazard experience is the most effective for reducing casualty losses. In the case of the Isewan typhoon disaster, the degree of human life loss for the coastal area of the delta, where safe places do not exist, was about five times as high as that for narrow coastal lowlands. The degree of human life loss for landslide disaster in rural areas is about three times higher than that in urban areas. In rural areas, especially in mountain villages, past hazard experience is handed down from generation to generation, and there exist closely united communities which promote emergency evacuation.

REFERENCES

Mizutani, T. (1982) Group Removal of Residents in Hazard-prone Areas, *Report of National Research Center for Disaster Prevention*, 29, 19–37 (in Japanese with English abstract).

Mizutani, T. (1984) Some Relationships between Intensity of Hazardous Natural Events and Amount of Disaster Damage, *Geographical Reports of Tokyo Metropolitan University* 19, 185–94.

Mizutani, T. (1989) Processes of Decrease, Migration and Recovery in Urban Population after Disasters, *Geographical Review of Japan* 62A, 208–24.

3

The Consequences of the 1972 Earthquake on the Urban Structure and Population Distribution of Managua

Jürgen Bähr

Two days before Christmas 1972 the city of Managua, Nicaragua, was devastated by several tremors that registered as high as 6.5 on the logarithmic Richter scale. Approximately 10,000 people lost their lives in the earthquake and the ensuing fires; another 20,000 were injured, many of them seriously, and approximately 50,000 were made homeless. Around 50,000 people lost their places of work, and in the following days more than 200,000 left the city for fear that more tremors might follow, seeking makeshift shelters in the countryside or in other large cities. In the ensuing period, the rubble was removed in the centre of the city, and the houses that were in danger of collapsing were torn down. But reconstruction was not begun immediately and has since been postponed time and again.

The earthquake of 1972 had long-term consequences for the structure of the city and the distribution of its population. In this chapter, I shall attempt to analyse some of these consequences.

GEOLOGICAL STRUCTURE AND EARTHQUAKES IN THE MANAGUA AREA

The severe earthquake of December 1972 was not the first to hit the city or to influence its development. Managua's location on the north-eastern escarpment of the Cordillera del Pacífico, which is 400–900 m high and consist of Pleistocene volcanic material, makes it particularly susceptible to earthquakes. Geologically, this mountain range may be described as a tilted block with its steep side facing north-east towards the depression and the volcanic zone in which the Nicaraguan lakes lie (Weyl, 1961). The faults forming its boundaries belong to the great north-west/south-east fault zone of the Nicaragua depression, in the middle of which lie the two largest lakes of Central America, Lake Managua and Lake Nicaragua. As late as the late Tertiary Era the Nicaragua depression was an arm of the sea separating the North American continent from the continent of South America. It was not until the uplifting and the volcanic activity during the late Pliocene and early Pleistocene that the depression became land and cut off the present-day Lake Nicaragua from the open sea.

Three main north/south or north-east/south-west faults run past or through the metropolitan area of Managua. The fault lines can be traced from the location of several volcanic lakes filled with water (*lagunas*). It is assumed that the movement of the blocks along these fault lines did not begin until the Quaternary, as a result of the relative lowering of the Nicaragua depression, and that the crustal movements are still continuing today.

For this reason, small and not-so-small tremors are not uncommon in Managua. In this century alone, 11 earthquakes have been registered that caused damage to buildings in the municipal area (Arce, 1973). The catastrophe of March 1931, with approximately 1,000 victims, had disastrous effects and, like that of 1972, levelled the entire downtown area of Managua.

URBAN DEVELOPMENT UP TO THE 1972 EARTHQUAKE

The 1972 quake caused a sharp break in urban development, primarily because the areas that were most strongly hit by the catastrophe were those bordering on the Plaza and the Central Market (see figure 3.1). Here approximately 600 blocks of houses collapsed almost completely. Only a few modern concrete constructions survived relatively unscathed. This meant that not only was the traditional business and administrative district destroyed, but also the most densely populated residential areas. To be sure, shortly after the earthquake the decision was made to

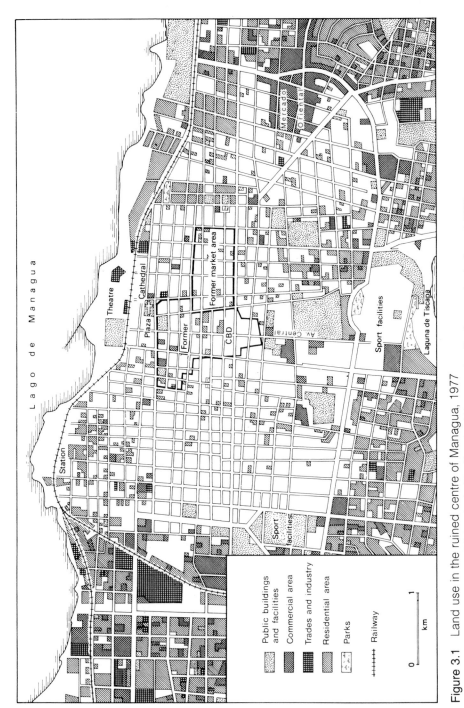

Figure 3.1 Land use in the ruined centre of Managua, 1977

Source: Information from Vice Ministerio de Planificacion Urbana and author's mapping in August 1977

rebuild Managua at the same location, because to relocate the capital completely would have by far exceeded the financial capacity of the country. Reconstruction was, however, not to occur spontaneously and without direction, but according to specific plans. Therefore the National Emergency Committee, which assembled on the morning after the earthquake, prohibited all construction in the old city centre for the time being. Later only the rubble was removed, so that the devastated area turned into a ghostly 'city of ruins', especially at night, in which only a few buildings continued to be used. However, it took much longer to adopt a binding urban development plan than was originally intended. With the revolution and the subsequent takeover by the Sandinistas (17 July 1979), the proposals that had been developed under Somoza were no longer valid. The discussion as to the future layout of the capital began again, and so far it has not reached a conclusion. The result was that many of the changes that were originally seen as only temporary have become permanent solutions. Many administrative offices moved to new locations. Business life reoriented itself to a great extent. And the most densely populated residential areas shifted from the city centre to peripheral regions.

Before we can fully estimate and classify the changes in structure and function of the different parts of the city since the earthquake, we must first give a brief summary of the development of the city until the catastrophe of 1972 (see in particular Sandner, 1969).

Managua is a city with no significant colonial past. It did not gain its special position until the present century. As late as the middle of the eigtheenth century there were only four dispersed settlements, populated primarily by Indians, in what is now the municipal area of Managua. Spanish settlers and mestizos gradually began to settle here after independence (1838). That a town charter was conveyed upon Managua in 1846, and that it even became the capital of the Republic of Nicaragua in 1858, despite its few inhabitants (approximately 5,000), was due only to the rivalry existing between the two leading cities of the country until that time, the trading centre Granada and the cultural centre León.

Significant impulses towards development came from the spread of coffee plantations, which began on the slopes of the Cordillera del Pacífico south of the city in 1853. In the following years Managua began to compete with León and Granada and to assume important trade functions.

Table 3.1   Population development of Nicaragua and Managua, 1906–1985[a]

	Nicaragua Total	% Urban	Departamento Managua Total	% of Nicaragua	Ciudad Managua Total	% of Nicaragua
1906	501,849	–	48,204	9.6	–	–
1920	633,622	–	74,696	11.8	–	–
1940	829,831	–	120,202	14.9	–	–
1950	1,049,611	35.2	161,513	15.4	109,532	10.4
1963	1,535,588	40.9	318,826	20.8	234,580	15.3
1971	1,877,952	47.7	485,850	25.9	384,904	20.5
1976	2,243,868	51.2	587,045	26.2	469,140	20.9
1985	3,272,064	57.2	903,998[b]	27.6	722,294[c]	22.1

[a] 1906–71 results of national census; 1976 and 1985 extrapolations.
[b] According to a 5% sample survey taken in 1984 the figure for 1985 is 1, 037, 062 (31.7%).
[c] No official figures available, calculation of the author based on the extrapolated figure for the department; according to the 5% sample survey the figure is 828, 613 (25.3%).
Source: Republica de Nicaragua (1975); Oficina Ejecutivo (1977); Instituto National de Estadísticas y Censos (1985).

After the Second World War, Managua became the leading city of the country. At that time Nicaragua began, with US support, to establish processing industries. The industrial sector (including building and construction industry), which accounted for only 13 per cent of the gross domestic product in 1955, had more than doubled its relative importance by 1978, to 28 per cent. In the process, the production of semi-finished and finished products increased at an above-average rate. The capital was given preference in the choice of location for new industrial firms. In the 1970s approximately 80 per cent of industrial production took place here, which, along with the expansion of the administrative machinery, led to a rapid increase in population. Whereas in 1906 the Municipio Managua had only 38,000 inhabitants still fewer than León (57,000), in 1971 it had more than ten times as many (431,000), and one out of five Nicaraguans already lived in the metropolis (in comparison, León in 1971 had 76,000.)

Parallel to the rapid increase in the number of inhabitants (table 3.1), was an equally marked expansion in area. Whereas up to about 1960 expansion had occurred predominantly in rings, more recently growth has progressed in distinct spearheads along the Carretera Interamericana Sur and Norte and along the street to Masaya (see figure 3.2).

Population development in the old city centre did not take place uniformly during this period. On the one hand, from approximately 1950 onwards, the first tendencies towards depopulation and city reconstruction became apparent. On the other hand, particularly in the vicinity of the covered market (Mercado Central), there was a marked increase in population density. This was achieved by building up the courtyards behind the rows of one-storey houses (for location see figure 3.1).

In Managua, as in other large Latin American cities, the business and administrative district had developed directly adjacent to the Central Plaza along the north/south axis of the Avenida Central (see figure 3.1). Until the 1960s two- and three-storey houses dating from the reconstruction phase after the earthquake of 1931 predominated here. Only a few high-rise buildings had been constructed.

Due east of the downtown section lay the central market district. In addition to the two big covered markets there were many shops, booths and stands. The streets around this Mercado Central with their densely built-up courtyards were an overpopulated residential area for the lower classes. Here especially a large proportion of the houses, including many still standing, were of wood or the so-called *taquezal*. This construction, which was used a lot after the 1931 eathquake, consists of a frame of thin wooden boards filled with stones and mortar or sometimes only with mud.

The method of construction, combined with the density of the buildings, were perhaps the most important reasons for the unusually large number of victims in the 1972 quake, and the damage amounting to several hundred million dollars. Most of the houses collapsed during the first strong tremor, so that the streets, which were too narrow to begin with, were soon filled with high mounds of debris blocking all escape routes. Since most of the housing was constructed of easily inflammable material, the fires that broke out at several locations spread rapidly, and the few fire-fighting appliances that were left intact could not be transported to the sources of the fires because the streets were blocked. The extent to which the destruction was related to the building material can be seen

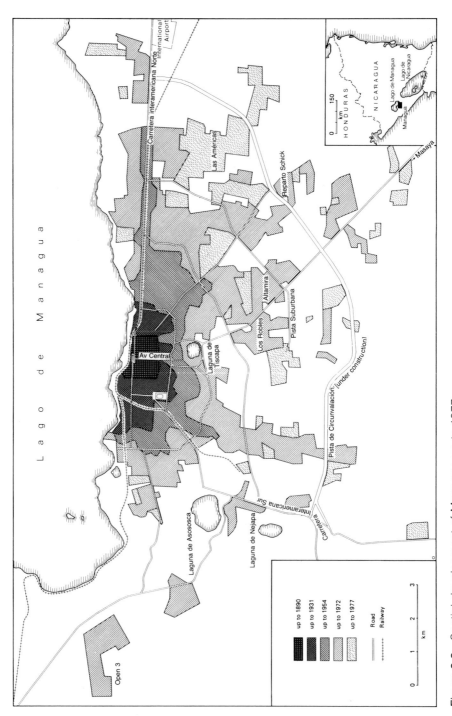

Figure 3.2 Spatial development of Managua up to 1977
Source: Sandner (1969) and unpublished documents from Vice Ministerio de Planificacion Urbana

Las Américas

Reparto Schick

Carretera interamericana Norte

International
Airport

Masaya

Altamira

Los Robles

Pista Suburbana

Laguna de
Tiscapa

Av Central

Pista de Circunvalación
(under construction)

L a g o   d e   M a n a g u a

Laguna de Asososca

Laguna de Nejapa

Carretera interamericana Sur

Open 3

▓	up to 1890
▓	up to 1931
▓	up to 1954
▓	up to 1972
▓	up to 1977
—	Road
+++	Railway

km
0   1   2   3

HONDURAS

NICARAGUA

Lago de Managua

Lago de Nicaragua

Managua

km
0   150

in the fact that a few modern concrete constructions, such as the Banco de América and the Hotel Intercontinental, were barely damaged.

THE CONSEQUENCES OF THE EARTHQUAKE FOR THE STRUCTURE AND FUNCTION OF THE DIFFERENT PARTS OF THE CITY

The postponed reconstruction of the old centre had consequences for the further development of the city. Three closely related points require attention in this respect:

1 At the periphery there soon sprang up extensive emergency constructions for the homeless, and shanty-towns, consisting in part of shacks built by the quake victims themselves.
2 The number of inhabitants and the population density in various parts of the city changed abruptly within a short period of time.
3 Many of the functions that had previously been concentrated in the downtown area shifted to other parts of the city.

I have already mentioned that at least 50,000 people lost their homes in the earthquake and more still left the city temporarily for the fear of further tremors. Thus within a period of only very few days the population figure for Managua dropped from 410,000 to only 170,000 (see table 3.2). Most of the families who fled from the city found temporary lodgings with friends or relatives in the vicinity. By the beginning of 1973, however, they had begun to return, and by the middle of 1973 the city's population had risen to over 250,000 again. Reconstruction had begun in the meantime but could not keep up with the influx, especially since it had been decided not to allow any new buildings or even makeshift housing in the residential areas around the Central Market that had been most densely populated before the earthquake. Instead, during 1973, with extensive support from the United States, the Banco de la Vivienda de Nicaragua constructed more than 11,000 temporary homes (settlement Las Américas; see figure 3.2) at the eastern edge of the city on the far side of Pista Suburbana, which represents the outer boundary of development zone 4. The plan was to turn them into permanent housing step-by-step in the following years.

Table 3.2 Population development of Managua from December 1972 to June 1976

Date		Inner city	Suburbs	City of Managua	Municipality Managua
22 Dec.	1972	398,503	10,693	409,196	457,396
31 Dec.	1972	157,249	12,560	169,809	217,189
28 Jan.	1972 3	195,721	16,840	212,561	286,355
30 May	1973	219,207	27,399	246,606	300,036
30 June	1973	227,772	29,220	256,992	310,453
31 Dec.	1973	313,408	39,027	352,435	407,925
30 June	1974	336,505	27,832	364,337	424,219
30 June	1975	402,252	19,665	421,917	463,218
30 June	1976	449,259	19,881	469,140	509,805

Source: Oficina Ejecutivo (1977).

These and other construction measures were not, however, enough to accommodate all of the victims of the earthquake, even temporarily, and simultaneously to keep up with the increase in population above and beyond the state registered in December 1972 (see table 3.2). Moreover, the poorest social strata often could not afford the newly built housing and therefore resorted to such measures as illegally occupying and sub-dividing land on which to build their simple wooden shacks. The largest squatter settlement, Población Open 3, developed in this manner at the previously very sparsely settled extreme western edge of the city. In 1975 almost 20,000 people were already living here rising by 1977 to approximately 30,000, according to estimates.

A total of 36 squatter settlements (*asentamientos espontáneos*) were counted in Managua in mid-1979 (MINVAH, 1983). Shortly before the takeover by the Sandinistas and before the election in 1984, the illegal occupation of land again reached a peak, because the people did not expect the government to intervene (Mathéy, 1985). According to data in MINVAH (1983) and in the study by Tapia (1984), between 1979 and 1981 alone 87.5 ha of land were occupied (22 new *asentamientos espontáneos*) and divided into 4,375 plots for about 25,000 people. The proportion of the population living in such settlements rose from 5.9 to 9 per cent.

The shifts in population triggered by the ban on reconstruction in the old centre of the city were not restricted to the lower classes, however. The wealthier classes had already begun to leave the residential areas near the old part of the city and move into the new

Table 3.3 Changes in gross population density in the different zones of Managua from 1971 to 1975

Zone	1971 persons/ha	1973 persons/ha	1975 persons/ha	Change 1971–5,%
Zone 1	143.7	0	23.1	−83.9
Zone 2	89.9	37.0	64.3	−28.5
Zone 3	23.2	17.2	28.3	+22.0
Zone 4	42.6	34.2	51.2	+20.2
Zone 5	13.4	12.2	26.1	+94.8
Zone 6	12.3	5.8	36.3	+195.1
Total	36.4	19.0	36.8	+1.3
Density gradient[a]	0.3774	0.1515	0.1454	−61.5
Central density[a]	154.0	42.9	50.7	−67.1

[a] According to $d_x = d_0 e^{bx}$ where x = distance to the Plaza d = population density b = density gradient d_0 = central density.
Source: Vice Ministerio de Planificación Urbana (1975).

exclusive suburbs at the outskirts of the city, and this tendency gathered momentum. Thus the two smart residential areas, Los Robles and Altamira along the street to Masaya (see figure 3.2), were developed mainly after the earthquake. Since 1979 development in these residential areas has been stagnating, as private construction has come almost completely to a standstill.

Since 1972 the population density has increased somewhat in a few limited areas of the old city centre. This is particularly the case in the 'new' market area that formed around the Mercado Oriental (see figure 3.1), which had existed previously, but had not been so important. In the middle of the 1970s conditions here were similar to the conditions that used to exist in the vicinity of the Central Market, with jammed streets, closely packed stalls and overpopulated living quarters in the former courtyards.

As a result of the shifts in population, the gross population density as a whole in Managua changed only slightly between 1971 and 1975 (see table 3.3). The values calculated for the individual zones, however, deviated much less from the average after the earthquake. Whereas, for example in zone 1 the population density decreased by 84 per cent, in zone 5 it increased by 95 per cent and in zone 6 by as much as 195 per cent. Thus a comparatively compact city with high central density had turned into a sprawling conurbation without a pronounced urban centre (see figure 3.3).

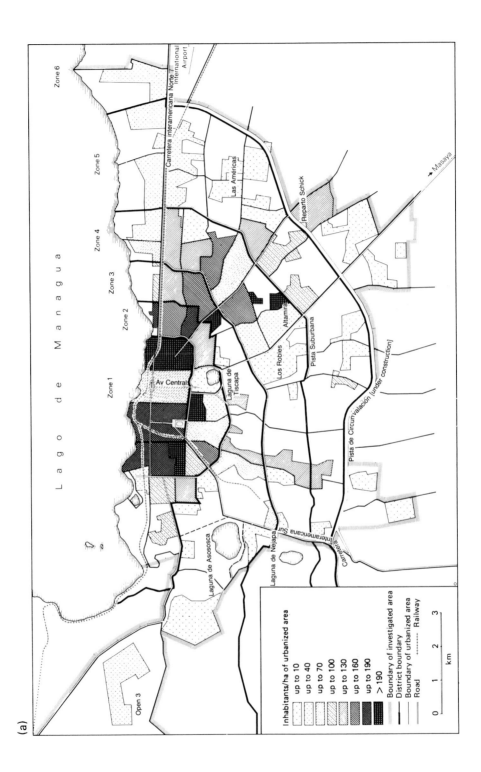

(a)

L a g o   d e   M a n a g u a

Zone 6
Zone 5
Zone 4
Zone 3
Zone 2
Zone 1

Carretera interamericana Norte
International Airport

Las Américas

Reparto Schick

Altamira

Los Robles

Pista Suburbana

Av Central

Laguna de Tiscapa

Pista de Circunvalación (under construction)

Carretera Interamericana Sur

Laguna de Nejapa

Laguna de Asososca

Open 3

Masaya

Inhabitants/ha of urbanized area

up to 10
up to 40
up to 70
up to 100
up to 130
up to 160
up to 190
> 190

Boundary of investigated area
District boundary
Boundary of urbanized area
Road
Railway

km
0   1   2   3

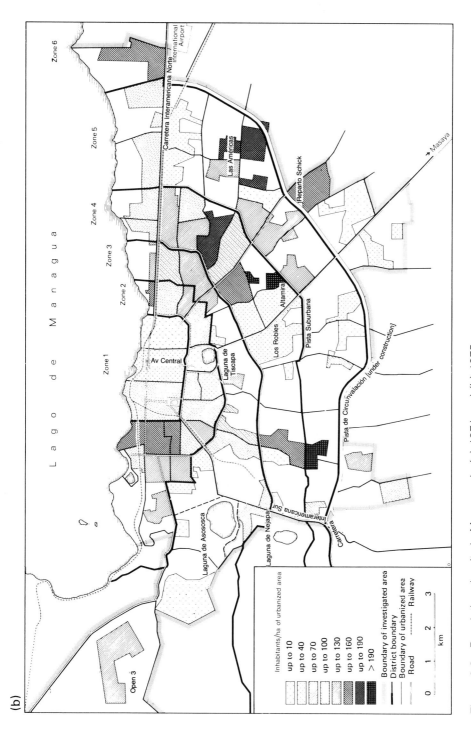

Figure 3.3 Population density in Managua in (a) 1971 and (b) 1975

Source: Vice Ministerio de Planificacion Urbana (1975)

Within the figure:

(b)

L a g o   d e   M a n a g u a

Open 3

Laguna de Asososca

Laguna de Nejapa

Av Central

Laguna de Tiscapa

Zone 1

Zone 2

Zone 3

Zone 4

Zone 5

Zone 6

Carretera Interamericana Norte

International Airport

Las Américas

Reparto Schick

→ Masaya

Altamira

Los Robles

Pista Suburbana

Pista de Circuivalación (under construction)

Carretera Interamericana Sur

Inhabitants/ha of urbanized area

up to 10
up to 40
up to 70
up to 100
up to 130
up to 160
up to 190
> 190

Boundary of investigated area
District boundary
Boundary of urbanized area
Road ------ Railway

0 1 2 3
km

Although there are no new population figures by district available, we can assume that this tendency has continued in recent times. Because reconstruction is still forbidden in the former city centre, population density in zone 1 is not likely to have changed significantly. The growth that has occurred has certainly benefited peripheral districts most of all. There has been no lasting improvement in living conditions here, though. Evidently immigration increased after the revolution much more than was assumed for a long time (see the comparison between the extrapolation of the population figures with the results of the sample survey for the middle of the 1980s in table 3.1); and as a result, residential areas for the lower classes have been in even shorter supply in the past few years. Statistics for 1984 show that 20 per cent of the families in Managua have no dwelling of their own, 15 per cent live in houses that are badly in need of repair, and another 30 per cent live in one-room shacks (Mathéy, 1985). The public water supply reaches only 63 per cent of the urban area, sewerage only 53 per cent (Loyman and Carmona, 1985).

The social structure of the metropolis, which is expressed at least approximately in the map of income distribution (figure 3.4 (a)), also changed considerably within a short period after the earthquake (Foucher, 1980). Partly this was due to the construction of emergency shelters and the emergence of shanty-towns at the edge of the city. But the steps taken to construct housing for the many middle-class families who were victims of the earthquake also played a role. These families, who had previously lived in central parts of the city, now moved to the periphery.

Only to the south of the old part of the city are there any remaining higher-class residential areas. This is particularly the case in the sparsely built-up region around Laguna Tiscapa, where the presidential palace is situated. For a long time this zone was completely unaffected by the spatial growth of the city, because the Somoza family owned extensive estates there that were still being used for grazing.

Today, the new exclusive suburbs lie at a considerable distance from the Plaza, being concentrated most strongly at the south-eastern and south-western periphery, where traffic connections are well-developed and convenient. Their development is distinctly sectoral and is oriented along the street to Masaya and the Interamericana Sur (partially outside the section shown in figure 3.4).

In the areas between these growth axes lie extensive residential areas for lower income groups. These include older settlements along the Interamericana Norte heading towards the airport, the 'Reparto Schick', which dates back to resettlement programme of the 1960s, the emergency shelters of the 'Población Las Américas' and the large shanty-town of 'Open 3'. Between them lie areas that have not yet been built up and estates of terraced houses built by state-owned construction agencies, so that the outskirts of the city today have a distinctly cellular structure. Thus the development trends that have been recognizable in the larger capital cities of Latin America for some time (see Bähr and Mertins, 1982) have intensified since the earthquake in Managua.

That Nicaragua's metropolis has developed into an agglomeration without a functioning urban centre is primarily due to the fact that the administrative offices, service institutions and businesses that were established around the Plaza and the Avenida Central were not able to begin reconstruction at their old locations and were forced to seek new sites. Only a few of the ministries and other government institutions, for example, the post office and the presidential palace, remained in the old city centre because damage to their buildings was slight. Others found at first temporary and later permanent quarters all over the city, some even outside the built-up area. Business life moved partly to the vicinity of the new main market (formerly the Mercado Oriental) and pártly out to the periphery. This process was accompanied by a discernible social segregation. The market and the surrounding streets are still the preferred shopping areas of the lower social classes. In contrast, the shops that catered to more sophisticated demands have completely left the central areas of the city and established themselves, much as in the United States, in new malls (*centros comerciales*) along the main arterial roads and particularly at important road junctions. Up to the end of the 1970s at least, not only the big department stores, modern speciality shops and fashionable restaurants were so located, but also snack bars, travel agencies, banks and some administrative departments. Recently this situation has changed somewhat; as a result of nationalization, supply problems and greater political insecurity, some institutions have been closed and some of their rooms are empty. Others, such as banks, were taken over by the state, and others still have had to limit their supplies.

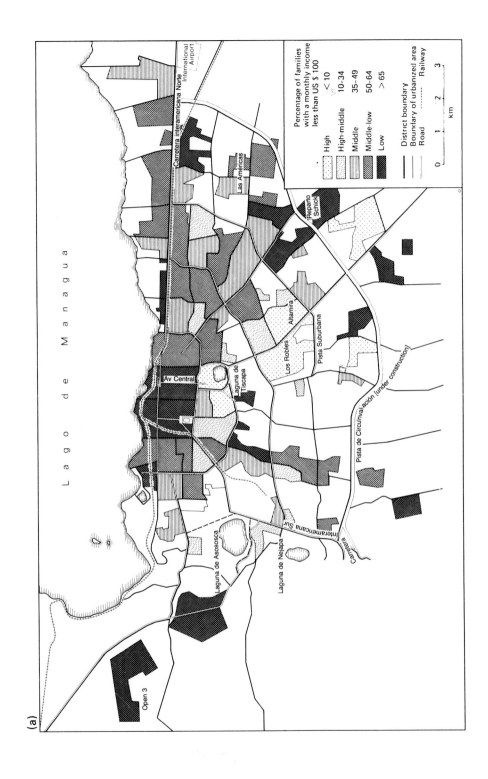

(a)

Lago de Managua

Open 3

Laguna de Asososca

Laguna de Nejapa

Av Central

Laguna de Tiscapa

Los Robles

Altamira

Pista Suburbana

Carretera Interamericana Sur

Pista de Circunvalación (under construction)

Carretera Interamericana Norte

International Airport

Las Américas

Reparto Schick

Percentage of families
with a monthly income
less than US $ 100

High   < 10

High-middle   10–34

Middle   35–49

Middle-low   50–64

Low   > 65

District boundary
Boundary of urbanized area
Road ········ Railway

0   1   2   3
km

(b)

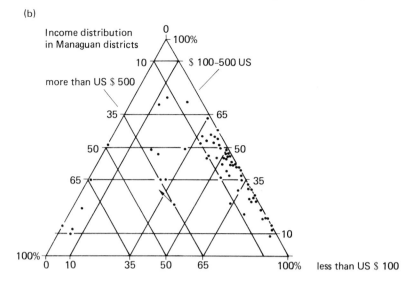

Figure 3.4   Income groups in the districts of Managua, 1975
Source: Carvajal and Velasco (1975)

The Somoza government even encouraged decentralized reconstruction with an ambitious programme in which the most important ring road and connecting routes were improved by 1976 at a
cost of $6.5 million, so that the new sub-centres can easily and
rapidly be reached by car. Those who are dependent on public
transport or who have to do their errands on foot – and according to
a poll taken in 1975 that is 88 per cent of all families – are not likely
to shop there. Thus the clientele of most of these malls is restricted
to the prosperous members of the population, if only for reasons of
accessibility.

THE FUTURE DEVELOPMENT OF MANAGUA

It is still difficult to make prognoses as to the future development of
Managua and its ruined downtown area. With the fall of Anastasio
Somoza the reconstruction concepts that were worked out in the
middle of the 1970s lost their validity. In the first drafts of these
plans three alternative possibilites were discussed:

1   Renewed concentration of shops and centralized institutions
    in the old city centre.

2 A decentralized distribution structure combined with the designation of the old part of the city as a residential area.
3 Conversion of the old centre into a government and administrative centre, moving the central business district to the road towards Masaya.

No final decision had been made when fighting broke out and Somoza was deposed in 1979. Shortly after the Sandinista takeover the new government passed a few laws affecting the future urban development of Managua, but a final reconstruction programme has yet to be adopted. With one exception, no concrete measures have been carried out, and therefore, there have been no fundamental changes in land use compared with the map of 1977 (figure 3.1). The one exception is the Proyecto Habitacional San Antonio (very simple housing, primarily in two-storey buildings, for about 400 families) that was completed in 1982 in the western portion of the ruined area.

The Decree 903 (Ley de Expropriación de Tierras Urbanas Baldias en el Casco Urbano Central de la Ciudad de Managua), proclaimed at the end of 1981, provides that all areas in the old city centre of Managua that are not built-up are to be expropriated, laying a basis for new large-scale planning. This task was entrusted to the Ministerio de Vivienda y Asentamientos Humanos (MINVAH), which presented the draft of a Plan Regulador de Managua in 1982 (see figure 3.5). According to this draft a future Centro de Managua is to emerge in the area that was devastated by the earthquake, comprising not only administrative departments and cultural institutions (Zona de Equipamiento de Gobierno) but also shops catering to both normal and specialized demands (Zona de Comercio General y Especializado). In an attempt to take the earthquake danger into account, buildings will not be constructed on top of active faults. To make up for this, the development in the remaining zones will be very dense.

It is not likely, however, that this plan will be realized in the foreseeable future. Not only the country's present economic problems and the consequent difficulty in financing such a project speak against it; the decentralized urban structure that has developed in the meantime does the same. Thus it is not very likely that the old city centre, which remains in ruins today, will be able to regain its former functions.

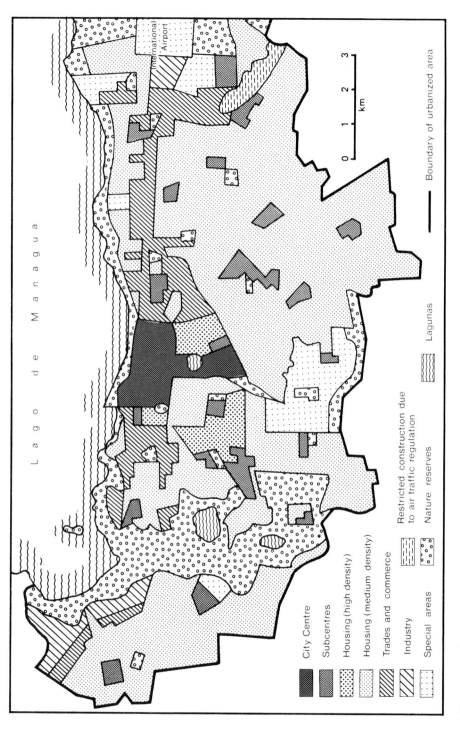

Figure 3.5 Plan Regulador de Managua (Proposal of Ministerio de Vivienda y Asentamientos Humanos)
Source: Peña and Klein (1984)

The following labels appear on the map:

L a g o   d e   M a n a g u a

International Airport

Boundary of urbanized area

0   1   2   3
km

City Centre
Subcentres
Housing (high density)
Housing (medium density)
Trades and commerce
Industry
Special areas

Restricted construction due to air traffic regulation
Nature reserves
Lagunas

REFERENCES

Arce, J. (1973) *Región de Managua. Tectónica y sismicidad (The Region of Managua. Tectonics and Seismicity)*, Catastro e Inventario de Recursos Naturales, Managua.

Bähr, J. and Mertins, G. (1982) A Model of the Social and Spatial Differentiation of Latin American Metropolitan Cities, *Applied Geography and Development*, 19: 27–45.

Carvajal, D. R. de and Velasco, J. (1975) *Ingreso, empleo y estructura espacial urbana de Managua (Income, Employment and the Urban Spatial Structure of Managua)*, Vice Ministerio de Planificación Urbana, Managua.

Foucher, M. (1980) Managua, ville éclatée, *Hérodote*, 17:32–52.

Instituto Nacional de Estadísticas y Censos (1985) *Anuario Estadístico de Nicaragua 1984 (Statistical Yearbook of Nicaragua 1984)*, Managua.

Loyman, M. and Carmona, M. (1985) *Proyecto 'Plan de saneamiento integral de barrios marginales en Managua' (Project 'Plan for the Integral Improvement of Shanty Towns of Managua')*, Working Paper, Jornadas Internacionales 'Renovación urbana y vivienda popular en áreas metropolitanas de América Latina', Hamburg-Hamburg.

Mathéy, K. (1985) Housing Policies in the Sandinista Nicaragua, *Triolog*, 6:42–8.

MINVAH (Ministerio de la Vivienda y Asentamientos Humanos de Nicaragua) (1983) La tierra en el desarrollo urbano: el caso de Nicaragua (The Land in Urban Development: the Case of Nicaragua), in Sociedad Interamericana de Planifecación (ed.), *Relacion campo-ciudad*, Ediciones SIAP, México, D. F.: 402–16.

Oficina Ejecutiva de Encuestas y Censos (1977) *Población de Nicaragua. Años 1971–1980 (The Population of Nicaragua, 1971–1980)*, Managua.

Peña, O. and Klein, J.L. (1984) Geografia de la población y cambio social en Nicaragua (Population Geography and Social Change in Nicaragua), *Revista Geográfica*, 99:145–66.

República de Nicaragua (1975) *Censos Nacionales 1971. Población por Municipios (National Censuses 1971. Population by Cities)*, Managua.

Sandner, G. (1969) *Die Hauptstädte Zentralmerikas: Wachstumsprobleme, Gestaltwandel und Sozialgefüge (The Principal Cities of Central America: Problems of Growth, Changing Form and Social Structure)*, Quelle and Meyer, Heidelberg.

Tapia, O. (1984) Die Tendenzen der Wohnungspolitik in Nikaragua von heute (Current Tendencies in Housing Policy in Nicaragua), in Bruno, E. , Körte, A. and Mathéy, K. (eds.), *Umgang mit städtischen Wohnquartieren unterer Einkommensgruppen in Entwicklungsländern*, Archimed, Darmstadt: 87–103.

Vice Ministerio de Planificación Urbana (1975) *Plan general de desarrollo urbano de Managua: Modelo referencial (General plan for the Urban Development of Managua. Reference Model)*, Managua.

Weyl, R. (1961) *Die Geologie Mittelamerikas (The Geology of Central America)*, Beiträge zur regionalen Geologie der Erde 1, Gebrüder Bornträger, Berlin.

4

Friuli: Ten Years After the Earthquake of 6 May 1976

Robert Geipel

THE EARTHQUAKE OF 1976

On 6 May 1976, at 9 p.m., an earthquake with a strength of 6.4 on the Richter scale and lasting for almost a minute took place in the area of Friuli in northern Italy. Its epicentre lay only about 5 km below the surface. The number of dead and wounded was very much affected by the particular time of day and the weather: most people were at home but out of doors because of the heat of the early summer evening. Nevertheless, 939 people perished in the wreckage of the 17,000 collapsing houses, and 2,400 were injured. The homes of 32,000 people were totally destroyed. Several hundred tremors, aftershocks and the heavy rain that set in immediately after the quake pulverized the already badly damaged buildings still further, making the homes of another 157,000 people uninhabitable. Altogether, an area of 4,800 sq km, embracing nearly 100 communes with a population of half a million, was affected by the catastrophe, and a zone 25 km across, containing 1,766 sq km, was totally levelled. The first, somewhat exaggerated, estimates placed the damage at 4,400 thousand million lire, or $6 thousand million.

The fears of Friulians that the fate of victims of Sicily's Val Belice earthquake of 1968 (about 80,000 were made homeless and put into barracks) might be repeated in their case gave rise to the motto *Dalle tende alle case* (straight from the tents into the houses – and not into barracks first).

At 11.30 a.m. on 15 September 1976 an end came abruptly to the four-and-a-half months of continuous and energetic rebuilding of houses and (especially) factories. After numerous light shocks, a second earthquake, at a strength of 6.1 on the Richter scale, struck Friuli. The number of homeless, which had decreased by the beginning of September to 45,000 because of the repair of less badly damaged buildings, and because people found shelter with friends and relatives elsewhere, swelled again to more than 70,000. Although the quake was weaker than the first on 6 May, the psychological effects were much worse. Bad landslides blocking escape routes out of the mountains, the loss of savings that had already been invested in reconstruction, the dangers of the prospect of the hard mountain winter, all overwhelmed the resistance capacity of a mountain population accustomed to privation. The Emergency Commissioner had to requisition hotels and apartments in the Adriatic coastal towns (occupied only during summer and standing empty in winter) as housing for the elderly, the disabled, and women and children; 32,000 of them were evacuated for the winter period to return to prefabs in their home villages in the spring.

Ten years after these events we resumed research in the disaster area, keeping in mind that a lack of longitudinal studies was mentioned by many authors describing disasters and disaster management. In 1987 we were able to take an overview of the whole process of reconstruction and the impact of the disaster on population, land-use, occupation and the psychological well-being of the Friulians.

Impact on Population and Housing-Stock

It is one of our findings that elderly people were killed during the May earthquake in a much higher proportion than should be expected from the overall demographic situation (see figure 4.1). This higher impact results from the fact that besides the weaker constitution and lower physical and psychological capacity of the elderly to overcome such hardship, the old city centres (*centro storico*) were occupied mainly by older people. In the disaster area 47 per cent of all buildings constructed before 1919 were destroyed compared to 8 per cent of those constructed after 1960. The older, poorer housing stock and its concentration in the centres inhabited by an elderly population was responsible for the many victims among the elderly.

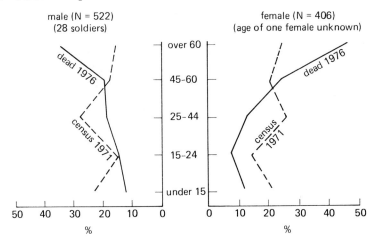

Figure 4.1   Mortality distribution associated with main shock, Friuli, 1976
Source: Data in the Church of S. Maria di Grazie in Udine and census data 1971 for Udine and Pordenone, ISTAT 1973

LARGE-SCALE CHANGES IN THE REGIONAL STRUCTURE

The Influence of Reconstruction Laws

The earthquakes of 1976 did not cause remarkable changes in the regional structure. The reconstruction laws aimed at the prevention of emigration from the disaster area. Compensation given to the victims had to be invested in the same location where the losses had occurred. Therefore emigration did not exceed the pre-earthquake trend of younger people leaving the mountain region in search of better working conditions. The 45 communes totally destroyed continued to follow this trend after 1976. After the sharp loss of about 1,000 persons in 1976, population stagnated at the level of that year. Neither among the communes nor among their respective fractions did population change in either the heavily or the less heavily damaged areas differ perceptibly between 1971 and 1981.

Change of Structure in the Agrarian Domain

In the mountain villages and in the hill country before the disaster the practice of part-time farming was dominant. The process of occupational dissociation was quickened by the earthquake. Stables were destroyed, cattle had been slaughtered or had to be sold. Reconstruction had to take into account whether stables and farm-buildings should be planned or given up for good. An attempt to preserve a semi-rural lifestyle, for instance through communal stables, communal herds of cattle with grazing rights proportional to the brought-in acreage of pasture land (as in neighbouring Slovenia) mostly failed.

It turned out that the earthquake also provided an opportunity to translate changed value-systems into reality. With the abandonment of agriculture, especially of cattle breeding, the capability of the communes to retain their own populations diminished. Moreover, agricultural know-how gets lost with the change of generations if it cannot be transferred from parents to children by showing how something is done. The image of Friuli as a mixed rural-urban society with strong links to its own land began to dissolve.

Transfer of Compensations as an Indicator for Inter-regional Migration

An example of the many crossroads of decision facing individuals and families after the disaster was the option either to invest the promised compensation for losses in the commune where the earthquake damage originated, or to transfer this compensation to another commune within the limited disaster area. The victims had this opportunity between 1978 and 1984. During this time, latent desires to move elsewhere, for instance into a village closer to the workplace, suddenly became possible of achievement with the entitlement to transfer the promised payment (state contributions) to such a place (*transferimento dei contributi*). With such an act of volition the already loosened links to the former home were severed completely, for after this a return to one's former home in the original place of residence was no longer possible. Mapping the direction and strength of such transfers of title deeds reveals inter-regional mobility and makes it possible to forecast future development of the alpine and pre-alpine parts of Friuli (see figure 4.2). Such mapping shows how the concept of the 'home area' slowly moves from the mountains to the plains (figure 4.3).

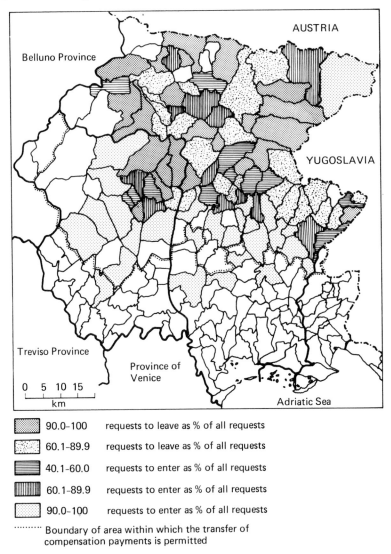

Figure 4.2 Requests for the transfer of compensation payments to another commune as a percentage of the total requests received

Speeding-up of Social Change: Viewpoint Baraccopolis

In the course of evacuation, repatriation into prefab towns and final return into the reconstructed or newly built home, regional and social differences and those specific to age-groups are evident. The

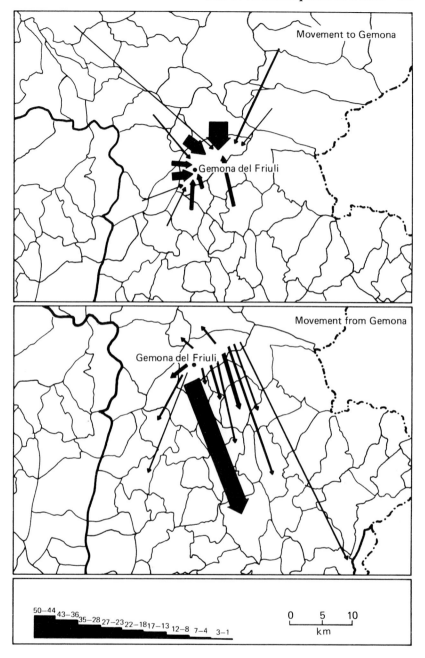

Figure 4.3 Gemona: relocation of persons receiving compensation payments since 1979

prefab town or *baraccopolis* becomes a focal point that collects and clearly shows the problems of regional society. Social change resulting from the disaster is accelerated. Processes normally spread out over a much longer period, maybe over generations, took place within a decade. The population had to react in quick succession to numerous decisions and their results. They had to decide between options that without the disaster would have been much less radical and much more within traditional patters. But now, even from people not used to decision-making, constant adaptions to overwhelming conditions were asked. Most people had to make these decisions even if they could not or would not overlook their consequences (e.g. high indebtedness in spite of threatening unemployment after the end of the period). Even more striking is the contrast to those not capable of making decisions, especially old and poor people who had to remain in the barracks. Those capable of decision-making, that is the productive age-cohorts, in the meantime have left not only the *baraccopolis* but possibly also the whole commune, as an example from Bordano shows (figure 4.4). As with similar work-oriented migrations, the active age groups are overrepresented in this transfer, so that increased ageing takes place in more remote mountain communes.

Slums of Hope and of Despair

Analysis of routine statistical material accumulated for electricity meter readings enables the assessment of the population of prefab towns over the course of the years. Such data enabled us to regard the *baraccopolis* as an experiment in an involuntary laboratory of social science. The speed of emptying the prefab towns (see table 4.1) enables us to draw conclusions about recovery capability in the various communes. This depends among other things upon the

Table 4.1   Population in prefab towns, 1977–1986

	1977	1978	1981	1985	1986
Persons in prefabs	65,500	61,200	38,900	25,800	20,535
Percentage of total population	25.5	24.1	14.7	9.9	7.8
Number of dwellings	20,400	21,700	15,700	12,200	9,727

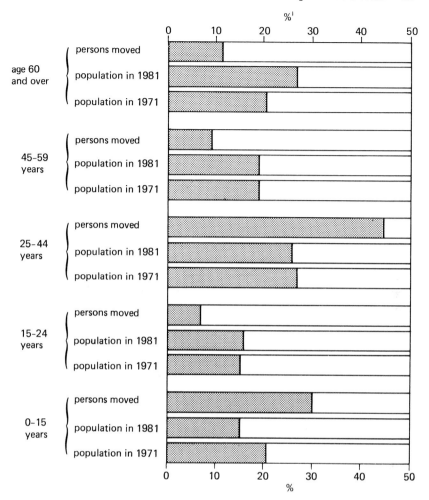

Figure 4.4   Moves with transfers of contributions from Bordano

degree of destruction, size of commune, economic situation and regional location (mountains, hillside, plains). Haas et al. (1977:67) gave an early warning against taking barrack settlements in disaster areas as necessarily mere transitional measures: 'Don't assume that all temporary housing will be temporary.'

Computer-lists on consumption of electric current in each barrack indicate whether its user is entitled to it free of charge or not.

Those who stay *con titolo* (with title) in a prefab belong to the handicapped group of the old, single and resigned people, who for the rest of their lives will have to stay in this abode. Anyone living in a prefab *senza titolo* (without title) does so in spite of a house or flat being ready and waiting which he or she will not accept for one of a variety of reasons, or is part of a new generation of barrack-dwellers who moved into an empty prefab as a squatter. Not all these squatters will have been previous residents of the commune. Perhaps they have come with a mobile construction gang to build the Villach–Udine freeway. Others are young families who left their parents' home and established their first household in a prefab, young adults who want to separate themselves from the family in search of independence. Small shops and workshops move into these prefabs, provisional arrangements of small enterprises typical of the economic history and entrepreneurial spirit of Friuli over decades, which have gained a new impetus during the reconstruction boom.

Thus in the remaining *baraccopolises* 'slums of despair' and 'slums of hope' meet, life-paths and generations overlap. While the giant building-site of Friuli is approaching its completion, some prefab towns (e.g. the biggest, Osoppo) have already totally emptied and show only the former foundation walls, leaving the huge task of removing these and redeveloping such sites to the status of farmland as before the disaster. In other towns like Venzone, where reconstruction aimed at the creation of a museum city, a replica or even a glorification of the former normal town to a national monument, the process of emptying the *baraccopolis* takes much longer. In Bordano, for example, finished settlements were not accepted because supply exceeded demand from the beginning or developed into over-supply, as many prospective inhabitants transferred their contributions to other communes and left.

SMALL-SCALE CHANGES IN THE REGIONAL STRUCTURE

Changes in the Housing Stock

Many other case studies demonstrate that residential accommodation built after a disaster shows a higher standard in respect to both size and equipment. If we look at the average change of dwelling space in Friuli between 1971 and 1981 within the 45 totally destroyed communes excluding rented apartments, growth of housing space is highest among the most severely damaged communes. Average housing space between 1971 and 1981 in the provinces of Udine and Pordenone grew from 82 sq m to 90 sq m per flat. But the mountain population diminished between the same period in favour of the plains. Growth in housing space during 1971–81 in the variously affected communes of the two provinces was as follows:

45 totally destroyed communes	11.3 sq m
42 badly damaged communes	9.4 sq m
48 lightly damaged communes	7.8 sq m
all other communes	5.2 sq m

Changes in the Types of Houses

The proportion of single family houses in all villages of the region was more or less the same before the earthquake (between 21 and 24 per cent). The dominant type was one- and two-family houses built wall-to-wall. Only the bigger towns like Gemona or Venzone had a relatively high proportion of multiple family dwellings, because of their traditional urban structure with higher density especially in the ancient city cores (more than 20 per cent). With the exception of Bordano (+4 per cent), this proportion diminished. The sub-jective image ('how it once was – how it should be to meet the Friulian ideal') influenced the reconstruction (assuming sufficient means) in that the realization of such dreams led to houses 'where you can walk around', instead of the formerly predominant row houses of high urban density. The proportion of one- and two-family houses built wall-to-wall diminished from 56.5 to 34.9 per cent, and free-standing one-family houses increased to 46 per cent in our sample.

Changes in Social Life

The destruction of their homes meant repeated transfers for the afflicted population: from ruins to tents, to hotel apartments on the Adriatic Sea, to prefabs in their village or elsewhere, and finally back to newly built houses. All this happened to people who hitherto (with the exception of the many guest-workers abroad) had rarely left their environs. The change of milieu meant not only a change of location but was connected for the people affected with the loss of familiar household objects, which had gradually to be replaced, to be fitted to the changing domiciles and finally to be integrated into the definite household. This procedure is a piece of mosaic in the process of loss of identity and its gradual recovery.

General Social Changes in Friuli

During the first phase of a disaster the number of conflicts is said to diminish, while conflict potential grows during the period of reconstruction, with formerly close social relations becoming weaker. Friulian observers of the development speak of a 'monetarization and commercialization of hitherto traditional links' (Strassoldo and Cattarinussi, 1978). After the pathos of altruistic aid and the solidarity of shared sorrows in evacuation towns and prefab camps has faded away, changes can be recognized among those who rendered the 'Friulian miracle' possible.

While surveys between 1976 and 1980 (Cattarinussi, Pelanda and Moretti, 1981) registered a growth in regional identity, interest in public welfare and the hope for a better tomorrow, statements of the mid-1980s point in the direction of 'Friuli has sold its soul.' Economic development (more jobs, of course mainly in construction; return of emigrants) has improved, the capability of the local administration is deemed high, and criticism is directed more against central government in Rome than against regional authorities. But signals of escapism cannot be ignored: alcoholism, drug abuse and criminality are growing, and egoism is replacing the former traditions of 'give and take' between neighbours. Among seven statements to be approved or rejected during Cattarinussi's interviews, 'less communication', 'more anonymity' and 'neighbourhood relations worse than before the disaster' found by far the greatest concurrence. These changes are mostly ascribed to the above-mentioned alterations in the layout of the settlement pattern: more one-family detached houses, more fences and walls inspired by journals on urban architecture, new and unknown neighbours, and so on.

Evaluation of the Dwelling Situation

Without doubt the people of Friuli in general are satisfied with their housing situation and also (but less) with their environment. In our four communes under survey (Gemona, Venzone, Osoppo, Bordano) the interviewees responded to our demand for a general assessment of their situation in respect to house/flat, neighbours and environment :

content	53.0 per cent
rather content	30.6 per cent
only partly content	7.6 per cent
slightly dissatisfied	8.2 per cent
totally dissatisfied	0.7 per cent

Semantic distinctions made to compare the pre-earthquake and the present situations in order to evaluate housing conditions versus environmental conditions indicate that the individual has gained greater welfare within his own four walls but lost in respect to environment and public affairs (see figures 4.5 and 4.6). Qualitative and quantitative improvements over former housing conditions are in contrast to losses within the neighbourhood (with exception of a 'more orderly layout'). People interviewed who live today at the same site as before 1976, might be most capable of assessing changes in environment. It is only the contrast of 'chaotic versus

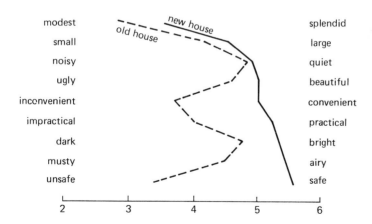

Figure 4.5 Evaluation of new houses after reconstruction and old houses before the earthquake

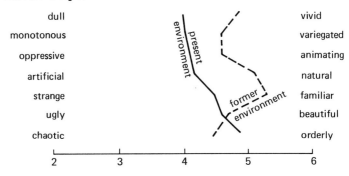

Figure 4.6   Evaluation of present environment after reconstruction and former environment before the earthquake

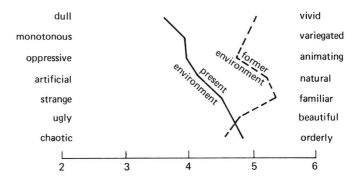

Figure 4.7   Comparison of former and present environment by persons who resettled at the same site

orderly' which speaks against the general bemoaning of the former, better environment (see figure 4.7).

The area outside the historical centre has hardly changed as to its environment. Substantial changes however concerned the city core. Expectations directed towards a reconstruction of the historical centres as locations of a vivid urban life ten years later proved to be illusory (see figures 4.8 and 4.9). As early as 1976, many services and public utilities had left the *centro storico* high upon Gemona's alluvial fan for locations closer to their customers, for example towards railway stations or bus stops along the big traffic artery in the valley of the Tagliamento.

The interruption of all social life in the historical centre during the long reconstruction period of about ten years (the length arising

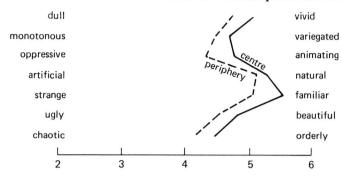

Figure 4.8 Evaluation of former environment by people living in the centre and in the periphery

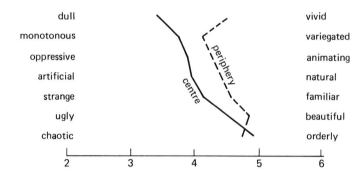

Figure 4.9 Evaluation of present environment by people living in the centre and in the periphery

from a later start because of more complications, longer duration of authentic, slower, rebuilding in the periphery with its 'normal' villas, therefore longer periods spent in prefab camps) is a severe impediment for those destined to return to the historical centres. They have been reconstructed for living conditions belonging to a no longer existing medieval society of big families with many children and servants, in contrast to the elderly childless couples who nowadays own monuments of the fourteenth century without corresponding incomes. The built environment of the historical centres lags behind the social changes.

CONCLUSIONS

The economic miracle of Friuli's reconstruction involving 44,000 single housing units has various sources: compensations from the Italian state on the basis of reconstruction laws, input of private savings, construction work done by the skilled owners themselves, high indebtedness and the aid of emigrant relatives who, if not returning themselves, offered their compensations to their relatives. The development of housing space has already shown that Friulians, at least quantitatively, live much better than before the earthquake. No wonder, because the Italian government pumped more than US$2.5 billion compensation money into the disaster area. After the failure of the Val Belice reconstruction, and under the critical eyes of neighbours from Austria and Yugoslavia, an example of efficiency had to be set in Friuli.

Assessment of the present-day environment in Friuli, however, must be based on both external factors (such as the housing situation) and internal factors (such as familiarity, neighbourhood, reminiscence of places of childhood, social well-being). In the hectic struggle of reconstruction, fixed upon the restoration of structures, this second aspect was entirely neglected. Monotonous structures, spatial distance between neighbours, extension of the sphere of intimacy, shopping in supermarkets along the thorough-fares far away from the historical centres all developed within less than ten years in Friuli. In the minds of the adults the social and psychological aspects of pre-earthquake times are still present (closeness to neighbours, intimacy, mutual aid), while the real environmental conditions are totally different (e.g. 'commercializing' of relations). The situation before 1976, seen from local perception, needs glorification and gets it by stressing Friulian culture, a political regional movement and the rural values of the past. 'Environment', under these aspects, is not merely something that can be measured by thousands of new houses. Environment appears more hostile than before the disaster, in terms of a disillusion about the visible achievements.

REFERENCES

Cattarinussi, B., Pelanda, C. and Moretti, A. (eds.) (1981) *Il disastro. Effetti di lungo termine. Indagine psicosociologica nelle aree colpite dal terremoto del Friuli*, Pubblicazioni dell' ISIG, Serie *Ricerche* 6, Udine.

Chiavola, E. (1985) Rehabilitation Strategies: The Friuli Case, paper presented at the international seminar, Learning from Earthquakes, Perugia, 11–13 April.

Cuny, F. C. (1983) *Disaster and Development*, Oxford University Press, New York.

Dobler, R. (1980) *Regionale Entwicklungschancen nach einer Katastrophe: Ein Beitrag zur Regionalplanung des Friaul*, Munchener Geographische Hefte 45, Regensburg.

Drabek, T. E. (1986) *Human System Responses to Disaster*, Springer Verlag, New York.

D'Souza, F. (1982) Recovery Following the South Italian Earthquake, November 1980: Two Contrasting Examples, *Disasters*, 6, 2:101–9.

Fabbro, S. (1985) *La Ricostruzione del Friuli*, Coop. Edit. Il Campo, Udine.

Foster, H. D. (1980) *Disaster Planning: The Preservation of Life and Property*, Springer Verlag, New York.

Friesema, H. P., Caporaso, J., Goldstein, G., Lineberry, R., McCleary, R. (1979) *Aftermath: Communities after Natural Disasters*. Sage, Beverly Hills/London.

Geipel, R. (1977) *Friaul: Sozialgeographische Aspekte einer Erdbebenkatastrophe*, Munchener Geographische Hefte 40, Regensburg.

Geipel, R. (1979a) Acceptance and Rejection of Earthquake, Landslide and Flood Hazards in Two Communes of Friuli/Italy, in *Papers of the International Symposium on Earthquake Prediction*, UNESCO, Paris, 2–6 April, Session IV-1, 1–15.

Geipel, R. (1979b) *Friuli: Aspetti sociografici di una catastrofe sismica*, Franco Angeli Editore, Milano.

Geipel, R., Steuer, M., Wagner, U., Gottschalt, F., Völkl, H. und Dobler, R. (1980) *Il progetto friuli – Das Friaul-Projekt*, Quaderni di ricostruire 1, C. Martin Internazionale, Udine.

Geipel, R. (1982a) The Case of Friuli, Italy. The Impact of an Earthquake in a Highly Developed Old Culture: Regional Identity versus Economic Efficiency, in Jones, B. G. and Tomazevic, M. *Social and Economic Aspects of Earthquakes*, Cornell University, Ithaca, 499–517.

Geipel, R. (1982b) *Disaster and Reconstruction: The Friuli (Italy) Earthquakes of 1976*, Wiley, Chichester.

Geipel, R. (1983) Katastrophen nach der Katastrophe? Ein Vergleich der

Erdbebengebiete Friaul und Süditalien, *Geographische Rundschau*, 35, 1:17–26.

Haas, J. E., Kates, R. W. and Bowden, M. J. (eds) (1977) *Reconstruction Following Disaster*, MIT Press Cambridge, Mass.

Hogg, S. J. (1980) Reconstruction following Seismic Disaster in Venzone, Friuli, *Disasters*, 4, 2:173–85.

ISTAT (Istitulo Centrale di Statistica) (1973) *11° Censimento Generale della Popolazione*, Roma.

Klinteberg, R. (1979) Management of Disaster Victims and Rehabilitation of Uprooted Communities, *Disasters*, 3, 1: 61–70.

Regione Autonoma Fruili–Venezia Giulia (1985) *Relazione sullo stato delle attivita regionali per la ricostruzione delle zone colpite dai sismi del 1976*, Trieste.

Rubin, C. B., Saperstein, M. D. and Barbee, D. G. (1985) *Community Recovery from a Major Natural Disaster*, University of Colorado Monograph 41, Boulder.

Stagl, R. (1981) Terremoto e ricostruzione secondo gli uffici tecnici dei 45 communi disastrati, *Ricostruire*, 15, 5:8–19.

Steuer, M. (1979) *Wahrnehmung und Bewertung von Naturrisiken am Beispiel zweier ausgewahlter Gemeindefraktionen im Friaul*, Munchener Geographische Hefte 43, Regensburg.

Strassoldo, R. and Cattarinussi, B. (eds) (1978) *Friuli–La prova del terremoto*, Milano.

Ventura, F. (1982) *The Earthquake in Campania and Basilicata (Italy) of 23rd November 1980 – The Nature of the State's Emergency Interventions and the Future Quality of Reconstruction*, ISIG, Gorizia.

5

The Impact of the Disaster in Mexico City, September 1985

Maria Teresa Gutierrez de MacGregor

Mexico is situated in a highly seismic region of the world; therefore the country is, and will continue to be, subject to earthquakes. So far, scientists have not been able to predict either the timing of earthquakes or their magnitude.

According to tradition and history, Mexico City (founded in 1325 as Tenochtitlan) has been afflicted by natural disasters, such as floods and earthquakes, since pre-Hispanic times. The damage done by earthquakes to Mexico City varies through time depending on their intensity, but it can be stated that, because of rapid demographic growth, their impact has become greater, reaching alarming proportions today in terms of the cost in lives and property as well as the resulting social and economic problems, which become greater and more numerous.

One of the most populous cities in the world, Mexico City is located in the centre of the country, at an altitude of 2240 m, on the bed of an old lake surrounded by mountains, some of which reach heights over 5,000 m, as in the case of Iztaccihuatl and Popocatepetl. Mexico City has become more vulnerable because of its rapid demographic spatial growth caused largely by the strong centralization of the country's main activities – economics, politics, administration, education, finances, etc, – which take place in the capital.

The effects of the partial destruction of the city caused by the earthquakes of 19–20 September 1985, though apparently forgotten, will continue rebounding for a long time because of their impact on the organization and planning of the city itself. Now, when the emotional shock has lessened, is the best time to try to explain, by means of papers and lectures, the reality of the city today and what positive or negative changes have been the outcome of the catastrophe as well as the policies that are being followed.

From time immemorial there has been a prophecy regarding Mexico City, the 'legend of the fifth sun'. The people of the sun, the Aztecs, believed according to their religion that life on earth had disappeared four times before, when the sun had gone down, and that only through sacrifice to the gods had it been reborn. These catastrophes, which their priests remembered, had taken place over long periods of time: the first time the world had ended when men had been devoured by tigers; the second, life was destroyed by hurricane-like winds; the third, by fire; the fourth, by an overwhelming rain that lasted several days; and the fifth, which is to end the period in which we are living today, is prophesied to take the form of an earthquake. According to tradition, catastrophe could occur every 52 years. Thus, on a given day, the fire was put out in every home and the population gathered at the Hill of the Star, located south of Mexico City, within the basin, and waited in prayer for some astrological signal that announced the danger to be over; then, there on the hill the new fire was lit and the priests handed out torches to the population so that passing from hand to hand, it would reach all homes (Caso, 1953).

It is strange that the priests should predict the destruction of their people, in the near future, through an earthquake. This, of course, lets us know that from time immemorial there were earthquakes in Tenochtitlan, today Mexico City. The earliest earthquake recorded which took place in Tenochtitlan, was in 1460 during the reign of Emperor Moctezume I (Manzanilla, 1986), but the strongest earthquakes felt in Mexico City took place in 1858, 1911, 1932 and 1957 (Rosenblueth and Meli, 1986), and the most recent were those which took place on 19 and 20 September 1985, the first with a magnitude of 8.1 on the Richter scale, the second registering 7.5.

The most frequent cause of earthquakes in Mexico City lies in a break located in the Pacific Ocean off the western coast of Mexico, where the Cocos plate goes under the North American plate. The Cocos plate moves approximately 5.0 cm a year in relation to the North American plate (See figure 5.1), this being one of the most

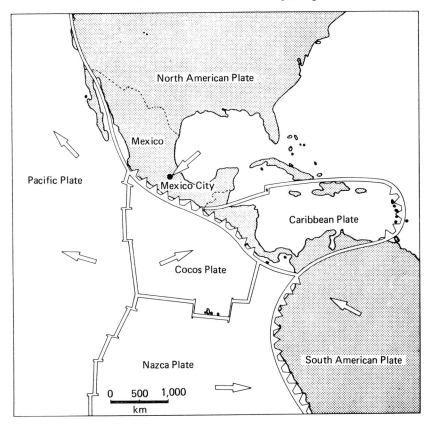

Figure 5.1   Plate tectonics affecting Mexico City

intensely active locations in the world. Great amounts of energy accumulate in the break and, when they are freed, cause the great earthquakes that afflict Mexico (Krishna, quoted by Tonda, 1986).

On 19 September 1985, the seismic wave travelled 400 km before reaching Mexico City at 7.19 a.m. It is thought that there were two physical factors that contributed to the magnitude of the catastrophe: the phenomenon of resonance when the seismic wave reached the sediment of the old lake that used to exist in Mexico's basin, which amplified the phenomenon, and the long duration of the vibration (Beck and Hall, 1986). In the zone of the break in the Pacific Ocean, energy continued to be freed through repeated quakes, the strongest of which took place the following day at 7.35 p.m.

In the past 50 years Mexico City has undergone unprecedented and anarchic demographic and spatial growth, from 1 million inhabitants in 1930 to 17 million in 1985, and from an area of 86.1 sq km to approximately 1,200 sq km. In 1985 its inhabitants represented 22 per cent of the country's total population and 37 per cent of its urban population. Over the past 15 years the metropolitan zone has grown annually by about 500,000 people and by more than 40 sq km (Garza, 1986). The tragic results of the earthquake in Mexico City were the more moving because of the high numbers of human losses due to the high demographic concentration in a mere 0.06 per cent of the nation's territory.

After the earthquake the extremely grave social tensions that existed in the capital were significantly accentuated by the great economic and social inequality among the inhabitants, where the most destitute and the groups with the lowest incomes were in general harmed the most. The earthquake sharpened the problems of a city that already suffered great deficiencies. Before the earthquake over 50 per cent of the population lived in unsatisfactory housing conditions; unemployment and underemployment affected over 40 per cent of the economically active population; and traffic jams caused the loss of 3 million man-hours per day (Gonzalez Salazar, 1986).

The greatest harm was done to the drinking-water supply, with the service reduced, within and outside the disaster area, to about 20 per cent of its usual volume, and to the transmission equipment for telephones and telegraphs, national and international, which worked at only 60 per cent of its capacity; even after a month had gone by only 40 per cent of the service had been re-established (CONACyT, 1986). The electricity supply was interrupted because the plants were damaged; the temporary suspension of the supply paralysed the underground and tram systems, and the traffic lights went out, causing traffic chaos.

It has been pointed out that Mexico City was not (nor is it) equipped with emergency centres situated at strategic points that would maintain the flow of, at least, the essentials: food, water, medicines and qualified personnel with rescue equipment. For this reason the civil population immediately improvised means of helping, before the government reacted. Rescue groups and brigades appeared with the intention of saving the people who had been caught under the debris. The solidarity of the Mexican people towards the victims ought to be stressed but, because there was neither a pre-established organization nor specialized equipment which would allow for greater efficiency and speed in rescue in cases such as these, the number of victims was higher than it should have been.

To quote Rosenblueth and Meli (1986): 'The city is divided into three zones: hills, the lake, and one of transition. The breaks affected the lake zone on a fringe where the land has a depth of between 20 and 35 m; in this zone the land is compressible, the waves were greatly amplified' (see figure 5.2). The greatest damage was done to buildings set on the old lake's alluvial deposits, which coincide with the centre of the city, not to the ones built on rocky soil (see figure 5.3).

Mexico City is so big that even though the earthquake was strongly felt everywhere, most of the population carried on with their usual tasks and did not realize what was happening until several hours later. Although the ravaged area is small (23 sq km) compared to the urban area (1,200 sq km), the disaster was outstanding because it affected one of the most vital and most densely populated areas in the city.

The earthquake took place in the morning, at 7.19 a.m.; if it had taken place later the number of deaths would have been higher, as seen from the data obtained from the Metropolitan Emergency Commission, which indicates that 5,727 buildings had been damaged, including 3,745 dwellings, 840 commercial buildings, 704 schools, 345 offices, 41 hospitals, 33 recreational buildings and 19 in the industrial sector (Galindo, 1985), where work usually begins at 8.00 a.m.

The data published about the disaster are contradictory, given the difficulty in evaluating the damages. For this reason, besides the data from the Metropolitan Emergency Commission, two other sources considered reliable were selected. First, the Economic Commission for Latin America, which stated that about 10,000 people died in collapsed buildings and 30,000 were injured; and that 30,000 dwellings were lost and 60,000 more must be repaired. It estimated that 150,000 people were left homeless and that, of these, about 30,000 were helped in shelters. The overall estimate of cost is that material losses reached $4,150 million. Secondly, Mendez (1985) cites the Department of the Treasury, which estimated the damages at $1,000–2,000 million, and the international consultants who esti-

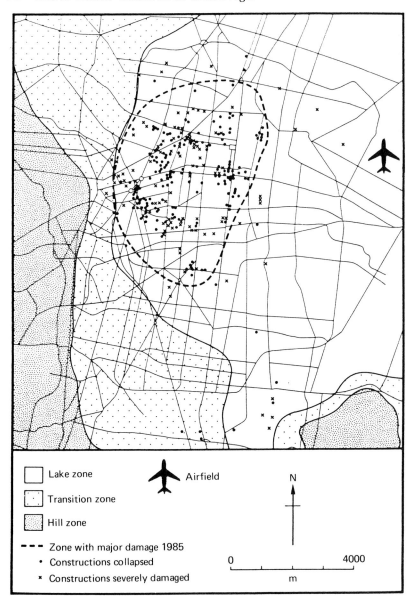

Figure 5.2   Subsoil zonation of Mexico City

mated them at $5,000 million. The lack of housing and the pressure from a large part of the population, which expressed its discontent in various ways, forced the President of Republic to decree in October 1985 an emergency measure expropriating 7,000 urban

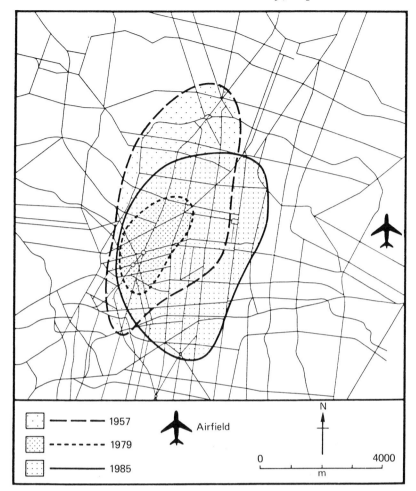

Figure 5.3   Location of earthquake damage zones in Mexico City

properties situated in the popular areas of the centre of Mexico City (Carrillo, 1985). This was such a significant move that it has been considered a historical precedent for urban expropriation in the country.

Some aspects of the catastrophe, such as emotional repercussions, are not easily measured. City people who, as a rule, are indifferent to what goes on around them, changed their attitude for several days and helped strangers. Unfortunately, this attitude did not last beyond three weeks; afterwards everybody returned to their usual behaviour.

International help was immediate. On 21 September, several specialized rescue brigades formed by experts from different countries arrived in Mexico City. Indeed, Mexico received help from 44 countries, socialist as well as capitalist, who provided food, medicines, medical supplies and equipment, demolition and rescue equipment, machinery, vehicles and clothes.

The earthquake emphasized that although the country is ruled by a federal government, the policy followed by every regime has been centralist in favour of Mexico City, and that the concentration of economic, commercial, administrative, political and financial activities in the capital makes it very vulnerable to both natural and man-made disasters. The last two regimes and the present one have all made proposals in favour of decentralization in order to decelerate growth in Mexico City, and as a result of the earthquake the government's interest in this has strengthened. On 9 October 1985 the National Reconstruction Commission was formed, including six committees; one of these is the Decentralization Committee, whose tasks are the following:

1   To specify the impact of the process of decentralization of the Federal Public Administration in social and economic activities.
2   To propose ways of stimulating the decentralization processes of education and the health services already at work.
3   To propose policies to decentralize economic activity in general as well as public services.
4   To analyse the ways of decentralizing higher education, science and technology.
5   To provide the means to select the cities which will be affected by decentralization.
6   To take into consideration the necessary relationship between decentralization, farming and animal husbandry production and regional development (Salinas de Gortari, 1986).

The urgency of the need to strengthen the decentralization process was noticeable during the establishment of the National Reconstruction Commission, when president Miguel de la Madrid (1986) stated:

The decentralization of national life needs to be supported by a reorganization of the Federal Public Administration in which the headquarters of the Secretariats will remain in the capital, but the resources, offices and, above all, power, will be decentralized as part of a greater process which includes higher education, industrial economic activity and services, commerce and finance.

Although the events that took place after the disaster hastened some of the actions tending towards decentralization, it is felt that the actions taken and the ones that will be taken have not shown, nor will they show, noticeable results, because even if some of the branch offices are decentralized, the amount of people moved will not be significant in a city where the number of inhabitants is estimated at 18 million in 1987 and whose growth is over half a million a year. To diminish regional inequalities effectively a great part of the federal budget should be invested in reinforcing development in the regions that are away from the country's central zone. But, most important, the population must be made conscious that natural disasters, with their tragic outcome, will continue to scourge the country and that, therefore, it should be ready, to the best of its abilities, to counteract their effect.

REFERENCES

Banamex (Banco Nacional de Mexico) (1985) *Exámen de la situación económica de México (Survey of the Economic Situation of Mexico)*, 61,719:434.

Beck, J. L. and Hall, J. F. (1986) Factors contributing to the catastrophe in Mexico City during the earthquake of September 19, 1985, *Geophysical Research Letters*, 13, 6:594.

Carrillo Arena, G. (1985) Coordinación de Vivienda Comisión Nacional de Reconstrucción, *Presidencia de la República* 241.

Caso, A. (1953) *El pueblo del Sol (People of the Sun)*, Fondo de Cultura Económica, México, D.F.

CONACyT y National Research Council (1986) Investigación para aprender de los sismos de septiembre 1985 en México (Investigation to understand the seismic activity of September 1985 in Mexico), *Informe técnico*, 20.

Galindo, M. (1985) Los sismos y el fracaso de la política económica (Earthquakes and the downfall of the economic policy), *Problemas del Desarrollo, Revista Latinoamericana de Economía*, Instituto de Investigaciones Economicas, UNAM, 16, 62–3:49.

Garza, G. (1986) Ciudad de México: Dinámica industrial y perspectivas de la descentralización después de terremoto (The City of Mexico: industrial dynamics and perspectives of the decentralization since the earthquake). *Descentralización Democracia en México*. Colegio de México:235.

González Salazar, G. (1986) Urbanismo, metropolización y subdesarrollo. Crísis Económica terremotos y politica económica (Urbanization, Metropolitanization and Underdevelopment. Economic Crisis, Earthquakes and Economic Policy. *Problemas del desarrollo: Revista Latinoamericana de Economía*, Instituto de Investigaciones Económicas, UNAM, 16, 62–3:175.

Madrid, M. de la (1985) Comité de Reconstrucción del Area Metropolitana de la Ciudad de México. Acuerdo que crea el Comité de Reconstrucción del Area Metropolitana de la Ciudad de México. (*Diario Oficial* 11 de octubre de 1985), Comisión Nacional de Reconstrucción, Presidencia de la República:52.

Madrid, M. de la (1986) Reconstrucción y Descentralización. Instalación de la Comisión Nacional de Reconstrucción. (*Diario Oficial* 9 de octubre de 1985), Comisión Nacional de Reconstrucción, Comité de Descentralización, Presidencia de la República:11.

Manzanilla, L. (1986) Relacion de los sosmos ocurridos en la Ciudad de México y sus efectos (Report on the seismic occurrences in the City of Mexico and their effects), *Revista Mexicana de Sociología* , Instituto de Investigaciones Sociales, UNAM, 48, 2:265.

Méndez Rodríguez, A. (1985) La politica urbana en la Ciudad de México (The urban policy in Mexico City), *Problemas de Desarrollo, Revista Latinoamericana de Economía*, Instituto de Investigaciones Económicas, UNAM, 16; 62–3:101.

Rosenblueth, E. and Meli, R. (1986) The 1985 earthquake: Causes and Effects in Mexico City, *Concrete International*:24–5.

Salinas de Gortari, C. (1986) Instalación del Comité de Descentralización. (*Diario Oficial* . 10 de octubre de 1985), Comisión Nacional de Reconstrucción, Comité de Descentralización, Presidencia de la Republica:23.

Tonda, J. (1986) México: zona de alta sismicidad, entrevista con Shri Krishna Singh (Mexico: Zone of high seismicity, interview with Shri Krishna Singh), *Información Scientifica y Tecnológica*, 8, 123:13.

6

Population Displacement due to Riverbank Erosion of the Jamuna in Bangladesh

K. Maudood Elahi

The shifting of major rivers in Bangladesh has long been a dominant enviromental problem affecting a sizeable population. Erosion by river is mainly hydrogeologic and when it is associated with a widespread flood, the magnitude of destruction is enormous. In Bangladesh, the rivers cause erosion due to their unstable character. This chapter concentrates on the river erosion due to the shifting of the Brahmaputra–Jamuna river and its impact on the human population. As background to the displacement mechanism of river erosion, this paper focuses first on the morphological behaviour of the Jamuna river, together with its shifting tendencies in recent times. The associated bankline shifts have been examined for the river using selected Landsat imageries, large-scale maps (C.S. maps), extensive field observation and anthropological investigation during 1984–6[1]. The consequent displacement of human population and habitat has been assessed for two census dates, 1961 and 1981, as well as by field survey data for two sample areas – Chilmari, in Kurigram district, and Kazipur, in Serajganj district, in northern and central Bangladesh respectively.

[1]A three-year research programme on the impact of riverbank erosion in Bangladesh was started in 1984 by the Departments of Geography of Jahangirnagar University (Bangladesh) and the University of Manitoba (Canada) sponsored by the International Development Research Centre (IDRC), Canada. Some preliminary data have been used in developing this paper. The author acted as the Principal Investigator of the research at the Bangladesh end.

THE JAMUNA RIVER

The Jamuna is the main river of Bangladesh, flowing from north to south and dividing the country approximately into two halves (see figure 6.1). It forms the lower part of the Brahmaputra–Jamuna drainage system. In the beginning of the nineteenth century, the Brahmaputra flowing through the Bengal upper delta deteriorated and started to flow through a new course; this became known as the Jamuna, but the upper reach still retained the old name. It is held that an abnormal flood in the late eighteenth century led to the change in the course of the Tista (a tributary to the Brahmaputra). This may have caused a diversion of the Brahmaputra into its present north-south channel, known as the Jamuna, though tectonic movements in the trough between the Barind and the Madhupur Tracts may have been partly responsible (Rashid, 1977).

The Brahmaputra–Jamuna river, one of the largest rivers of the world and originating in Tibet (China) as Tsang Po, is 2,700 km long and drains an area of about 600,000 sq km of which less than 10 per cent lies within Bangladesh (figure 6.1). As it passes through China and India, cutting through the Himalayas, it maintains a more or less stable course, but as soon as it enters the Bengal basin it assumes a braided pattern consisting of several channels separated by small islands/sandbars, called *chars* within the course. During the last 200 years or so, the channels have been swinging between the main valley walls. As a result, during monsoon seasons, extensive overbank spill, bank erosion, bankline shift and *char* land shifts have become typical for the Jamuna.

Data available for recent decades indicate that the bank spill from the Jamuna during the 1966 flood reached a maximum of about 7 per cent of its total discharge of 689,000 m^3/s between Bahadurabad and Aricha, and in 1974 it reached about 10 per cent of its total discharge of 908,000 m^3/s at Bahadurabad. The average annual flow of the Jamuna is 19,250 m^3/s (GOB/JMBA, 1986).

BANKLINE CHANGES AND THE EROSION PHENOMENON

The Jamuna is typically a braided river consisting of several channels; these can change courses in a short period of time, and islands

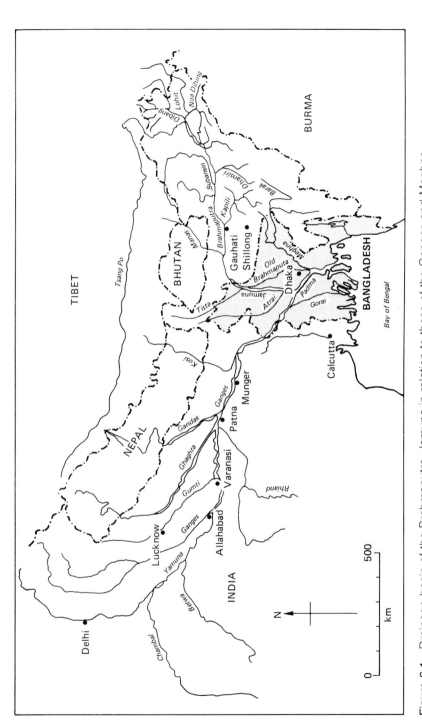

Figure 6.1   Drainage basin of the Brahmaputra–Jamuna in relation to those of the Ganges and Meghna

that have remained in position for many years may disappear in the course of a major flood. Moreover, as it flows through the alluvial plain, its banks are being actively eroded, involving both lateral and vertical erosional processes.

During the last 200 years, the Jamuna has been very active, shifting laterally between valley walls, so that some reaches are now as much as 19 km apart (Khan and Rashid, 1985). The bankline changes and overall width of the river have been studied dating back to 1830 (IECO, 1964; Coleman, 1968; and Huq, 1983). From these studies the following conclusions, as to the morphological change of the Jamuna may be made:

1   rates of bank erosion and deposition are very high, but there are places where erosion exceeds deposition;
2   the rate of erosion of the left bank is lower than that of the right bank. There has been a tendency for the Jamuna to migrate in a westerly direction, causing widespread erosion along the right bank.
3   shoals and *chars* also change positions over time; in some places *chars* often disappear following a flood;
4   major flow channel swings during the monsoonal floods and the formation of new channels are common features.

Recent Changes in the Jamuna Bankline

The sequential Landsat data of recent years indicate a striking braided pattern of the Jamuna and the pattern is ever-changing. This is reflected in figure 6.2, which shows the changing braided channels of the lower Jamuna in post-monsoon season for the years 1973, 1976, 1980 and 1984, and indicates the extent to which the banklines are affected by the channel shifts and erosion in various places. It is seen that both Chilmari (not covered entirely in figure 6.2) and Kazipur, together with the other places, lie in the active erosional zone of the river.

At Chilmari, the width of the river is about 12.5 km. The general behaviour of the river is causing the Jamuna to exert pressure on its right bank at Chilmari, where the administrative headquarters were eroded away during the late 1970s. The bankline at Kazipur is also under the threat of active erosion, and the administrative headquarters there were eroded away in 1980. The average annual rate of

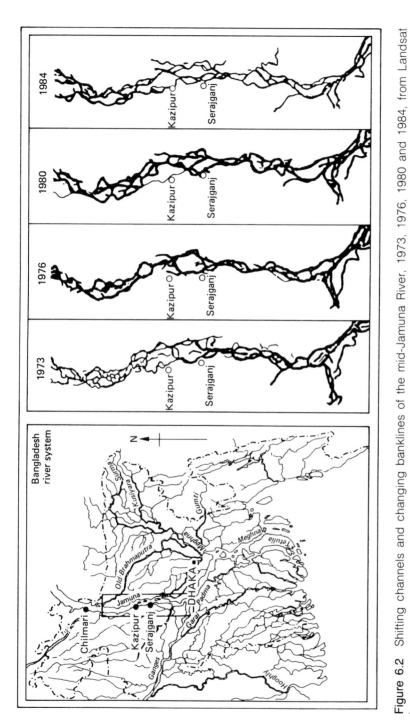

Figure 6.2 Shifting channels and changing banklines of the mid-Jamuna River, 1973, 1976, 1980 and 1984, from Landsat imagery

erosion is about 244 m (Khan and Rashid, 1985). The Landsat imageries show that a minor offshoot channel parting from the main flow some 16 km upstream of Kazipur is diverting the water flow to cause bank erosion in the Kazipur area. There are permanent *chars* between the channels with human habitation, many subject to periodic erosion. For both the areas, bankline and *char* land erosions are attributed to the meandering nature of the channels within the valley walls of the Jamuna, a process most likely to continue because of the unconsolidated alluvial deposits of the Jamuna flood plain. Both field observation and the interpretation of recent remote sensing data support this view, and the bankline delimitation using Landsat imageries (1976–84) indicates that the river is shifting further westward.

Riverbank Erosion and its Impact on Human Population

A detailed study at micro-level was conducted during 1984–6 to investigate the extent of the impact of bankline erosion on selected aspects of human habitat in Chilmari and Kazipur. For this purpose, a field survey was conducted in Chilmari and Kazipur *upazilas*[2] and population data were also collected from the census sources for 1961 and 1981 (GOP, 1964; GOB, 1985).

In both Chilmari and Kazipur a large number of *mouzas* are affected by bank erosion. Forty *mouzas* out of a total of 60 and 117 respectively in the Chilmari and Kazipur *upazilas* under study were found to have been liable to active erosion during the period under investigation (see table 6.1). Total amounts of gross land erosion in Chilmari and Kazipur were 6,849 and 17,445 acres respectively. The amounts of land accreted were too small in both the areas, so in sum erosion greatly exceeded accretion in both the *upazilas*.

The worst affected *mouzas* were in the unions of Astamirchar, Raniganj and part of Ramna in Chilmari; and Char Girish, Subhagachha and Khas Rajbari in Kazipur (see table 6.2). In addition, most *char mouzas* and those along the bankline are liable to erosion at some time or other within a given period. Although the 245 km

[2]A *mouza* is an area surveyed and recorded for the purpose of revenue administration. An individual village or a group of villages, depending on population, comprises a *mouza*. A number of *mouzas* forms a union, a number of which constitute an *upazila* (sub-district). The next administrative unit in the hierarchy is the district.

Table 6.1 Extent of erosion and accretion in Chilmari and Kazipur *upazilas* by unions and number of *mouzas* affected, 1961–1981

Unions	Total mouzas	Unaffected mouzas	Eroded mouzas	Acres	Accreted mouzas	Acres	Erosion–accretion balance
CHILMARI[a]							
Nayarhat	10	0	8	2,938	2	29	− 2,909
Chilmari	10	0	9	52	1	13	− 39
Astamirchar	22	1	18	3,840	3	563	− 3,279
Raniganj	5	2	3	13	0	0	− 13
Thanahat	7	7	0	0	0	0	0
Ramna	6	4	2	6	0	0	− 6
Total	60	14	40	6,849	6	605	− 6,246
KAZIPUR[b]							
Sonamukhi	9	9	0	0	0	0	0
Chalitadanga	12	12	0	0	0	0	0
Gandhail	9	7	1	17	1	46	+29
Maijbari	8	5	2	392	1	7	− 385
Kazipur	10	6	4	2,628	0	0	− 2,628
Subhagachha	8	2	5	561	1	9	− 552
Khas Rajbari	15	4	4	116	7	75	− 41
Char Girish	21	0	16	8,617	5	632	− 7,985
Natuapara	8	2	4	1,087	2	6	− 1,081
Tekani	8	0	3	2,999	5	1,217	− 1,782
Nischintapur	9	1	1	1,028	7	3,493	+ 2,465
Total	117	48	40	17,445	29	5,485	− 11,960

[a] Total area covered by survey: 51,950 acres.
[b] Total area covered by survey: 76,674 acres.

Table 6.2 Proportion of erosion-affected areas in the *mouzas* by unions in Chilmari and Kazipur *upazilas*, 1981

| Unions | *Percentage of area of mouzas eroded* | | | | |
	Below 20	*20–40*	*40–60*	*60 and over*	*Total mouzas*
CHILMARI					
Nayarhat	6	1	0	1	8
Chilmari	9	0	0	0	9
Astamirchar	8	0	0	10	18
Raniganj	3	0	0	0	3
Thanahat	0	0	0	0	0
Ramna	2	0	0	0	2
Total	28	1	0	11	40
KAZIPUR					
Sonamukhi	0	0	0	0	0
Chalitadanga	0	0	0	0	0
Gandhail	1	0	0	0	1
Maijbari	1	1	0	0	2
Kazipur	1	1	1	1	4
Subhagachha	3	2	0	0	5
Khas Rajbari	3	0	0	1	4
Char Girish	1	0	0	15	16
Natuarpara	3	1	0	0	4
Tekani	2	0	1	0	3
Nischintapur	0	0	0	1	1
Total	15	5	2	18	40

Bangladesh Water Development Board (BWDB) embankment protects the bankline *mouzas* from flood, it is hardly an effective deterrent to bank erosion, and therefore, breaches in the embankment as a result of erosion are not uncommon. In recent years, *mouzas* like Uari, Patoari and Kharkharia in Chilmari, and Dhekuria, Meghai, Maijbari and Khudbandi in Kazipur are under the ravage of active erosion. In all, 13.0 and 15.6 per cent of the net areas of Chilmari and Kazipur respectively were eroded away in the 20-year period to 1981. This trend of bank erosion has been more or less sustained during the 1980s.

The consequent impact of bank erosion in the *mouzas* in both areas is immediately reflected in the variations in the changes in population. A review of the variations is made for the 1961–81

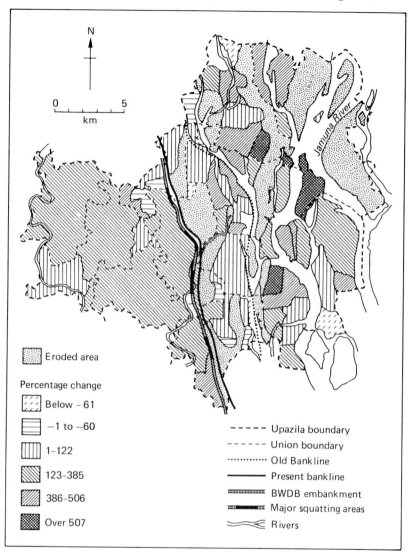

Figure 6.3 Kazipur: percentage population change, 1961–81

census period. As expected, the highly erosional *mouzas* registered negative to very low rates of change in population. Most *char mouzas* are of this nature (see figures 6.3 and 6.4). Some relatively stable *char mouzas* have registered high to extremely high positive changes in population. This characteristic is pronounced in both the *upazilas*. The reasons for this situation may be explained by the

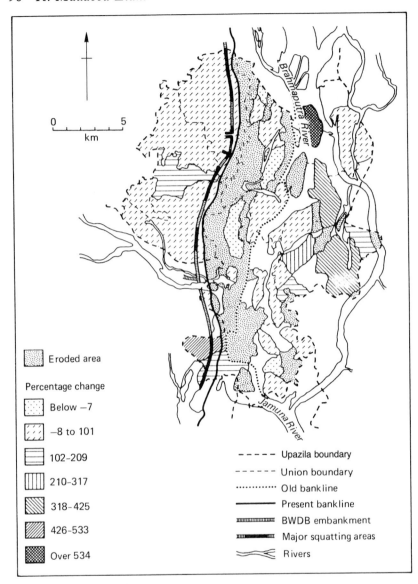

Figure 6.4   Chilmari: percentage population change, 1961–81

availability of relatively fertile land and by the possibility of growing at least one good crop in the *char* immediately after the monsoonal flood.

The bankline and the mainland *mouzas* of Chilmari registered
medium/low to medium/high variations of population indicating

that the population dynamics are more or less stable (see figure 6.4). But the low level of population change compared to Kazipur is quite distinctive. This is related to the pysical and economic characteristics of the *upazila*. Chilmari is a remote *upazila* with poor communications, slowly developing physical infrastructure and chronic food shortages. It has the record of two severe local famines within a decade, in 1974 and 1984. The high mortality level, particularly infant mortality, has long been affecting the natural growth of the population, and some out-migration of population may also have affected the change in the population increase.

In Kazipur, a fairly high increase in population is marked in the bankline and mainland *mouzas* and at least one *mouza* recorded a very high increase. This situation may be explained, in contrast to Chilmari, by a less mobile population and by the agricultural potential of the area. It may be mentioned here that the areas of high to very high population changes, as in some bankline *mouzas* and a number of *char mouzas* in both the *upazilas*, have been the result of the movement of some displaced population into the *mouzas* affecting the rates of population increase in a positive way. It is also worth mentioning here that a number of *mouzas* where bank erosion is quite active, in both Chilmari and Kazipur, had still registered high or very high population changes (see figures 6.3 and 6.4). This is due to the existence of the BWDB embankment near an erosion-prone area offering shelter to a sizeable number of households of displacees – many living there for years in the hope that some day they will have access to the emergent land.

This analysis of population variation in Chilmari and Kazipur *upazilas* is based on the assumptions of the lack of any significant in-migration of population from outside (in fact, any hazard-prone *upazila* is an unattractive place for in-migration in Bangladesh), and of the internal process of population adjustment within the area. The spatial variations of population remarkably influence those of households in both the *upazilas*. This is borne out by the high degree of association between the proportions of variations of population and households in the *mouzas* during 1961–81. The regression values for Chilmari and Kazipur were 0.700 and 0.715 respectively.

DISPLACEMENT OF POPULATION: THE CASE OF THE DISPLACEES

Besides the recorded changes in population and households influenced by riverbank erosion in the Jamuna flood plain, the
phenomenon of population dislocation is evident through the extensive squatting settlements along the river and in nearby areas. Most
of these displacees have suffered household-level dislocation and
family disintegration due to short- or, more often, long-term socio-
economic and demographic disruption, and many have experienced
multiple displacement during their lifetimes.

Riverbank erosion, often associated with abnormal flooding,
creates human misery, damaging crops and properties and dislocating various social and economic linkages. Had population dislocation been caused only by flood, economic recovery would be
possible within a predictable time, but the victims of riverbank
erosion suffer the entire loss of their land, the main sustenance of
the farming households in rural Bangladesh. In general, economic
recovery is not possible by the next monsoon, even if a farmer has a
little land left. The situation in the erosion-prone areas is thus one
of continuing gradual economic deterioration of the people affected.

As a result of the abnormal 1984 flood and associated bank
erosion along the Jamuna flood plain, more than 40,000 households
were affected in nine *upazilas* in Kurigram district. In Chilmari
alone, about 500 households took shelter along a 4.6 km stretch of
the BWDB embankment near Ramna and Dakshin Uari. In Kazipur
upazila, nearly 900 households had joined the existing squatting
settlements on the BWDB embankment. There are no statistics as
to the exact number of people living on the 245 km long embankment from Kaunia (Rangpur) to Hurasagar (Pabna). However,
according to an estimate by the BWDB, about 7,000 households
were living on the embankment in 1982. This seems to be an
underestimate as a higher figure was returned for the Kazipur–
Serejganj area alone. In Chilmari–Kurigram area, the bank erosion
of the Tista and the Brahmaputra–Jamuna has uprooted nearly
5,000 households during the past decade or so. Chilmari
alone lost about 13 per cent of its total area dislocating about 20
per cent of its population. Some households have been the victims
of the phenomenon more than once, and many live in makeshift
shelters on the BWDB embankment. There are major concen-

trations of squatters, contributing to slum developments, in Patoari, Uari, Ramna, Kharkharia and Bhasanpara Bhatirpara *mouzas*.

The very presence of about 8,000 uprooted families living on the 86 km stretch of the BWDB embankment from Kazipur to Chouhali via Serajganj alone testifies to the magnitude of the problems in the mid-Jamuna flood plain (Zaman and Bablu, 1985). They were uprooted from their villages over the past few years by bank erosion along one of the worst erosion affected areas in the whole flood plain and probably in the whole country. About 23 per cent of the total area of Kazipur was eroded, dislocating about 16 per cent of its population in 1981. Eight villages and the administrative head-quarters of Kazipur have been eroded away in the past seven years or so. It has been estimated that about 18,000 people were displaced due to riverbank erosion in Kazipur *upazila* during 1974–81, of whom a little over 12,000 stayed in the same *upazila* on the roads, BWDB embankment and *Khaslands* (common land) (Haque, 1985). The flood of 1984 made the situation worse. Kazipur *upazila* sources reported that a total of 29,000 households were affected by the flood, many being erosion victims from *char* areas (Zaman and Bablu, 1985). In Kazipur, the major slum and squatting settlements are located in Subhagachha, Maijbari, Meghai and Khodbandi *mouzas* and around Banglabazar.

As a result of bank erosion of the Jamuna in and around Serajganj town, the squatters number about 5,550, and they live in slum conditions on the railway track (abandoned due to erosion threat) and the BWDB embankment. Moreover, an estimated total of 70,000 households have taken refuge on the BWDB embankment along the Jamuna from Kaunia (Rangpur) to Hurasagar (Pabna) alone. The number of the displacees taking shelter in these areas is increasing and there are rare instances of people moving out from the embankment or roadsides after they had once settled down (Elahi, 1987).

The principal occupations of the displacees are mostly in the informal sector of the local economy, including wage labour, both agricultural and non-agricultural. The farming displacees survive on the *kod* tenure arrangement, taking fixed-term lease of land from big farmers, and many are engaged in share-cropping. About 53 per cent of all displaced households are thus engaged in agricultural occupations. Some engage in small and seasonal businesses and in some households one or more members have moved out to nearby towns to supplement family income.

The housing conditions of the displacees in squatting settlements, as expected, are very poor. The houses mostly occupy the inner side of the embankment overlooking the river, as the outer slope is usually adjacent to privately owned lands. The local administration does not seem to recognize their existence and is unaware of the exact number of the slum dwellers and the squatting population living on the embankment and other peripheral lands in rural areas. To the local administration, as the slums do not definitely exist as a 'village', they have no geographic or administrative entity. Hence, virtually no developmental measure reaches these displaced people. Moreover, a number of non-governmental organizations (NGOs) working in nearby areas have no programme for these people since their activities are guided by the specific guidelines of local development in rural areas. The displacees are not easily absorbed in the local *samaj* (the social unit) and are often subject to hatred from local communities and generally looked down upon as potential threat to the local stable populace and to the existing resource base. To others, their existence is merely regarded as the potential reservoir for urban squatting in the country.

CONCLUDING REMARKS

The above discussion merely outlines the extent of bankline shift and associated bank erosion of the river Jamuna. The resultant impact on human habitat has been examined, taking Chilmari and Kazipur *upazilas* as case study areas. It has been found that the erosion phenomenon has a direct bearing on differential population change and on related human occupancy and bankline settlements of the displacees. A striking aspect of human occupancy in the erosion-prone areas is the development of rural slums inhabited by the displacees, the victims of riverbank erosion. The BWDB flood protection embankment along the right bank of the Jamuna is almost permanently inhabited by these people. The explanation of this situation is that they generally tend to stay on in areas closer to the original places of residence, hence the very high population increase in a number of *char mouzas* in the Jamuna. Hope of recovery of land in emerging *char* areas and desire to live with their own *samaj* make them relatively less mobile and often almost permanently settled in the rural slum conditions. Although many tend to survive by dint of enduring physical hardship, shared poverty and economic sufferings, the quality of life, living and habitat conditions tend to deteriorate beyond normal comprehension.

The current state of land use and the land tenure system in rural Bangladesh leaves a pessimistic future for the displaced population. The existing rules governing *char* lands in Bangladesh (Presidential Order no. 135 of 1972) provide that all newly emergent lands previously lost by flooding should be restored not to the original owner but only to the government. The objectives of this order were (1) to recover all such lands from the control of the local landlords (*jotdars*) and (2) to redistribute newly emergent lands among the landless and small peasants who have less than 8.5 acres of land for resettlement locally. In reality, inequalities in land ownership coupled with local power struggles and violence mean that the resettlement programme is either hindered or delayed. And in practice, the displaced households have little access to these lands. On the other hand, with over 50 per cent of all rural households in the country being functionally landless (BBS, 1981)and with little hope of their reabsorption within the rural economy in a substantial way, these slums gradually assume a semi-permanent feature in the rural landscape and act as the sources of potential urban squatting. Under these circumstances, the sooner an economic rehabilitation and land reallocation policy for the benefit of the displacees, particularly in the erosion-prone areas, is adopted, the better. One way to do this would be the recovery of all *khas* land allegedly occupied by the big farmers and the influential villagers, and redistribute these to the landless displaced population. Secondly, the newly emerged *char* lands that are also allegedly occupied by the local landlords and politically influential persons in rural areas (Zaman, 1985) should be recovered for distribution amongst the rural displacees. These two measures alone would effectively pave the way for both physical and economic rehabilitation of these people, and would help to arrest their gradual townward drift. As interim measures the following three suggestions could also be considered. First, since the BWDB embankments are often damaged by the squatters through the growing slum construction, and the BWDB's efforts to evict them have never been successful, the dwellers in these areas could be trained to maintain, and entrusted with the responsibility of maintenance of a given stretch of embankment. This could include a large-scale programme of tree plantation and regular repair of the embankment with a view to strengthening it. Secondly, construction of low-cost housing with sanitary and clean drinking water facilities, as has been done in the coastal cyclone-prone areas, should be initiated in order to improve the displacees' living environment. In this, both the relevant government machinery and the NGOs could play very effective roles. And thirdly, the landless displacees could be organized at the local level for employment in alternative economic activities.

Failure to formulate and implement a positive policy for rehabilitation of these people will make the rural resource base and living conditions only more vulnerable in the face of the ever-increasing proportion of rural landlessness and rural squatting in the country.

REFERENCES

BBS (Bangladesh Bureau of Statistics) (1981) *Statistical Yearbook of Bangladesh*, Dhaka.

Coleman, J. M. (1968) Brahmaputra River: Channel Processes and Sedimentation, *Sedimentary Geology*, B: 129–239.

Elahi, K. M. (1987) Rural Bastees and the Phenomenon of Rural Squatting due to Riverbank Erosion in Bangladesh, Seminar on Shelter for Homeless, Urban Development Directorate, Government of Bangladesh, Dhaka.

GOB (Government of Bangladesh) (1985) Census Data for Chilmari and Kazipur Upazilas, Bangladesh Bureau of Statistics (unpublished computerized release of 1981 census data).

GOB/JMBA (1986) *Jamuna Bridge Appraisal Study*, Rendel Palmer and Tritton, NEDECO and Bangladesh Consultants Ltd, Dhaka.

GOP (Government of Pakistan) (1964) *District Census Report, 1961*: Pabna and Rangpur, Ministry of Home Affairs, Dhaka.

Haque, C. E. (1985) Impact of Riverbank Erosion in Kazipur: An Application of Landsat Data, REIS Workshop, Jahangirnagar University, Dhaka.

Huq, N. (1983) *Application of Remote Sensing Technology for Detecting Fluvial Changes of the Ganges and Brahmaputra-Jamuna River Courses in Bangladesh* , SPARRSO, Dhaka.

IECO (Intenational Engineering Company) (1964) *East Pakistan Water and Power Development Authority Master Plan*, California, 2 vols.

Khan, A. R. and Rashid, A. (1985) Morphological Processes and Erosion Phenomenon of Brahmaputra Right Bank and Bhola Area of Lower Meghna Estuary, REIS Working Paper, Jahangirnagar University, Dhaka.

Rashid, H. er. (1977) *Geography of Bangladesh*, University Press Ltd., Dhaka.

Zaman, M. Q. (1985) Endemic Land Conflict and Violence in Char Villages of Bangladesh, REIS Workshop, Jahangirnagar University, Dhaka.

Zaaman, M. Q. and Bablu, A. I. (1985) Rural Bastees: a Socioeconomic Background to the Squatters on the Jamuna Right Bank Embankment, REIS Workshop, Jahangirnagar University, Dhaka.

7

The Hazard Potential of Drought for the Population of the Sahel

C. R. de Freitas

INTRODUCTION

The Sahel, a strip of land stretching across most of Africa along the southern edge of the Sahara Desert, is the world's casebook on drought and desertification. The horror of suffering from drought-induced malnutrition and famine, the countless lives lost and the amount of aid given are now familiar themes. Human and physical processes that determine the drought hazard for the people in the area have been the focus of a large amount in interdisciplinary research. However, the links between population and the environmental processes are complex and much remains to be done.

This chapter reassesses current knowledge on the drought hazard in the Sahel with a view to identifying the potential for and susceptibility to drought-related disasters in the region. The risk to human communities from the drought hazard is reviewed in terms of socio-economic, cultural and environmental factors involved and their links with population. Patterns of causality are traced, aimed at highlighting the way in which societies respond to climate variability as well as the way in which this response may affect vulnerability to drought.

An attempt is made to show that the impact of drought on population in the Sahel is inextricably linked to feedback processes between the atmosphere and the land surface as modified and used by the very population that is at risk. It is argued that the initiative in the hazard lies with nature and therefore the potential for disaster, or potential impact intensity on population, is broadly set by natural forces.

A theoretical reference state is depicted schematically in figure 7.1(a). It shows that the impact on society of physical events of variable magnitude, in the present case climate or rainfall, depends on the vulnerability of the society to that variable outside a zone of insensitivity to significant damage. Impact or damage depends, therefore, as much on the vulnerability of the society as it does on the magnitude of the physical event itself. However, it is argued that in the Sahel, the severity of the impact is largely a function of the size, distribution and land-based activity of the population. The degree of risk to the population, therefore, will depend on the socio-economic, cultural and political forces that provide a context for the climatic events.

In contemporary societies in the developing countries of Africa the effects of drought seem to be repetitious, probably because the effects of climatic variability are aggravated by rising population and the absence, or reduced scale, of demographic responses that in earlier times served to reduce the size of the population greatly over the short term and suppress population recovery rates. There also exists the added effect of human-induced feedback processes that accentuate and even perpetuate drought phases.

Figure 7.2 provides a conceptual framework for a discussion of the drought hazard in the Sahel. It traces linkages between the climatic context of drought, human response to the hazard, environmental degradation and demographic impact that collectively affect feedback processes that ultimately modify both the vulnerability and susceptibility of the population to drought.

THE CLIMATE CONTEXT

During this century, great droughts have occurred in the Sahel in 1910–14, 1940–4 and, most recently, in 1968–, one which has not yet ended. Because the period 1968–73 was so dry it became known as 'the Sahelian drought', but it is in reality part of a two-decade-long fluctuation of rainfall over all of sub-Saharan Africa. In fact, there is a persistent downward trend in rainfall, well below long-term mean values (see figure 7.3). The climatological record shows that desiccation of the Sahel began in the late 1950s, preceded by a ten-year

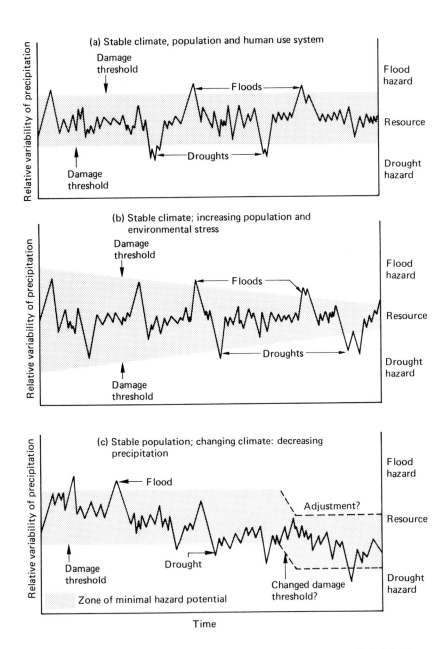

Figure 7.1 Hazard thresholds in relation to precipitation in the Sahel for three different scenarios: (a) dynamic equilibrium of climate, population and human use of the environment; (b) stable climate with increased stress on the environment from modern farming methods, overgrazing, depletion of vegetation for fuel, etc. and (c) stable population along with climatic change towards

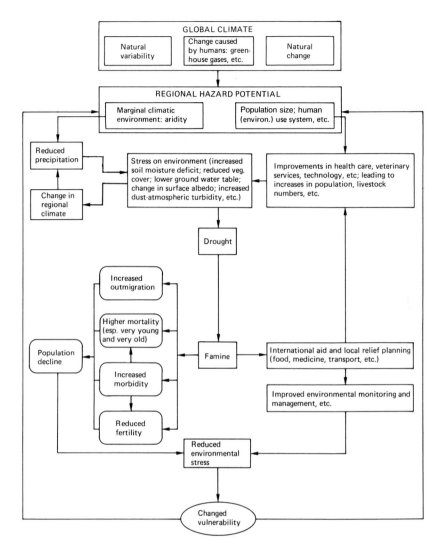

Figure 7.2 A conceptual framework for the drought hazard in the Sahel, showing linkages between the climatic context of drought, environmental degradation, demographic response and vulnerability to the hazard

drier conditions. The shaded area shows a zone where damage from variation in precipitation is negligible.

Source: (a) is adapted from Burton and Hewitt (1974) and Heathcote (1985)

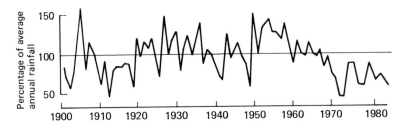

Figure 7.3   Rainfall variability since 1900 for all available rainfall stations (33) in the Sahelian zone
Source: Nicholson (1985)

period when rainfall was well above normal. The end of the colonial period came just as the deterioration in climate was beginning, and many countries in this part of Africa were in the throes of settling into their recently acquired independence. According to Hare (1983), the decade of relatively high rainfall may have misled African statesmen into believing that lasting change had occurred.

Wherever relatively long rainfall records exist, the data show that drought is part of the normal climate of the Sahel. This is not surprising since rainfall in semi-arid regions is highly variable in time and space. However, Nicholson (1980, 1981) has shown that, unlike rainfall regimes in semi-arid areas of the globe generally, Sahelian droughts display remarkable spatial coherence in that droughts often occur over the whole sub-Saharan belt simultaneously. This increases the areal extent of the damage and the impact potential for individual countries as well as the region as a whole.

In some areas there are signs of two-to-three-year rhythms in rainfall overridden by larger amplitude variations of 10 or 30 years, but the evidence is too weak for useful prediction (Landsberg, 1975; Hare, 1983). There is also a tendency for both dry years and wet years to persist in groups of two or more consecutive years (Landsberg, 1975). This, as will be discussed below, increases the regional hazard potential, since there can be increased cultivation and grazing during wet years resulting in severe overloading of the carrying capacity of the land during subsequent dry periods.

These perturbations of climate are best thought of as climatic variability (see figure 7.2). Climatic change, on the other hand, is said to exist when a distinct signal is visible above short-term variation. It is now widely accepted by climatologists that the stability of world climate is being threatened by the build-up of 'greenhouse' gases from human pollution, mainly carbon dioxide, and that climatic change resulting from this is currently under way. Whether the potential effect on dry climates in the sub-tropics over the next 100 years or so will be significant is difficult to assess. Furthermore, it is difficult to distinguish between natural and human causes of climatic change. It is clear, nevertheless, that short-term climatic changes, referred to as climatic fluctuations, have occurred in the Sahel. The data show, for example, that such an episode currently exists.

CAUSAL PROCESSES

Accurate data are hard to come by, but recent population growth rates in the Sahel have been estimated at more than 2.5 per cent per annum, giving an annual increase in population in the region of around 1.5 million (Grainger, 1982). Furthermore, the populations of nomads are increasing as fast as the urban and sedentary rural populations. This growing number of people and their use of the land has had a significant impact on the environment of the Sahel.

The fact is that drought is a climatological problem whereas desertification is part of an ecosystem structure where there is both drought and stress on the land, essentially as a result of overpopulation. This interaction with the environment is shown schematically in figure 7.4. Since most of the non-urban population engages in subsistence farming and herding, the amount of rainfall determines the carrying capacity of the land. Desertification sets in when the numbers of people and livestock exceed the carrying capacity. In pre-colonial Africa, the number of grazing livestock and the size of the area cultivated increased with rainfall. As a dry cycle began, overgrazing and overcultivation resulted in severe environmental stress and degradation. Carrying capacity decreased and population declined accordingly as people either died or moved away.

In modern times, on the other hand, when carrying capacity began to decline, aid in the form of medicine, food and shelter suppressed the death rate, morbidity and the need for out-migration. The continued presence of large numbers of people might even reduce carrying capacity still further. A larger and more resilient population remained, providing an elevated base from which increased growth could continue when rainfall temporarily increased again. In any event,

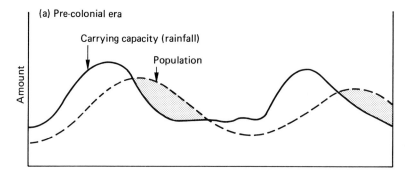

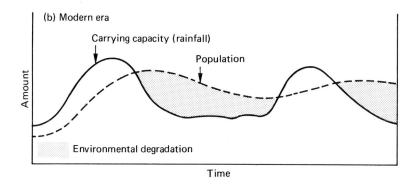

Figure 7.4 Relationships between rainfall, population and environmental stress in the Sahel, given: (a) traditional subsistence farming and land use and (b) modern agriculture with external aid and support systems
Source:　adapted from Oliver and Hidore (1984)

the result is an even larger population than before. Stress on the land is such that plant cover is destroyed beyond the minimum required for the prevention of severe soil erosion. The more fertile top soil is removed, less soil remains and therefore less moisture is retained. The soil dries out and soil temperatures increase further, speeding drying and collapse of the system.

More specifically, stress on the land results from 'deforestation', overgrazing and overcultivation, each of which is directly related to population. Deforestation, or more precisely in this context, the removal of woody vegetation, results from the growing population's use of wood for fuel. For example, in Niamey, the capital of Niger, 90 per cent of the people cook with wood or charcoal (Tinker, 1983). High oil prices discourage the use of kerosene, which was seen as an alternative 15 years ago. According to Talbot (1986), fuel wood provides an energy source for 80 per cent of the African population.

In the developing countries of Africa, rangelands comprise over half the land area and support a large human population that is dependent, in one way or another, on grazing livestock (Talbot, 1986). Overgrazing of these rangelands results from five main factors. First, population growth has meant an increase in the number of nomadic herdsmen and thus in the number of animals. Second, better veterinary care and assistance provided by government agencies in reducing livestock diseases have resulted in lower animal mortality. Third, widespread drilling of wells has allowed more animals to be watered than the land can support in periods of drought. Fourth, many nomads have moved to the major towns where they hold lucrative government jobs. According to Tinker (1983), they often invest this money in animals in their family's herd. Fifth, population growth in the agricultural zone has led to pressure for more land. There is a decrease in the area available for grazing as agriculturalists steadily encroach on the traditional grazing lands to farm soil that is too arid to be permanently cropped.

These are not the sole causes of desertification, but they produce land which, when drought occurs, has lost the capacity to protect itself. Moreover, it is an important part of the chain of processes in the system that feeds back on itself, reaffecting the vulnerability of the population and, ultimately, the future drought hazard or damage potential. Aspects of this chain are illustrated in figure 7.2 and discussed below.

In wet years there is expansion and intensification of grazing and cultivation of land that is otherwise marginal. During the next relatively dry year there is an excessive demand on water stored in the soil. The soil dries and becomes susceptible to wind erosion and eventually blows away. Even if the rains were to return, what soil remains is washed away by sheet erosion and gullying. Most important, if such changes affect a large area, positive feedback processes to which regional climate is highly sensitive are set in motion, accentuating the existing anomalies in climate.

The key factor is stability of air. When the atmosphere is stable upward motion of air is discouraged. Even in humid airstreams, rainfall will not occur unless stability is overcome. It is the widespread, persistent atmospheric subsidence associated with the subtropical high-pressure belts that accounts for most of the large areas of arid and semi-arid climate of the world, including those of northern Africa. These high-pressure belts migrate towards the poles in summer and towards the equator in winter.

Rain is brought to the Sahel by the African summer monsoon. This is an annual cycle dominated by the northward advance of rain-bearing, oceanic air over the land affecting an area between the sea and the southern boundary of the sub-tropical high-pressure belt in the north. The Sahel is at the far northern edge of this area and the problem is that the summer monsoon does not always reach far enough north. Should the migration of the sub-tropical air advance only one degree of latitude less than normal, large areas of the Sahel experience a great reduction in rain. In recent years the northward movement of the rain-bearing air has been less than normal and, in effect, the dry Sahara climate is moving south.

A major cause appears to be change to ground surface albedo, that is the reflectivity of the ground with respect to solar radiation, as a consequence of degradation of vegetation. Bare or sparsely covered terrain has a higher albedo than a vegetated surface. The additional reflection of solar energy results in a radiation deficit and associated cooling. This in turn leads to subsidence of air which expands as it descends, drying and warming in the process and inhibiting cloud formation. Thus, the increased reflectivity of the terrain causes the effects of the sub-tropical high-pressure belt to extend outward from the Sahara in the north further into the Sahel, leading to drying. The dry conditions result in a further loss of vegetation, causing increased reflectivity and subsidence of dry air even further to the south, and so on (Otterman, 1974; Charney, 1975; Charney, Stone and Quirk, 1975; Laval, 1986).

Schnell (1975) suggests that the lack of vegetation cover leads to a scarcity in the atmosphere of rare ice-forming nuclei of biological origin that are required to trigger precipitation in clouds (de Freitas and Woolmington, 1980). Another contributing factor may be the increase of airborne dust from the bare soil being exposed to wind erosion. It has been known for some time that very large amounts of this dust originate in the Sahara and its surrounds and it occurs in such large quantities in the atmosphere that it can affect visibility as far west as the Caribbean (Rapp, 1974). This dust in the atmosphere reduces incoming solar radiation and heating of the land surface which in turn leads to a reduction in convectional activity and rainfall brought about by rising warm air.

In each case, or in combination, the effect is that a decrease in rainfall is exacerbated by processes resulting from environmental stress caused by large human populations that trigger processes in the atmosphere, which enhances dryness, which feeds back on itself. The net result is an expansion of desert margins or, at the very least, conditions under which a 'natural' drought prolongs itself.

DEMOGRAPHIC IMPACT

It is surprising that there is no well developed body of theory on the complex inter-relationships of climate, drought and population. Attention has often been focused on the feedback links between population and food supply, and more frequently famine, usually as a way of explaining population stagnation or a dramatic increase in mortality. Often the demographic impact of drought extends beyond the dramatic mortality crisis of famine. The significance of what happens is equally important to both the subsequent human use system and the regional climate, the interactions of which are crucial to the hazard potential in the area or regional vulnerability to the drought hazard.

The periodic impact of drought and famine on the population of the Sahel leaves marks on its size and demographic composition. Reliable data are hard to come by, but the conventional view is that mortality rises and fertility falls during a drought. The demographic consequences, however, may be more complex than this, depending on the social, cultural and economic structure of traditional societies as well as the magnitude, frequency, duration and areal extent of drought. It is likely that the demographic consequences will be more subtle than vast fluctuations in mortality; rather, a set of conditions in which fertility and mortality vary less dramatically and result in a small but persistently positive growth rate (Caldwell, 1975; Faulkingham and Thorbahn, 1975; Watkins and Menken, 1985).

Mortality

In the context of Malthusian theory, as a population exceeds its resource base during drought it is reduced in size by increased mortality due to famine. Released from stress when the rains return, the population will again grow at an increasing rate until the next drought. The connection between drought and food availability is well established, but that between food availability and mortality rates is not. The impact of drought on its victims may take forms other than death by starvation. If mortality rates do increase it may be from deaths brought about by an increase in infectious diseases as a result of the body's weakened nutritional state (Galloway, 1986). This may result directly from factors that accompany the breakdown of hygiene, but also indirectly from the degradation of water supply and disposal systems, crowding in refugee camps that facilitates cross-infection and conditions resulting from poor sanitation and inadequate medical services.

The duration of the drought is also important. Watkins and Menken (1985) develop the point that the intensity of the mortality crisis is defined not only by the increase in death rates over those in normal times, but also by the length of time during which death rates were elevated. The effect on the annual death rate is reduced in a drought of short duration. Likewise, the intensity, spatial extent and frequency of drought will affect mortality rates. The actual number of deaths will also depend on the size of population in question. Conditions in the Sahel have become characterized by desiccation and drought of long duration, moderately high intensity and large areal extent where, collectively, large numbers of people are affected.

Nevertheless, mortality rates in the Sahel have been suppressed by large-scale and well organized food and medical aid. For example, as early as 1980 there were 400 relief agencies in this part of Africa (Watkins and Menken, 1985). Net losses due to out-migration are also reduced since the larger the population and area affected the more likely there are to be impediments to cross-border movements.

The demographic consequences of drought and desiccation will also depend on the rapidity with which the population can recover. This will depend on the differences between birth and death rates towards the end of the drought period, as well as on the age and sex patterns of mortality, which, in turn, can affect fertility. In the Sahel mortality rates rise most among the very old and very young. Because of this the demographic effects are shorter-lived than if the greatest losses were among women of early child-bearing ages.

Watkins and Menken (1985) report that the greatest rise in death rates during the Bangladesh famine of 1974–5 occurred among children aged 1–11 months, children aged 5–9 years and people over 45 years of age. There is a high death rate during the first month of life. However, the very young generally are not as sensitive to death from starvation and malnutrition as are some others. This is due to the quality and quantity of breast milk that is often sufficient for the very young until the mother is nearly starved, so that they will be affected after their elders have succumbed (Watkins and Menken, 1985).

The ability of the population to recover after drought will also depend on the sex composition of deaths. It appears that in most circumstances in the Sahel, mortality rates are lowest for women and young adults so that the capacity for reproduction and population recovery is preserved.

Fertility

Fertility usually declines during drought and famine. The reasons for a decline in fertility include increased stillbirths or foetal losses, amenorrhoea and loss of libido from malnutrition and stress, postponement of marriage, separation of spouses associated with temporary migration in response to drought, decreased coital frequency from stress and separation and increase in voluntary birth control. In the 1974–5 Bangladesh drought, fertility rates fell off by the same proportion in all age groups so that there was no age-related shift as there is in mortality (Ruzicka and Chowdhury, 1978). The evidence suggests that the same thing occurs in the Sahel (Caldwell, 1975).

There is also evidence that fertility increases after a famine, giving rise to a post-drought rebound in population. This may be due to an increase in the number of marriages after the famine because of remarriage of those whose spouse had died during the famine or, for others, because marriage was delayed until after the drought.

From the evidence, it seems that drought in the Sahel does not have a pronounced effect on population stability (Caldwell, 1975). Classic Malthusian conditions, whereby a population is reduced in size by a crisis, does not occur. Population growth continues, as does stress on the environment, so that with time there is increased sensitivity and vulnerability to even normal rainfall variability (see figure 7.1(b)). During the next stage the amplifying effects of drought and climate lead to severe degradation of environmental resources, in turn leading to desertification.

Migration

Migration has been one of the most important ways in which people respond to the drought hazard in the Sahel, in that it enables huge numbers to survive the drought. Very large numbers of people moved from the north (Caldwell, 1975) to areas further south where conditions were initially better. The effect was a spreading of heavy exploitation of the land from the arid core along with the positive feedback mechanisms resulting from environmental stress and degradation that enhance desiccation and lead to desertification.

Migration in the Sahel was of two basic types. First, movement of an entire group along with their herds to less stressed land. The traditional way of life was maintained and, if conditions improved, they would return to their origin (Birks, 1978), thus re-establishing the potential for renewed stress on the land during the subsequent drought. The cycle would begin again, but with population steadily growing all the time. Second, movement that was initially intended as a temporary measure but became permanent when drought conditions failed to improve as desertification set in. According to Caldwell (1975) and Colvin (1981), large numbers of people were involved. Consequently, there is a major redistribution of population.

This large-scale redistribution of population is a major adjustment to the drought hazard. In the region of origin there is a permanent or long-term relief from the pressures of large numbers of people and livestock. Exploitation may now occur at a level which the land-based resources can sustain, dampening or eventually breaking the cycle of positive feedback processes that perpetuate drought and ultimately reducing vulnerability to the hazard. An alternative interpretation of this is illustrated in figure 7.1(c), in which the adjustment phase is one of changed level of use that is less demanding, rather than a discrete adjustment to a changing climate of reduced precipitation. The effect is the same since the variability in precipitation does not exceed that range of values within which it provides a basis for effective management of the land resource base.

CONCLUSION

It is clear that variations in climate affect population growth and structure and that, in the present context, severe drought and famine produce major changes in basic demographic processes that are not in keeping with classic Malthusian theory. There are also important feedback effects. Yet demographers often limit their discussion of climate to a sentence or two. They focus their attention on most socio-economic and cultural aspects of the human use system treating climate as a possible explanatory variable in the simplest of terms. This may be because there is no well developed body of theory that can be used to provide a conceptual framework for examining interrelationships between drought and population, or climatic hazards and population generally. The demographic context of the drought hazard in the Sahel in many ways provides and on-going empirical base from which a theoretical framework may be calibrated and tested.

Clearly, a major objective of all this is to ameliorate the impact of the hazard through identification and understanding of the processes involved and their interaction. Development aid may not be enough, especially if the societies subjected to on-going climatic stress are viewed as passive victims of external forces. Often the problem stems from a failure of societies to adapt to their specific circumstances, or the failure to combine relief aid and disaster planning with appropriate development strategies.

REFERENCES

Birks, S. (1978) The Mountain Pastoralists of the Sultanate of Oman: Reactions to Drought, *Development and Change*, 9: 71–86.
Burton, I. and Hewitt, K. (1974) Ecological Dimensions of Environmental Hazards, in Sargent, F. (ed), *Human Ecology*, North-Holland, Amsterdam: 253–83.
Caldwell, J. C. (1975) *The Sahelian Drought and its Demographic Implications*, American Council on Education, Overseas Liaison Committee paper 8, Washington, DC.
Charney J. G. (1975) Dynamics of Deserts and Drought in the Sahel, *Quarterly Journal of the Royal Meteorological Society*, 101: 193–202.
Charney, J. G., Stone, P. H. and Quirk, W. J. (1975) Drought in the Sahara: A Biogeophysical Feedback Mechanism, *Science*, 187:434–5.

Colvin, L. G. (1981) Senegal, in Colvin, L. G. (ed), *The Uprooted of the Western Sahel*, Praeger, New York: 83–112.

de Freitas, C. R. and Woolmington, E. R. (1980) Catastrophe Theory and Catastasis, *Area*, 12:191–4.

Faulkingham, R. H. and Thorbahn, P. F. (1975) Population Dynamics and Drought: A Village in Niger, *Population Studies*, 29:463–7.

Galloway, P. R. (1986) Long-Term Fluctuations in Climate and Population in the Preindustrial Era, *Population and Development Review*, 12, 1:1–24.

Grainger, A. (1982) *Desertification*, Earthscan, London.

Hare, F. K. (1983) *Climate and Desertification: A Revised Analysis*, World Meteorological Organization, United Nations Environment Programme, WCP 44, Geneva.

Heathcote, R. L. (1985) Extreme Event Analysis, in Kates, R. W., Ausubel, J. H. and Berberian, M. (eds), *Climate Impact Assessment*, SCOPE 27, Wiley, Chichester: 369–401.

Hugo, G. J. (1984) The Demographic Impact of Famine: A Review, in Currey, B. and Hugo, G., *Famine as a Geographical Phenomenon*, D. Reidel, Dordrecht: 7–31.

Landsberg, H. E. (1975) Sahel Drought: Change of Climate or Part of Climate? *Archiv fur Meteorologie, Geophysik und Bioklimatologie*, B, 23:193–200.

Laval, K. (1986) General Circulation Model Experiments with Surface Albedo Changes, *Climatic Change*, 9:91–102.

Motha, R. P., Le Duc, S. K., Steyaert, L. T., Sakamoto, C. M. and Strommen, N. D. (1980) Precipitation Patterns in West Africa, *Monthly Weather Review*, 108:1567–78.

Nicholson, S. E. (1980) The Nature of Rainfall fluctuations in Subtropical West Africa, *Monthly Weather Review*, 108:473–87.

Nicholson, S. E. (1981) Rainfall and Atmospheric Circulation During Drought and Wetter Periods in West Africa, *Monthly Weather Review*, 109:2191–208.

Nicholson, S. E. (1985) Sub-Saharan Rainfall 1981–1984, *Journal of Climate and Applied Meteorology*, 24: 1388–91.

Oliver, J. E. and Hidore, J. J. (1984) *Climatology : An Introduction*, Charles E. Merrill, Columbus.

Otterman, J. (1974) Baring High Albedo Soils by Overgrazing: A Hypothesized Desertification Mechanism, *Science*, 186:531–3.

Rapp, A. (1974) *A Review of Desertification in Africa – Water, Vegetation and Man*, Secretariat for International Ecology, SEIS 1, Stockholm.

Ruzicka, L. T. and Chowdhury, A. K. (1978) *Vital Events and Migration, 1975: Demographic Surveillance System-Matlab*, vol. 4, Cholera Research

Laboratory, Scientific Report 12, Dacca. Cited in Watkins and Menken, 1985.

Schnell, R. C. (1975) *Biogenic Ice Nucleus Removal by Overgrazing: A Factor in the Sahelian Drought*, Final Report to Directors, Rockefeller Foundation, MS, NCAR, Boulder.

Talbot, L. M. (1986) Demographic Factors in Resource Depletion and Environmental Degradation in East African Rangelands, *Population and Development Review*, 12, 3:441–51.

Tinker, J. (1983) Deserts: Fending Off Disaster, *People*, 10:8–11.

Watkins, S. C. and Menken, J. (1985) Famines in Historical Perspective, *Population and Development Review*, 11, 4:647–75.

8

The 1984 Drought and Settler Migration in Ethiopia

Aynalem Adugna

The 1984 settler migration in Ethiopia was unprecedented in terms of magnitude. About half a million people were resettled in just one year. The migration was an emergency response to the severe famine that besieged the entire country. It was also considered by the government as a lasting solution to the population problems that were supposedly the results exclusively of natural disasters. The major senders were the severely-hit areas in the north. These certainly deserved to be the centres of out-migration; were there, however, areas that were readily habitable to host the half million in-migrants?

Politicians spoke with varying tones and journalists made varying news about the 1984 Ethiopian famine. Newspapers and radio and television programmes were busy reporting on the drought and famine as one of the phenomenal events of the 1980s. Thousands of deaths occurring daily, congestion of relief camps, exodus to neighbouring countries and so on made headlines. Most were unequivocal in their statements that this was a misfortune brought upon Ethiopians by the 1984 drought; but is it possible that just one year's failure of rains can produce a disaster of this magnitude? Can famine strike at once with all populations falling victims in a period as short as one year? The answers are obviously no. Two things are thus evident. First, the 1984 drought and famine was not a sudden outbreak, but only a phase in the series of major and minor droughts post-dating the disastrous famine of 1972–3, which itself was not the beginning. In fact, some researchers point out that 'famine has always been inherent in the Ethiopian socio-economic set up' (Bahru Zewde, 1976). Secondly, apart from the natural factors, a number of social, economic and political factors were responsible for the famine. Those who concluded that the famine was the result of natural factors alone were therefore as mistaken as those who believed that it was merely a result of the ineffectiveness of measures taken by the government.

THE SCOPE AND CONSEQUENCES OF THE DROUGHT

On a national level the scope and consequences of the 1984 drought varied from region to region depending on the duration of the drought and also on the frequency of previous droughts. Locally, its effect varied according to the socio-economic position of individuals. A work on previous droughts in Ethiopia suggests that 'the impact of drought upon the people is dependent upon their resources, some survive and maintain their economic independence for some time whereas others, especially the poor, can not do so' (Wood, 1976:74). On a national scale, the magnitude of the drought in 1984 was such that 13 of the 14 administrative regions, locally known as *kifle hagers*, were affected although to a varying degree, the only exception being Wellega *kifle hager* (RRC, 1984a). The worst hit area was northern Ethiopia, covering the administrative regions of Wello, Tigray and Eritrea. Harerge in the east and Bale and Sidamo in the south were also severely hit (see table 8.1). In Wello alone, about 2.6 million persons were reported to be needing immediate assistance. In Tigray, the affected population was about 1.4 million. In Gonder, 11 per cent of the population did not have enough to eat or, indeed, had nothing at all. The report by RRC (1984a) states that during the two months of October and November 1984, 2.5 million people in ten *kifle hagers* were being supplied with emergency food in 195 food distribution centres. There were also 20 large shelters and 41 intensive feeding centres for malnourished children and lactating mothers, but only a third of the affected population were actually receiving food aid in relief centres. The rest stayed in their homes fighting hunger on their own, so that the unsuccessful ones were forced to give in and die a silent death, The economically better-off survived to the next rainy season. In big relief centres of Wello, such as Korem, up to 100,000 persons were being supplied with food, and in Kobo and Alamata

Table 8.1   Number and percentage of population in Ethiopia affected by the 1984 drought and famine, by *Kifle Hager*

No.	Kifle Hager	Total population, 1984	No. of people affected	Percentage of total
1	Wello	3,609,918	2,587,420	71.6
2	Tigray	2,409,700	1,429,390	59.3
3	Eritrea	2,704,000	827,000	30.6
4	Gonder	2,905,362	346,500	11.9
5	Sidamo	3,790,579	532,500	14.0
6	Gamogofa	1,248,034	106,330	8.5
7	Harerge	4,151,706	864,340	20.8
8	Shewa	9,503,140	779,820	8.2
9	Arssi	1,662,233	76,460	4.6
10	Bale	1,006,491	120,920	12.0
11	Gojam	3,244,882	76,120	2.3
12	Keffa	2,450,369	90,000	3.7
13	Illubabor	963,327	25,000	1.1
14	Wellega	2,369,677	–	–
	Total	42,019,418	7,861,800	18.7

Source: Relief and Rehabilitation Commission (1984b)

another 120,000. It may also be noted that a third of the affected population were in Wello. The inadequacy of available shelter and accessibility of the affected areas were the major problems in stepping up the relief effort once the food began to be made available by donor governments and agencies. Diseases resulting from very low night temperatures and overcrowding were aggravating the already high mortality situation. Unfortunately, mortality is the least known phenomenon of the time, for the one major reason that there are no obtainable data.

According to a recent study by Aynalem and Kloos (1987), in the absence of government intervention, the choice of relief centres was dictated mainly by distance and availability of information. In addition, what the drought victims planned to do after the drought strongly influenced their choice of initial destinations. Those who hoped to return back home did not travel long distances. In Wello and Tigray for instance, most of the people leaving their homes did not go outside their respective *kifle hagers*. In Tigray, centres like Mekele, Axum, Adwa and Wikiro were hosting tens of thousands

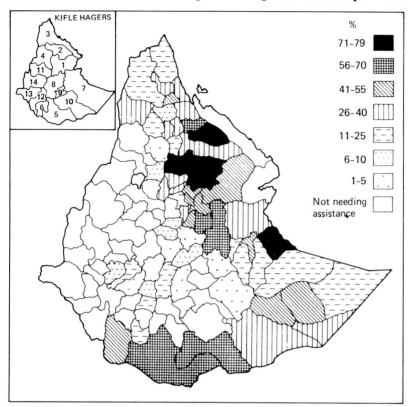

Figure 8.1 Percentage of the rural population needing food assistance in 1985, by *awraja*. Inset: the *kifle hagers* of Ethiopia: 1 Wello; 2 Tigray; 3 Eritrea; 4 Gonder; 5 Sidamo; 6 Gamogofa; 7 Harerge; 8 Shewa; 9 Arssi; 10 Bale; 11 Gojam; 12 Keffa; 13 Illubabor; 14 Wellega

of refugees. In northern Shewa, similar numbers of migrants flocked to Debre Birhan, Debre Sina and Karakore towns. The numbers of relief centres and refugees in them were a reflection of how severe and widespread the famine was. The spatial variations (see figure 8.1) in intensity of famine by *awraja* (subdivisions of *kifle hager*) were due primarily to the differences in degree of vulnerability already existing in rural Ethiopia, which in turn were dependent upon the frequency and duration of previous droughts and famine. Equally or perhaps more important contributors are other problems that are social, economic and political in origin, including:

1 internal wars, as in northern and south-eastern Ethiopia;
2 difficulty of access to the people needing help because of lack of transport;
3 difficulty of reaching the continuously moving nomadic people, especially in southern, south-eastern and north-western Ethiopia;
4 absence of studies and reliable data to determine the magnitude of problems faced by local populations and the amount and type of assistance needed (Mesfin Wolde Mariam, 1984).

Although their effects were localized, other disasters such as forest fire, hail storms, plant and animal diseases, outbreaks of crop pests and epidemics were also experienced in various regions. Political problems arising from political tensions also seemed to have acquired greater vehemence in the face of the drought and famine.

Both the loss of human life and the damage inflicted upon the economy by the 1984 drought and famine were unprecedented in recent history. The dominant eonomic activity in Ethiopia is agriculture, engaging close to nine-tenths of the population. Of the total area of the country (1,223,600 sq km), 15 per cent is under crops and 50 per cent is used for grazing and browsing (Eshetu Chole and Teshome Mulat, 1987). Unfortunately, agriculture is the economic sector least resistant to the vicissitudes of nature. Even the slightest change in the environment affects production of the type of agriculture practised in Ethiopia, where the techniques used for cultivation are primitive and where agriculture is almost entirely for subsistence.

Surveys were not made in Eritrea and Tigray to estimate crop production because of political problems, but as shown in table 8.2, agricultural production in 1984 was less than that for 1983 in all other *kifle hagers*. In the worst hit *kifle hager*, Wello, crop production in 1984 was only 28 per cent of the 1983 production. Illubabor suffered the second greatest production shortfall, although it is outside the traditional drought zones and rainfall amounts there are amongst the highest in the country.

Although not among the areas reported to be receiving food aid, Wellega too suffered greatly from a reduced crop production which led to scarcity of food and a sudden rise in food prices. The considerable reductions in production in Harerge, Gamogofa,

Table 8.2   1984 agricultural production in Ethiopia as a percentage of 1983 production, by *Kifle Hager*

Kifle hager	%	Kifle hager	%
Arssi	87	Illubabor	45
Bale	66	Keffa	64
Gamogofa	58	Shewa	73
Gojam	93	Sidamo	58
Gonder	86	Wellega	69
Harerge	57	Wello	28

Source: RRC(1985).

Sidamo and Bale were to be expected because these are drought-prone regions. Moreover, 'when we note that 1983 itself was a drought year in many regions, we can understand the magnitude of the 1984 shortfall' (RRC, 1985a: 2). The least affected *kifle hagers* in terms of crop production were Arssi, Gojam and Gonder (see table 8.2).

In addition to agricultural surveys, the food prices in some markets were studied, though only three crops – *teff* (*Eragrostis abyssinica*, the most important staple food crop in Ethiopia), maize and barley – were emphasized. The rise in the prices of these food grains was in most cases proportional to the magnitude of production decrease. The highest price increase, of about 400 per cent for *teff*, was, for instance, recorded in Dessie market of Wello (see figure 8.2), the region that experienced the maximum shortfall in food production. Similarly, high rises in the price of *teff* were witnessed in selected markets in Harerge and Shewa. The situation in Tigray and Eritrea may not have been less severe. However, nothing definite can be said about these two areas because of lack of data. According to RRC's (1985a:6) assessments, 'the level of prices in all regions were abnormally high', irrespective of the fact that food grains were not shipped in significant quantities from relative surplus regions to deficit regions. The main explanation for this is that 1984 was a disaster year for all regions and hence crop production was lower than normal everywhere. It may also be noted that the price rise was not limited to *teff*. All other crops were sold at higher prices than normal in all administrative regions. What is considered normal here is the average of the three to five year prices for the years preceding 1984. In the summer of 1985 the food

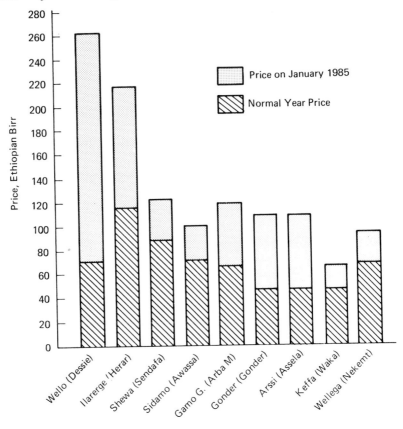

Figure 8.2 Market prices of *teff* in selected markets of ten *kifle hagers*, January 1985

problem had reached critical levels even in the capital, Addis Ababa, leading to a change of diet, at least temporarily, from *teff* to rationed wheat, rice, maize and some exotic foods like spaghetti.

It was immediately obvious that something extraordinary had to be done to deal with these problems. But what was to be done? This was a subject of heated debate internationally, though there appeared to be a unanimity among local politicians on measures to be taken. Western relief agencies accused their respective governments of being insensitive to human sufferings and insisted that their governments' disfavour of the political line followed by Ethiopia should not preclude the giving of emergency food and long-term development aid. Food shipments soon began to arrive in

Ethiopia in large quantities, although not large enough to feed all the starving population. Development aid, however was, a luxury that Ethiopia was not entitled to enjoy. But was it or is it possible to feed people in camps indefinitely? If not, what other alternatives exist?

In October 1984 the Ethiopian government came up with a decision that lent favour to the already existing view that resettlement was the only solution to the problems arising from drought and famine (RRC, 1979). According to the new 'emergency plan', over a million people were to be moved from the drought-affected regions in the north to the 'unused' areas in western and south-western Ethiopia.

THE 1984–1985 PLANNED RESETTLEMENT

Planned resettlement is a recent phenomenon in Ethiopia, dating back only to the 1950s (Eshetu Chole and Teshome Mulat, 1987). Historically, many of the settler movements have been spontaneous (Wood, 1982, 1985). This has helped to redress population/resource disequilibrium arising from continuous use and settlement of some areas with other areas remaining insufficiently used. However, it is difficult to ascertain if there is any utilizable land in Ethiopia that is still unused, although this is a popular view in government (RRC, 1985b). According to Agrey-Mensah et al. (1984), two opposing views prevail in Ethiopia regarding this subject: 'At one extreme, it might be said that there is no suitable land which is not occupied and utilized, though perhaps at very low levels of productivity, by the existing population. At the other extreme, [it is claimed that] there are indeed areas which are utilizable and unoccupied.'

The problem arises partly from the difficulty of identifying the criteria for classification. Nevertheless, it may be stated here that land that is readily utilizable with available local technologies or without requiring high financial, material and other inputs is very scarce. Through the centuries, the various population groups have managed to colonize and settle in previously avoided ecologies, thus bringing all conceivably cultivable land under sedentary cultivation. Where the environmental possibilities did not allow settled agriculture (in the areas that are currently claimed to be unused) shifting cultivation, nomadism and in places hunting–gathering or a combination of all or some of these, provided an alternative means of deriving the means of sustenance. It can, therefore, be argued that although the Ethiopian population is not optimally distributed any major or minor operation designed to restructure the existing pattern will have to involve huge technological, financial and human resource inputs if areas that are not readily habitable are to be made habitable. More than anything, this requires careful planning based on research and thorough feasibility studies. Unfortunately, most of the resettlement operations in Ethiopia lack these esssential components of viable resettlement work. The recurrence and severity of population problems arising from natural, social, economic and political causes militated against their adoption. Agrey-Mensah et al. (1984:v) in their studies of special settlement schemes, summarize the situation as follows:

> The planning of settlements has not been adequate as they appear to have been conceived as emergency responses to crisis. Sites were not chosen both from the point of view of settlers who had to live there, and from the point of view of potential for agricultural production. No preliminary surveys were undertaken to assess the suitability of the sites from continuous cropping. As a result no special measures were taken to maintain the productivity of the soils, leading to lower yields than projected in the plans.

In consequence, the dependence of settlers upon government aid for food, clothing, housing, farm implements, etc. stretches over a longer period than envisaged in resettlement plans, which according to the National Revolutionary Campaign and Central Planning Supreme Council (NRCCPSC, 1984a:5) is two to three years. The government is thus faced with continuous problems of catering for the needs of those already settled and of resettling those who are in relief centres. This is a very costly undertaking for a third world government that is already beset by more socio-economic problems than the majority of nations in the same category. It is in this light that the 1984 planned resettlement should be seen. It may be noted, however, that the term 'planned' here has a dubious meaning. It was government-planned in the sense that it did not result from the wilful and self-financed movement of individuals from their homes to resettlement sites. On the other hand, the fact that the resettlement was an emergency operation implemented at short notice makes it difficult to consider as an action based on a well-thought-out plan. For lack of a more appropriate term, we will consider the 1984 population redistribution as an emergency redistribution.

One of the objectives of the ten-year (1984–93) perspective plan of Ethiopia is to intensify the population redistribution effort and resettle far more persons than were resettled during the previous decade (NRCCPSC, 1984a). It was envisaged that 85,250 households would be resettled over the ten-year period. The plan for 1984 and 1985 was to resettle 6,050 and 6,600 households respectively. Each household was to be allotted 2.5 ha of land, half of which would be cultivated with government assistance during the first year.

In the face of the 1984 drought and famine, mounting concern over the sudden rise in the number of 'famine deaths' and the inadequacy of food aid given by donor governments, the government quickly prepared a new 'emergency plan' (NRCCPSC, 1984b). According to the December issue of the NRCCPSC publication, 300,000 household heads, or a total of 1,500,000 people, were to be resettled in just one year (see also RRC, 1985b). Thus, the government's plan to resettle persons on a modest scale was, according to Desalegn Rahmato (1986) 'overtaken by events'. In consequence, he adds, 'planned resettlement was quickly replaced with emergency resettlement'.

The plan was to be implemented in two phases. Phase one had a target of relocating 50,000 households in the thinly populated highland areas and this was completed in January 1985 (RRC, 1985b:188). The resettlers were distributed among 1,307 peasant associations in Wellega, Illubabor and Keffa administrative regions (RRC, 1985c). This resettlement, which focused on the traditionally favoured *dega* (highland) areas of the country is designated as *sigsega* or 'integration' resettlement. The second phase, described as 'more challenging' (RRC, 1985b), was concerned to resettle 250,000 households in the hitherto sparsely populated and less favoured lowlands in the geographically marginal areas. Of these, 150,000 households or about 750,000 persons were already resettled towards the end of 1984 (RRC, 1985b). This is designated as *medebegna* or 'conventional' resettlement.

Settlers were drawn from five *kifle hagers*: Wello (50 per cent), Tigray (33 per cent) and the rest from Shewa, Gonder and Gojam.

Wellega *kifle hager* was the major recipient, followed by Illubabor, Keffa, Gojam and Gonder, all in south-western and north-western Ethiopia (see Aynalem Adugna and Kloos, 1987). This was undoubtedly the largest population redistribution ever undertaken in the country. But what is the implication of this large-scale movement in an economy that is too feeble to nurture all the displaced until they become self-supporting? 'Inevitably migration on such a historic scale has implications that extend beyond the limited scenarios of productivity and land utilization sketched out by the economic planners and will, indeed, have a profound impact on the entire social and cultural fabric of modern Ethiopia' (Hancock, 1985:25). Some pessimists like Clay and Holcomb (1985) concluded that the emergency resettlement was a futile exercise and that a new catastrophe is imminent. In his report of a 15-week study in 1985–6 of Pawe resettlement site in western Ethiopia, Sivini (1986) stressed that 'the resettlement . . . is involving notable human costs higher than those caused by famine'. He also pointed out that the 'highly critical situation' in Pawe was caused mainly by the hostile lowland climate which is foreign to highland settlers and the widespread attack of malaria. Mortality varied from one week to another during his study, generally decreasing away from the rainy season. For the period under study, he calculated a weighted child (aged 0–5) mortality rate of 522 per thousand, and mortality rates of 269 for children aged 6–13 and 131 for persons aged 14 and over. It is difficult to state whether this was an ephemeral phenomenon resulting from the grave challenges posed by the untamed environment then subsiding as time went by, or if it is a commonplace occurrence. The major obstacle is the absence of data. According to government reports, however, the settlers in all resettlement sites are leading a 'new' and 'better' life. Newspapers and radio and television broadcasts are full of reports intended to confirm this.

CONCLUSION

Looked at in every respect, the years 1984–5 mark a unique episode in the history of settler migration in Ethiopia, but above all the magnitude of the drought and famine, and the migration of half a million persons it generated, are unprecedented.

The number of out-migrants from areas was not always proportional to the magnitude of the problems as measured by the percentage of persons needing immediate food assistance. Eritrea, for instance, did not send settlers, probably because of the possible political consequences, although it was the third worst affected area. There were also areas, like southern Shewa, that saw unexpectedly high out-migrations; Shewa was the third major supplier of migrants and yet only 8 per cent of its population were reported to need help in 1984.

Identification of settlement sites was done within a short period of time, and hence it cannot be expected that rational evaluations of the possible human and ecological consequences were made. Moreover, the overall resettlement effort was under great strain because the settlement sites were planned to be developed by the settlers themselves, contrary to expectations that this should have been done before. It is not therefore unreasonable to accept some of the reported human consequences, including the very high infant and child mortality rates, especially for the periods immediately after resettlement. Nevertheless, it would be wrong to conclude that the 1984 resettlement did not bear any positive results. A lot of resources are still being poured into the resettlement effort to help the resettlers regain the self-reliance they long for and prize so much. Whether this objective is being met or will be met requires further research before it is substantiated.

Decision on resettlement and its implementation was made hastily and the previously important spontaneous movements were not very common. This ran counter to suggestions based on evaluations of similar operations preceding the reference period that spontaneous out-migration should be encouraged.

Although drought and famine seemed to be widespread phenomena, especially in northern Ethiopia, their effects closely paralleled the already existing socio-economic stratification in rural villages, and therefore the degree of vulnerability of individual households. Even within the households, the effect differed depending on 'factors such as age, social status, and gender' (McCann, 1985:22).

Persons of all ages were moved to resettlement sites, although most of the household heads were in the 20–40 age group. Studies conducted at settler destinations also show that there is not much sex imbalance. This is because of the government's decision that whole families should be moved. Previously, especially under spontaneous movements, male household members out-migrated first, to be joined by their family members later. Thus, the age–sex structure of people resettled during the 1984–5 period does not show any significant difference from the general age–sex structure in rural Ethiopia. It may however, be noted that family separation during the process of movement was not uncommon.

The facts of resettlement in Ethiopia are still in the unfortunate state of vagueness, scarcity and inaccessibility. It is therefore, natural that this chapter should focus on peripheral information commonly available in libraries. Given the present state of affairs it is also extremely difficult to prophesy what is the future of the resettlement sites, and of the million people living in them.

REFERENCES

Agrey-Mensah, et al. (1984) *An Evaluation of the Ethiopia Resettlement Program*, Ethiopian Highland Reclamation Study, Working Paper 5, Ministry of Agriculture, FAO.

Aynalem Adugna and Kloos, H. (1987) Settler Migration, *Ethiopian Journal of Development Research* (forthcoming).

Bahru Zewde (1976) Historical Outline of Famine, in Hussein, A. M. (ed.), *Rehab: Drought and Famine in Ethiopia*, African Environmental Special Report 2, International African Institute, London.

Clay, J. B. and Holcomb, B. (1985) *Politics and Ethiopian Famine*, Cultural Survival Inc., Cambridge.

Daniel Gamachu (1985) Peripheral Ethiopia: A Look at the Marginal Zones of the Country, in Treuner, P., Tadasse, K. M. and Teshome Mulat (eds), Regional Planning and Development in Ethiopia, Institute für Raumordnung und Entwicklungsplanung, Universität Stuttgart.

Desalegn Rahmato (1986) Some Notes on Settlement and Resettlement in Metekel Awraja (Gojam province), paper prepared for the ninth International Conference on Ethiopian Studies, Moscow.

Eshetu Chole and Teshome Mulat (1987) Land Settlement in Ethiopia, in Oberai, A. S. (ed.), *Land Settlement Policy and Population Redistribution in Developing Countries: Achievements, Problems and Prospects*, ILO, Geneva.

Hancock, G. (1985) *Ethiopia: the Challenge of Hunger*, Gollancz, London.

McCann, J. (1985) The Social Impact of Drought in Ethiopia Oxen Households, and Some Implications for Rehabilitation, paper for discussion at the Walter Rodney African Studies Seminar, Boston University African Studies Centre.

Mesfin Wolde Mariam (1984) *Vulnerability to Famine in Ethiopia, 1950–1977*, Vikas, New Delhi.

NRCCPSC (National Revolutionary Campaign and Central Planning Supreme Council) (1984a) *The Ten-Year Perspective Plan* (In Amharic), Addis Ababa.

NRCCPSC (1984b) *Program of Action to Solve Problems Caused by Drought* (in Amharic), Addis Ababa.

RRC (Relief and Rehabilitation Commission) (1979) *Resettlement – Lasting Solution to People in Drought-Affected Areas*, Addis Ababa.

RRC (1984a) *Report of the Problems Caused by the 1983 and 1984 Drought* (in Amharic), Addis Ababa.

RRC (1984b) *Review of the Current Drought Situation in Ethiopia*, Addis Ababa.

RRC (1985a) *Early Warning and Planning Service, Monthly Report*, Addis Ababa.

RRC (1985b) *The Challenges of Drought: Ethiopia's Decade of Struggle in Relief and Rehabilitation*, Addis Ababa.

RRC (1985c) *Data on Number of Farmers in Integration and Conventional Settlement Schemes by Age and Sex and Kifle Hager*, Addis Ababa.

RRC (1985d) *The 1986 Food Supply Prospect*, (Supplement), Addis Ababa.

Sivini, G. (1986) Famine and the Resettlement Programme in Ethiopia, unpublished paper, University of Calabria.

Wood, A. P. (1976) Farmers' Response to Drought in Ethiopia, in Hussein, A. M. (ed.), *Rehab: Drought and Famine in Ethiopia*, African Environmental Special Report 2, International African Institute, London.

Wood, A. P. (1982) Spontaneous Agricultural Resettlement in Ethiopia, 1950–74, in Clarke, J. I. and Kosinski, L. A. (eds), *Redistribution of Population in Africa*, Heinemann, London.

Wood A. P. (1985) Population Redistribution and Agricultural Settlement Schemes in Ethiopia, 1958–80, in Clarke, J. I., Khogali, M. M. and Kosinski, L. A. (eds), *Population and Development Projects in Africa*, Cambridge University Press, Cambridge.

9

The Indirect Effects of Famine on Population: Case Studies from the Republic of the Sudan

A. Trilsbach

INTRODUCTION

The famine disasters which affected Ethiopia, Sudan and other sub-Saharan states during the mid-1980s are well known. Throughout the world, images of starving and disease-ridden peoples appeared on television screens, and famine-related charities were boosted by a new international consciousness to provide 'aid' for starving people. There is no doubt that the numbers of people affected directly by the disaster were high, a figure measured in millions regardless of which definitions are used.

After a brief review of some of the direct consequences of the drought and famine, this chapter attempts to identify some of the less obvious impacts of the 1984–5 famine disaster in the Republic of the Sudan and to look at some of the indirect effects which faced the population more widely.

DIRECT EFFECTS

Sudan has always been vulnerable to environmental disaster and the influx of refugees from neighbouring states. Since achieving independence in 1956, civil war within the country and its neighbours has seen a regular ebbing and flowing of refugees to and from Uganda, Zaire, the Central African Republic, Chad and Ethiopia (especially Eritrea). In each case the arrival of refugees in Sudan has placed pressure on traditional Sudanese hospitality, symbolized by an informal 'open door' refugee policy. The economic, social and resource costs of hosting refugees have been well documented, especially in the context of pressure on food demands, but in the past Sudan has been able to absorb many of the new arrivals into its labour markets, especially during times of peak agricultural pressure such as during harvests.

The scale of the 1984–5 crisis introduced new factors into the Sudanese economy and society. In the country generally, it was estimated that one in three of the population was affected directly by the famine, but in central and northern areas almost everyone felt some impact, ranging from starvation to escalating inflation and other indirect effects. Upwards of one million 'external' refugees (mainly from Ethiopia but with significant numbers from Chad) were supplemented by a similar number of 'internal' refugees (mainly from the western provinces of Darfur and Kordofan and form the Kassala and Red Sea areas of eastern Sudan). Data from North Kordofan Province help to illustrate the magnitude of the crisis. By the end of the year 1.2 million people were completely destitute, while an even greater number were affected by hunger and/or the partial loss of livelihoods (Sudan Government, 1985). The most immediate and direct strain was the need for food, especially for staple products such as sorghum and wheat, and for clean water. However, the impact of the famine was felt throughout the country and even in those parts not affected by famine or by civil war directly, the consequences were clear.

INDIRECT EFFECTS

It is possible to highlight a number of indirect consequences of the famine; these can be considered broadly under the following five headings.

Land-Use Conflicts

The widespread loss of pasture and reliable drinking points forced many pastoralists to seek alternative emergency supplies, sometimes resulting in conflicts between neighbouring population groups.

This was not a new phenomenon and even in moderately dry years conflict over land and water allocation could occur, as witnessed at El Muqeirinat in western White Nile Province in 1979 (Trilsbach, 1983). However, the period from 1983 saw an escalation of the problem to a scale hitherto not witnessed.

The problem can be illustrated by a case study of farmers in the area transcending the boundary between the provinces of North and South Kordofan. The failure of the rains in the southern part of North Kordofan led to pastoralists having to face either a loss of animals or the need to sell them at extraordinarily low prices as the market became saturated (Trilsbach and Ahmed, 1986). The only possible alternative was to move to areas with relatively improved grazing resources. This led to severe land use conflicts in the Nuba Mountains area of South Kordofan between the native farmers and the pastoralists from North Kordofan. Conflict was greatest where livestock interfered with the semi-successful rain-fed grains which were grown. Fortunately, the tension was eased with improved rains in southern North Kordofan in 1985, after which most of the pastoralists were able to return to their traditional territory.

Disruption of the Employment Market

Many of the large-scale agricultural schemes in central Sudan, both irrigated and rain-fed, have relied on seasonal labourers for key agricultural operations such as harvesting. It is well known that westerners (from Nigeria, Chad and Darfur) participating in the *hajj* to Mecca have provided a considerable amount of labour, working in return for money to assist with the next stage of the pilgrimage (Nasr and Duffield, 1980). The severity of the drought and subsequent famine forced many rural Sudanese and international refugees to seek alternative paid employment simply to survive. The flood of labour on to the market disrupted the traditional system by making jobs more difficult to obtain and by depreciating prices.

One clear example of the disrupted employment market was seen on the Rahad Irrigation Scheme in the east–central Sudan. For at least four years before 1984 hired labour was paid a wage of 75 piastres for picking a *guffah* of cotton. This was supplemented with a large supply of *dura* (*Sorghum vulgare*), the staple food, and reasonably acceptable accommodation. In 1984 there was a considerable labour surplus from 'internal' refugees (mainly from the Tendelti and Umm Ruwaba areas of west–central Sudan). The oversupply of labour allowed the employers to reduce wages. In that year most temporary labourers were paid only 50 piastres per *guffah*, with little or no *dura* supplement and the provision of very poor-quality accommodation (Rahad Scheme Administration Office, personal communication). The employers were able to reduce their input costs further because, in addition to paying lower wages, the surplus of labour meant that there was no need to look for labour or to provide transport. A consequence was that those labourers employed, mainly 'internal' refugees, were exploited, while more traditional labour forces either found jobs difficult to obtain or had their income reduced below the normal expectation. In general, wages have returned to earlier levels since 1985.

Price Variations

As expected at times of supply shortage, consumers faced large increases in the price of many basic items, especially foods such as staple grains – *dura* (*Sorghum vulgare*), *dukhn* (*Pennisetum typhoideum*), wheat and bread derivatives – sugar, eggs and meat. During 1984, in most areas grain prices at least trebled, and even this increase was exceeded in some places, often for considerable periods of time. It is worth stressing here that, even in those areas most devastated by famine, food was always available in towns. Its price, however, often precluded any opportunity for poorer families to purchase it and such people had to rely on famine assistance from charitable organizations. A dilemma for many rural people was that while basic foodstuffs were increasing in value, saleable assets especially livestock were decreasing. It has been noted that many livestock died in the drought and, apart from those who could find new grazing land – often in conflict with others – many pastoralists were forced to sell their animals. The scale of the crisis and the poor condition of most animals meant that pastoralists in many areas were forced to sell their animals simultaneously (Trilsbach and Wood, 1986). The consequent flooding of the market meant that animals were sold for pitiful sums, and this can be demonstrated by figures obtained from the large livestock market at El Obeid in North Kordofan (see table 9.1).

These prices demonstrate the full potential impact of inflation on

Table 9.1   Average prices for livestocks at El Obeid market

Animal	1983[a] £S	1984[a] £S	1985[a] £S
Goats	50	5	150-170
Sheep	70-100	7-10	200-300
Cattle	200-300[b]	35-50[b]	600-1500[b]
Camels	2000-3000	800-1000	2000-4000

[a] End-of-year prices.
[b] The higher price mainly for the best milking cows.
Source: Livestock records at El Obeid market.

the rural society at the peak of the crisis. The fact that livestock values soared in 1985 was of little comfort for pastoralists. Most of them sold their animals when prices were at their lowest (1984) and were trying to restock their flocks and herds when prices were at their highest (1985). These wildly fluctuating prices had implications for many rural traders in general, because the need for food and basic survival items reduced the amount of money in the trading system and sales of non-essential items decreased (see Trilsbach, 1987). This was commented on with some indignation by hardware sellers in El Obeid and Umm Ruwaba, and their views were echoed throughout Sudan and across a wide range of commercial traders.

Family Burdens

Comments have already been made with reference to the impact of drought and famine on stimulating new and extended population migrations of both a temporary and a permanent nature. It is hardly surprising that many families facing disaster turned to relatives for financial and material support when the crisis was at its greatest. In common with many African and Islamic societies, in Sudan this response was eased by the network of extended families. Most of the 'internal' Sudanese refugees had relatives living in the principal towns and cities, most notably in the extensive residential areas of Omdurman in the Three Towns capital of Sudan (Khartoum, Khartoum North and Omdurman). It is impossible to estimate the number of refugees that descended upon relatives in the Omdurman area, but it probably exceeded 100,000; an estimated 40,000 arrived from the province of North Kordofan alone (Sudan Government, 1985). Many of the migrants were forced to dwell in small courtyard areas of existing houses or in temporary shanty quarters at the western fringes of the city. At the peak of the recent famine, although some international charities were offering considerable basic help, the vast majority of migrants expected to receive a basic living at the expense of relatives residing permanently in the city. This expectation of support is a fundamental aspect of northern Sudanese culture and few migrants would have felt any sense of guilt or obligation towards their hosts. The host families were bound by tradition to assist their 'guests' and this in turn placed considerable burdens on their shoulders, especially financial, as food prices were often as high in urban areas as in rural ones. Many found it difficult to improve incomes by extending their 'urban' working hours, as many of the migrants were able to undercut their wages, especially in less skilled jobs. Once again a consequence was a reduction in the money supply and a general slump in commerce and trade.

Exploitation

Comments so far in this chapter have highlighted problems of food shortage, inflation and poverty. It is important to note, however, that some individuals were able to make vast profits by exploiting the desperate situation which many people faced. Comments about farmers on he Rahad Scheme have already alluded to this situation, but other examples demonstrate that this was more widespread. A clear example was witnessed on the fringes of El Obeid in late 1985. Many of the 'internal' refugees in North Kordofan migrated to the nearby towns when the crisis emerged during 1984. However, whereas many of the males left the province to seek work in the economically more advanced areas of the capital and Gezira Province, many of the women and children were left behind (Trilsbach and Ahmed, 1986). In effect these female-dominated refugee communities became a very cheap source of urban labour. Most of the women were forced to engage in urban service jobs such as housemaids, for which they were paid as little as £S1 per day – enough to buy a small amount of bread and maybe some okra and dried onions; often, this had to feed as many as five children and one or two elderly people. So some urban dwellers, especially merchants, were able to offset some of their trading losses by recruiting cheap labour.

An additional category of exploiters were food hoarders. It is well known that some ruthless merchants had stored grain for several months before the famine crisis to boost prices, and hence profits. Further evidence indicates that corruption amongst several government officials resulted in much 'charity' food being diverted into the hands of merchants who were able to sell it at inflated prices.

CONCLUSIONS

This chapter has considered a number of points under the general heading of the indirect impacts of famine on population. In some cases the responses have been contradictory, such as increasing poverty for some and profits for others. A simpler understanding of some of these facts can be achieved with reference to figure 9.1. Of particular note are the bold arrows, which single out the paths used by the exploiters. In this chain, the exploiter's path ends up with the profit, whereas all others lead to poverty. The diagram is very simplified and does little to consider external influences such as government policy and international factors, but it does help to demonstrate the relationships between the various points mentioned in this chapter.

A final comment refers to the longer-term impact of the famine disaster on population. In some cases the impacts described have appeared to be short-term, but how true is this? At this late stage it is worth considering the influence of large-scale international relief agencies. At the height of the famine, many of the traditional rural food producers were forced to abandon their livelihoods to seek alternative employment and sources of food. To some extent the food shortages were offset by international relief supplies. An alarming consequence of this has been that since the peak inflation of 1984–5 food prices have been sufficiently low to discourage many of the traditional farmers from returning to their farms; potential profits are minimal while potential hazards seem to be extensive. This suggests that the food production system has been transformed quite radically, and unless some financial incentives can be secured, the whole of the rural economy will have undergone a long-term shift. What implications this has for trading and employ-

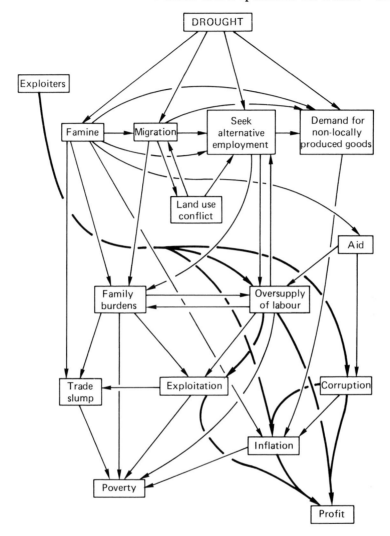

Figure 9.1   Indirect consequences of famine

ment systems is too early to judge, but it would seem that the long-term indirect impacts of famine may be quite significant.

REFERENCES

Nasr, A. A. and Duffield, R. R. (1980) *A Bibliography of West African Settlements and Development in the Sudan*, University of Khartoum Monograph Series 13.

Sudan Government (1985) *The Strategy of Kordofan Regional Government to Combat Desertification and Alleviate the Effects of Drought*, Ministry of Finance and Economy, Department of Planning and Economy, Khartoum.

Trilsbach, A. (1983) *Desertification and Rural Change in Central Sudan*, unpublished PhD thesis, University of Wales (Swansea).

Trilsbach, A. and Ahmed, M. M. (1986) *The Aftermath of the 1984 Sudan Famine: Some Observations from North Kordofan in 1985*, Report to the University of Khartoum, Dept. of Geography.

Trilsbach, A. and Wood, S. (1986) Livestock Markets and the Semi-Arid Environment: A Case Study from Sudan, *Geografiska Annaler*, 68B, 51.8.

Trilsbach, A. (1987) Environmental Change and Village Societies West of the White Nile, in Lawless, R. I. (ed.), *Middle Eastern Villages*, Croom Helm, London.

10

China: The Demographic Disaster of 1958–1961

A. J. Jowett

Famine is no stranger to China, for this is Mallory's 'land of famine' (1928), a land whose population in the century prior to 1949 appeared to be held in check by the Malthusian controls of famine, disease and war. Yet in the post-1949 era, China's apparent success in feeding a rapidly expanding population (542 million in 1949, 745 million in 1966 and 1046 million in 1985) is regularly quoted as a prime example of how effective political management can harness available resources, overcome environmental constraints and deliver such improvements in the production and distribution of food supplies that famine and malnutrition are eliminated. Thus, while it is widely acknowledged that famine was a constant threat to the people of China in the pre-1949 era, there is little acknowledgement that famine continued to afflict China after the communists came to power in 1949. In part at least these views are in need of serious revision, for in what has become known as the 'three bitter years' (1959–61) China suffered one of the most devastating famines ever recorded. Yet outside China there is little awareness of the famine of 1959–61. Restricted access, limited and misleading data, plus Chinese denials combined to conceal the existence and true extent of the disaster for almost 20 years. Nowadays, with the benefit of policy changes and press relaxation in the post-Mao era and in particular with the growing availability of census data, statistical yearbooks and academic journals, we have access to the basic economic and demographic data from which to re-assess Chinese developments since 1949. Even before they released the statistical

Table 10.1   Production of food-grains in China, 1956–1965

	Foodgrain[a] total m. tons	Production per capita kg/person	Rice m. tons	Wheat m. tons	Potatoes[b] m. tons
1956	192.75	306.8	82.48	24.80	21.85
1957	195.05	301.7	86.78	23.64	21.92
1958	200.00	303.1	80.85	22.59	32.73
1959	170.00	252.9	69.37	22.18	23.82
1960	143.50	216.7	59.73	22.17	20.35
1961	147.50	224.0	53.64	14.25	21.73
1962	160.00	237.8	62.99	16.67	23.45
1963	170.00	245.8	73.77	18.48	21.39
1964	187.50	266.0	83.00	20.84	20.13
1965	194.53	268.2	87.72	25.22	19.86

[a] Unprocessed food-grains including cereals, soyabeans and potatoes.
[b] Potatoes are converted into a grain equivalent form by equating 4 tons of tubers with one ton of grain; after 1963 the conversion ratio is 5:1.
Source: Statistical Yearbook of China, 1983.

yearbooks, the Chinese had already confirmed the existence and dimensions of the disaster of 1958–61. The noted economist Xue Muqiao (1981), reported that a serious famine had afflicted rural China; Sun Yefang (1981), director of the State Statistical Bureau, revealed that China's death rate had risen from 10.8 per thousand in 1957 to 25.4 in 1960; and the journal *Jingji Guanli* (*Economic Management*) indicated that some 20 million people had died of famine between 1959 and 1962 (Domes, 1985). Thus, what for 20 years had been the view of a very small minority of outside observers, was eventually acknowledged as the official view of the Chinese government.

THE AGRICULTURAL DISASTER

Table 10.1 shows that total food-grain production declined dramatically in 1959 and 1960, bottomed out in 1960–61 at a level almost 30 per cent below that of 1958, recovered only slightly in 1962–3 and took until 1965 to regain the level of 1957. In per capita terms production declined from 303.9 kg of unprocessed grain in 1956–8 to 220.3kg in 1960–1 and recovered to only 241.8 kg in

1962–3.In a country which was self-sufficient in grain, where over 85 per cent of calorie intake was derived from cereals and where, in good years, food consumption probably averaged only 2,100 kcal per person per day, the decline of 56.5 million tons in food-grain production between 1958 and 1960 was bound to have a dramatic and disastrous impact. Just how disastrous can be gauged from the fact that in 1956–8 10 million tons of grain supported about 33 million people and in 1960 China was faced with a shortfall of almost 60 million tons, if net exports are added to the production decline.

While the precise causes of the agricultural disaster remain in dispute, it is generally agreed that a combination of man-made and natural disasters precipitated the harvest failures of the late 1950s and early 1960s. The collectivization of agriculture; the arrival of the communes and the initiation of the Great Leap Forward in 1958; the excessive level of grain procurement from 1958 to 1960; a massive reduction of manpower, with the agricultural labour force down from 193.1 million in 1957 to 154.9 million by the end of 1958; an equally disastrous decline of traction power, with the number of draught animals down from 57.2 million in 1954 to 38.2 million in 1961; a decline of over 20 million ha in the land sown with food-grains – all combined to drain China's low technology, labour-intensive agriculture of its resources and incentives with the result that food production declined dramatically. The political, economic and technical shortcomings of the Great Leap Forward were exacerbated by natural disasters. Floods and drought, arising from the unreliability of monsoon rainfall, have been the traditional mechanism for triggering famine in China. It was therefore no surprise that the government of the day should ascribe the agricultural failures of 1959–61 to the unprecedented bad weather of that period. However, in apportioning blame for the agricultural disasters the peasants of Hunan province reported in 1962 that 30 per cent of the production difficulties were caused by natural calamities, while 70 per cent resulted from man-made factors (Liu Shaoqi, 1969). Twenty years later that view was echoed by Luo (1981) who concluded that 'human factors' played a more decisive role than the 'forces of nature'. A more detailed account of the background to the famine is provided by Ashton et al. (1984), Bernstein (1984), Jowett (1985) and MacFarquhar (1983).

Table 10.2   Calorie and protein availability per person per day in China, 1956–1965

	Calories			Protein		
	Total kcal	% derived from		Total gm	% derived from	
		Grain	Animal products		Grain	Animal products
1956	2,148	88.2	3.5	55.5	83.7	6.8
1957	2,124	88.4	3.8	57.3	83.6	7.2
1958	2,128	87.2	4.5	56.3	83.1	7.6
1959	1,770	86.4	4.6	47.5	81.2	8.3
1960	1,509	87.0	4.0	41.0	80.6	8.0
1961	1,619	87.9	3.1	44.3	83.0	6.4
1962	1,710	89.5	2.9	46.6	84.1	6.1
1963	1,825	88.8	4.0	47.4	82.7	7.8
1964	2,001	88.6	4.3	51.6	83.2	8.1
1965	2,025	88.4	4.6	54.6	84.0	8.0

Sources: The above data have been generated by using the total annual food availability calculated by Piazza (1983) and the population data provided by the State Statistical Bureau (1984).

FOOD CONSUMPTION

Given that food-grains provide 85–90 per cent of China's calorie intake and 80–85 per cent of its protein intake, the nutritional well-being of the population is critically dependent on the domestic grain harvest. China's international grain trade in the decade 1956–65 varied from net exports of 4.16 million tons in 1959 to net imports of 4.75 million tons in 1964. As such, the grain trade represented no more than 2.5 per cent of domestic production.

Though the Chinese have recently released food consumption data for the years since 1977 there is a general lack of official information on calorie and protein intake for the period of 1949–77. In the absence of official data we are dependent on western estimates, and in particular on the World Bank's food balance sheets for the years 1950–81 (Piazza, 1983). A revised form of the World Bank data for the period 1956–65 appears in table 10.2.

It should be remembered that Chinese data refer to food availability and not to food consumption. Smil (1986) calculates that food consumption in China is about 15 per cent below the level of food availability. Actual consumption is lowered by losses incurred in household storage, food preparation, cooking and left-overs.

Food availability is estimated to have declined from around 2,150 kcal per person per day in 1957 to 1,500 kcal in 1960, and to have recovered to 2,025 kcal in 1965. If these figures are close to reality, and they accord with other Western estimates (Smil, 1985), they imply devastatingly low levels of average food intake for the years 1959–62, and especially 1960. By way of comparison, recent FAO data suggest that daily food consumption for 1982–4 in some of the problem areas of Africa was 1,657 kcal in Ghana, 1,749 kcal in Mali, and 1,781 kcal in Uganda. The World Bank's estimate for Ethiopia was 1,758 kcal in 1981.

Some measure of the nutritional deprivation in China at the time of the famine is to be found in refugee reports which record among their dietary items chaff, grass, leaves, tree bark, roots and many wild plants. Widespread reports of starving beggars and occasional incidents of cannibalism are to be found in the literature (London and London, 1976). Nutritional diseases and disorders, famine oedema, beri beri, night blindness, famine diarrhoea and inflammatory disorders of the liver were widely reported (Aird, 1969; W.K., 1961).

DEMOGRAPHIC RESPONSE TO FAMINE

China's demographic response to the famine of 1959–61 appears to correspond closely with the general model postulated by Bongaarts and Cain (1982) for developing countries. According to Chinese data, the impact of the famine was such that by 1960 the soaring death rate surpassed the plummeting birth rate and China's population went into decline. Over the two years 1960–1 China's official view is that the total population declined by about 13.5 million. Using revised forms of China's demographic data, it can be shown that over the four years 1958–61 China suffered some 25–30 million more deaths and experienced some 30–35 million fewer births than might have been expected under normal conditions. As such the magnitude of China's demographic disaster ranks it as one of the worst in the history of the world. The following discussion examines the impact of the 1959–61 famine on China's mortality and fertility with some brief comments on the natural growth rate and age structure of population.

Table 10.3 Crude death rates and annual number of deaths in China, 1953–1967

	Crude death rate, per thousand				Annual deaths, m.	
	SSB(1)	Banister(2)	Coale(3)	Hill(4)	SSB(1)	Banister(2)
1953	14.00	25.77	25.5	23.8	8.14	15.05
1955	12.28	22.33	22.4	20.9	7.47	13.55
1957	10.80	18.12	19.0	19.1	6.88	11.47
1959	14.59	22.06	23.3	32.8	9.72	14.43
1960	25.43	44.60	38.8	29.5	16.96	29.02
1961	14.24	23.01	20.5	21.2	9.40	14.83
1963	10.04	13.81	13.0	17.1	6.85	11.73
1965	9.50	11.61	11.1	13.1	6.79	9.51
1967	8.43	10.47	9.9	11.0	6.36	8.38

Sources: 1   State Statistical Bureau (1984); 2   Banister (1984); 3   Coale (1984); 4   Hill (1985); data in this column are for 'fiscal years'. 1953 = 1953–4 (mid-year to mid-year)

Various western institutions, such as the US Bureau of Census and the World Bank, have reconstructed China's population data in order to get the best demographic fit from the various strands of available information. Having taken account of omissions (military personnel), under- and overenumeration, clustering of ages and the conflict between Chinese and western calendars, differing reconstructions have been published by authors such as Banister (1984), Coale (1984), Hill (1985) and Kincannon and Banister (1984).

Famine and Mortality

Such was the severity of the famine that, according to Chinese data, the annual number of deaths peaked from less than 7 million in 1957 to almost 17 million in 1960 and then declined equally dramatically to less than 7 million in 1963 (see table 10.3). The associated death rate rose from 10.80 to 25.43 per thousand and fell back to 10.04 per thousand (see figure 10.1). Western reconstructions of China's demographic data imply a substantial underenumeration of mortality amounting to about 38 per cent of deaths (57.4 million) in the inter-censal period 1953–64 and about 16 per cent (21.5 million) between 1964 and 1982 (Coale, 1984). Using reconstructed mortality figures, Banister calculates that annual deaths rose from 11.5 million in 1957 to 29 million in 1960, with a peak death rate of 44.6 per thousand (see table 10.3). My own calculations show the excess deaths over the four years 1959–62 to be (a) 16.5 million using China's official data, or (b) 25.0 million using Coale's mortality reconstruction of (c) 31.5 million based on Banister's reconstructed death rates. Employing slightly more refined techniques, Ashton et al. (1984) estimate that China's excess deaths numbered 29.5 million.

Under famine conditions the demographic sub-groups exposed to the highest risk of mortality are normally assumed to be infants, children and the elderly. Current estimates suggest that by 1960 infant mortality may have doubled, rising to almost 300 deaths per thousand live births, while life expectancy at birth was probably halved, falling to less than 25 years in 1960 (Banister, 1984). Lavely's study (1984) of a single commune in Sichuan province shows infant mortality to have risen from less than 50 per thousand in 1955 to almost 400 per thousand at the height of the famine. Such was the rise in mortality among the young that for the whole of China the median age for deaths dropped from 17.6 years in 1957 to 9.7 years in 1960 (Wang, 1984). Though Hill's data (1985) show infant mortality to have exceeded 200 per thousand in 1958–9, 1959–60 and 1961–2, he concluded, somewhat surprisingly, that the brunt of the mortality increase in the famine years was borne not by the children but by the over-40s.

Our knowledge of the regional variations in famine mortality is very limited, but it is apparent that the situation in rural China was far worse than in the cities. The unreasonable level of grain procurement in 1959 and 1960 appears to have ensured a higher level of food supplies for the cities, especially the major cities, at the expense of the countryside. Furthermore, the less developed provinces of the interior carried far higher levels of mortality than the more developed coastal provinces. However, as revealed in table 10.4 and figure 10.1, all areas of China for which data are currently available show evidence of famine mortality. The increase in the death rate is marginal in the case of Shanghai, substantial even in the coastal provinces of Liaoning and Jiangsu and massive for rural China as a whole and inland provinces such as Henan. Famine mortality shows both regional and temporal variations, with the peak level of mortality falling somewhere in the triennium 1959–61. That the death rate for the whole of China should have more than

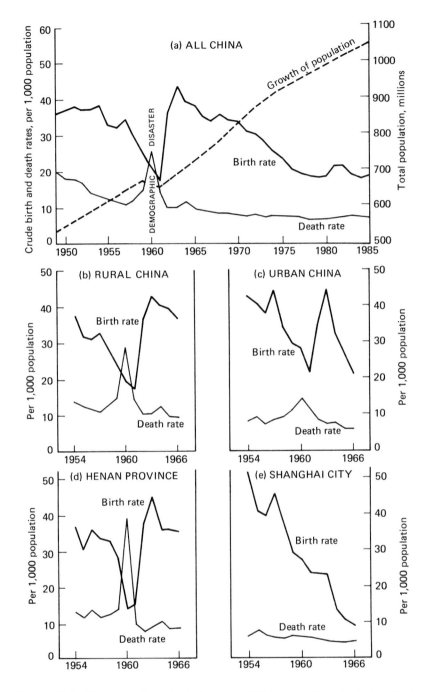

Figure 10.1 Vital rates for selected areas of China and for selected periods

Table 10.4   Increased mortality in China in response to famine: selected regional examples

Source	Area	Period [a]	Crude death rates (CDR) [b] per thousand	Increase in CDR [b] per thousand
1	Shanghai (city population)	1958–59	5.8 – 6.4	0.6
1	Shanghai (total municipality)	1958–59	5.9 – 6.9	1.0
1	Shanghai (rural counties)	1957–59	7.4 –10.6	3.2
2	China (urban population)	1957–60	8.5 –13.8	5.3
3	Xinjiang (province)	1958–59	13.0 –18.8	5.8
4	Liaoning (province)	1957–61	9.4 –17.5	8.1
5	Jiangsu (province)	1957–60	10.2 –18.6	8.4
2	China (total population)	1957–60	10.8 –25.4	14.6
2	China (rural population)	1957–60	11.1 –28.6	17.5
6	Henan (province)	1957–60	11.8 –39.6	27.8

[a] From the minimum rate in the 1950s to the maximum rate during the famine.
[b] In the absence of information which would permit a reconstruction of provincial death rates, the material presented in table 10.4 is that derived from official Chinese sources. As discussed in the text, Chinese deaths in the 1950s were markedly under-reported and actual levels of mortality are likely to have been substantially higher than shown in table 10.4. Reconstructed death rates for China's total population are included in table 10.3.
Sources: 1   Shanghai Municipal Statistical Bureau (1984); 2   State Statistical Bureau (1984); 3   I am indebted to Yuan-Qing Li for this information; 4   Liaoning *Economic Statistics Yearbook* (1984); 5   Wang and Luo (1983); 6   Henan Population Geography (1983). I am indebted to William Lavely for providing me with graphs of the birth rates and death rates in Henan Province, 1954–79.

doubled in the period 1957–60 is a harrowing indication of the severity of the famine. Even in the relatively more prosperous coastal provinces of Jiangsu and Liaoning the death rate rose by more than 80 per cent; in Henan province the death rate trebled and Anhui province appears to have suffered even more tragically with a reported death rate of 68 per thousand in 1960 (Bernstein, 1984). A detailed account of Liyuan Commune in Anhui province, where half the population died of starvation or fled the area, is provided by Bernstein (1983). In the far west of China, Xinjiang province appears to have avoided the worst effects of both the drought and government policies and thereby records, by the

Sources: China (total, rural, urban): State Statistical Bureau (1984); Henan Province: Lin and Chen (1983); Shanghai City: Shanghai Municipal Statistical Bureau (1984)

standards of the day, a relatively modest rise of 45 per cent in its death rate. However, it is something of a mystery of why Xinjiang's death rate should have peaked in 1959 when the low point in provincial grain production did not occur until 1961.

Famine and Fertility

While it is self-evident that famine increases levels of mortality, it is less evident that famine generates major declines in fertility. Yet there is much evidence to show that famines are associated with large reductions in the birth rate. In China, as elsewhere, the high points of famines are associated not only with peak rates of mortality but also with the low points of conceptions. Such correlations were seen during food shortages in seventeenth- and eighteenth-century Europe and are particularly well documented in the case of the Dutch famine of 1944–5 (Stein et al., 1975; Stein and Susser, 1978). As a result of the wartime famine, births in the affected Dutch cities were reduced to about one-third of the expected number, with the substantial decline in fertility beginning some nine months after the onset of acute starvation.

A variety of mechanisms appear to link nutritional deprivation with temporary infertility. Substantial increases in the reported cases of amenorrhoea (the cessation of menstruation and presumably of ovulation) are the normal accompaniments to famine, and famine amenorrhoea appears to be one of the major causes of temporary sterility (Le Roy Ladurie, 1975). Several other factors contribute to reduced fertility at times of famine. As Bongaarts and Delgado (1981) report:

> Any or all of the following factors could be important: a physiological change in a woman's ability to ovulate, conceive, or complete pregnancy due to malnutrition; a disturbance of the reproductive system resulting from the psychological stress associated with famine conditions; an involuntary reduction in coital frequency due to physical weakness, lack of interest, or separation of spouses; and a voluntary control of fertility through abstention, induced abortion, or contraceptive practice.

Reduced libido in both males and females, decreased coital frequency and a reduction in the production of sperm are characteristic features of famine strickened populations (Keys et al., 1950). The possibility of increased foetal wastage in severely malnourished women is a matter of some dispute (Gopalan and Naidu, 1972; Stein and Susser, 1978). Separation of spouses while searching for food is a normal response to famine conditions, as is a reduction in the marriage rate. Thus, a combination of biological, psychological and behavioural mechanisms appear to explain the dramatic decline of fertility at times of famine.

China's fertility response to the famine of 1958–61 appears to conform to the general pattern outlined above. Famine amenorrhoea, which was widely reported in China (Alsop, 1962), generated widespread temporary sterility. Figure 10.1 shows that while the death rate peaked in 1960 the birth rate reached its low point in 1961. One might infer that the highest level of mortality and the lowest level of conceptions coincided with the height of the famine in 1960, materializing as very low levels of fertility in 1961. Chinese and western data relating to fertility in the decade 1955–65 are summarized in tables 10.5 and 10.6. Famine conditions were responsible for a halving of fertility between 1957 and 1961, with the total fertility rate (TFR) declining precipitously from 6.405 to 3.287. Even in urban China the TFR was lowered by almost three points. Western reconstructions of China's demographic data suggest that the crude birth rate declined from over 40 per thousand in the mid-1950s to around 22 in 1961, with the annual number of births falling from over 27 million in 1957 to around 14.5 million in 1961.

Table 10.5   Fertility data of China, 1955–1965

	Total Fertility Rate(1)			Crude birth rate(2)		
	National	Rural	Urban	National	Rural	Urban
1955	6.261	6.391	5.665	32.60	31.74	40.67
1957	6.405	6.504	5.943	34.03	32.81	44.48
1959	4.303	4.323	4.172	24.78	23.78	29.43
1960	4.015	3.996	4.057	20.86	19.35	28.03
1961	3.287	3.349	2.982	18.02	16.99	21.63
1962	6.023	6.303	4.789	37.01	37.27	35.46
1963	7.502	7.784	6.207	43.37	43.19	44.50
1965	6.076	6.597	3.749	37.88	39.53	26.59

Sources: 1   Renkou yu Jingji (1983); 2   State Statistical Bureau (1983).

Table 10.6   Annual births and crude birth rate in China, 1955–1965

	Birth, millions			Crude birth rates, per thousand		
	SSB(1)	Banister(2)	Hill(3)	SSB(1)	Banister(2)	Hill(3)
1955	19.84	26.36	24.82	32.60	43.04	40.4
1957	21.69	27.39	25.80	34.03	43.25	40.3
1959	16.50	18.67	18.88	24.78	28.53	28.9
1960	13.92	17.41	14.72	20.86	26.76	22.7
1961	11.90	14.46	20.88	18.02	22.43	32.1
1962	24.64	26.80	33.81	37.01	41.02	50.8
1963	29.59	33.57	30.71	43.37	49.79	44.7
1965	27.09	27.89	28.51	37.88	38.98	39.4

Source: 1   State Statistical Bureau (1983). Annual births are calculated from crude birth rates and mid-year population totals. 2   Banister (1984); 3   Hill (1985); data in these columns are for 'fiscal' years; 1955 = 1955–6 (mid-year to mid-year).

Calculations of the number of births which were lost or postponed as a result of the famine are particularly sensitive to assumptions of how fertility would have developed in the absence of the disaster. Nevertheless there is a growing consensus that some 33–35 million births were lost or postponed as a result of the famine. Age-specific fertility rates plotted for 1957 and 1961 (figure 10.2) show that fertility declined at all ages. Such a uniform reduction in fertility among both the younger and the older married women of China supports the view that the restriction of childbearing arose from famine-induced sub-fecundity rather from a large increase in the use of contraception. Postponement of marriage during the famine years – the total female first-marriage rate declined form 0.918 in 1956 to 0.738 in 1959 (Renkou yu Jingji, 1983) – was an additional factor which depressed levels of fertility in 1960–1.

Previous experience indicates that periods of famine-induced infertility are often followed by a phase of hyper-fertility. This was certainly the case in China, for in 1963 the TFR rose to 7.502 and the crude birth rate probably reached 50 per thousand (tables 10.5 and 10.6). Studies by Stein et al. (1975) have shown that infertility and infecundity caused by starvation are rapidly reversible. Famine apparently causes no lasting damage to a population's ability to reproduce. Even with small increases in food intake, populations existing at very low calorific levels have witnessed an immediate physiological recovery of normal ovulation, fecundity and sexual

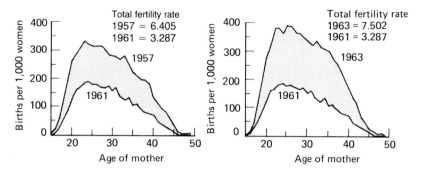

Figure 10.2   Age-specific fertility rate of China, 1957, 1961 and 1963
Source: Renkou yu Jingji (1983)

activity. China in the early 1960s conforms to this pattern of development. Small increases in food-grain production, a growing government awareness of the severity of the famine, a lower level of grain procurement and the switch from being a net exporter to a net importer of grain combined to raise the average food availability in 1962 by some 200 kcal per person per day above the disaster level of 1960 (table 10.2). While food availability in 1962 was still 20 per cent below the level of 1956–7, the marginal increase in food consumption was apparently sufficient to trigger off the hyper-fertility conditions of 1963. In the immediate post-famine period a substantially larger number of women than normal were susceptible to pregnancy. Under normal nutritional conditions many of China's married women in the 1950s would not have been at risk of conceiving because they were either pregnant or because they were breastfeeding a recently born infant and hence experiencing periods of temporary postpartum anovulation. The onset of famine significantly changed these demographic conditions. During 1960–1 the low level of conceptions greatly reduced the number of pregnant women and the high level of infant mortality greatly restricted the number of breastfeeding mothers. Thus by 1962 an abnormally high number of women were exposed to pregnancy. The recovery from infecundity combined with the resumption of normal sexual activity produced a high level of conceptions in 1962 and nine months later this yielded the peak level of fertility in 1963. Some 33.5 million babies were born in 1963 and in the three years from

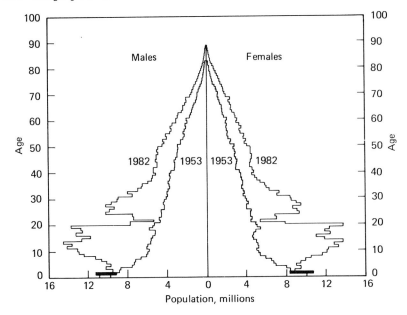

Figure 10.3   Age structure of population of China, 1953 and 1982
Source: Population Census Office (1985)

mid-1962 to mid-1965, over 90 million births were recorded. Plots of age-specific fertility patterns for 1961 and 1963 (figure 10.2) show that fertility rose at all ages. An additional factor fuelling high fertility in 1963 was the abnormally large number of marriages undertaken in 1962. The total female first marriage rate rose from 0.738 in 1959 to 1.189 in 1962 as marriages postponed during the famine were combined with the resumption of a normal marital pattern. The post-famine 'baby-boom' was, however, short-lived, and China's outstanding demographic achievement of the past 20 years has been the large and rapid decline of fertility (see figures 10.1 and 10.2).

The dramatic decline of fertility in 1961 and its precipitous rise in 1963 is a characteristic feature of almost all the provinces of China (see figure 10.1 and table 10.5). In Liaoning, a more developed province with more reliable demographic data, the birth rate dropped from 41.9 per thousand in 1957 to 17.3 in 1961 and then soared to 49.1 in 1963. In the capital Beijing, data for the municipality show that over the same period, the birth rate dropped from 42 per thousand to around 25 and then recovered to almost 44 (Gong, 1985).

Table 10.7　Size and natural rate of increase of population in China, 1955–1965

	Total population, millions		Natural increase rate of population, per thousand			
	National, SSB(1)	National, Banister(2)	National, Banister(2)	National, SSB(1)	Rural, SSB(1)	Urban, SSB(1)
1955	614.65	606.73	20.71	20.32	19.14	31.37
1957	646.53	633.22	25.13	23.23	21.74	36.01
1959	672.07	654.35	6.47	10.19	9.17	18.51
1960	662.07	650.66	−17.84	− 4.57	− 9.23	14.26
1961	658.59	644.67	− 0.58	3.78	2.41	10.24
1962	672.95	653.30	27.00	26.99	26.95	27.18
1963	691.72	674.25	35.98	33.33	32.70	37.37
1965	725.38	715.55	27.37	28.38	29.47	20.90

Sources:　1　State Statistical Bureau (1984); year-end population totals. 2　Banister (1984); mid-year population totals.

Famine and the natural growth rate of population

While all sources are agreed that at the height of the famine the death rate exceeded the birth rate, the extent of China's population decline is a matter of some disagreement. The internal inconsistency of China's Household Registration data becomes particularly apparent in 1960–1. Population totals show a decline of 10 million in 1960 and a further decline of 3.48 million in 1961 (see table 10.7). Yet table 10.7 shows that only in one year, 1960, did the death rate exceed the birth rate. Rates of natural increase for 1960 and 1961 are −4.57 and +3.78 per thousand based on the published birth rates and death rates but −14.99 and −5.27 when calculated from the recorded population totals. Western reconstructions of the available data shows that China's population declined in both 1960 and 1961, with a total reduction of some 5–10 million.

The contrasting severity of the famine in rural and urban China is registered in the minimum growth rates of population which, using official data, were −9.23 per thousand in the countryside but +14.26 in the cities. Currently available data show that the regional response to the famine varied from the city of Shanghai with a minimum growth rate of + 17.9 per thousand to Henan province with −25.6 (table 10.8).

Table 10.8   Vital rates, selected regions of China

Region	Year[a]	Total population, millions	Vital rates, per thousand[b]		
			CBR	CDR	NIR
Shanghai (City population)	1961	6.41	23.8	5.9	17.9
Shanghai (Municipality)	1961	10.53	22.4	7.7	14.7
China (Urban population)	1960	103.73	28.03	13.77	14.26
Xinjiang (Province)	1959	6.16	29.87	18.84	11.03
Shanghai (Rural counties)	1961	4.12	20.4	10.5	9.9
Jiangsu (Province)	1960	42.46	18.6	18.6	0
Liaoning (Province)	1961	25.19	17.3	17.5	− 0.3
China (Total population)	1960	662.07	20.86	25.43	− 4.57
China (Rural population)	1960	531.34	19.35	28.58	− 9.23
Henan (Province)	1960	48.50	14.0	39.6	−25.6

[a] The year with the minimum natural growth rate of population.
[b] Note as in Table 10.4 on p. 145.
Sources: See Table 10.4.

Famine and the age structure of population

Single-year age-distribution data, from the 1982 census, are available for the whole of China and for the provinces of Hebei, Henan and Zhejiang. As seen on figure 10.3, China's 1982 population pyramid is deeply scarred by the demographic disaster of 1958–61. Over the period 1957–65 the rapidly fluctuating number of annual births, trimmed by variable rates of survival, appears as a series of peaks and troughs on the age structure of population. Such is the variation in the size of the cohorts that in 1982 there were 19.5 million 24-year-olds, only 10.7 million 21-year-olds but 27.4 million 19-year-olds. The dearth of population in the 20–23 age group, survivors from the births of 1959–62, is a clear indication of the extent to which the severity of the famine impinged on Chinese levels of fertility and mortality.

In terms of the regional variation in the impact of the famine, the evidence from the 1982 age structure of population (table 10.9) supports the earlier view that the demographic damage was nationwide rather than localized, that inland provinces suffered more than the coastal regions and that Henan province was severely affected. Thus the demographic trough is eroded far deeper into the population pyramid of inland Henan than into the pyramid of coastal

Table 10.9   Cohort ratios, mid-1982 census data (number of 19 year olds = 100)

Age	Year of birth	China(1)	Hebei(2)	Henan(2)	Zhejiang(2)
15	1966/7	83.1	75.1	84.6	75.2
17	1964/5	89.2	88.4	79.5	88.3
19	1962/3	100.0	100.0	100.0	100.0
20	1961/2	57.1	45.8	53.1	59.7
21	1960/1	39.0	39.3	24.8	45.5
22	1959/60	52.3	64.7	41.6	61.5
23	1958/9	52.2	60.8	41.2	52.5
25	1956/7	68.9	77.2	63.1	71.9
27	1954/5	71.8	78.5	69.2	71.6

Sources: 1   Population Census Office (1985); 2   Population Census Office (1982).

Zhejiang. Henan, with a 1982 population of 74.42 million, had 2.11 million 19-year-olds but only 0.52 million 21-year-olds, whereas among Zhejiang's 28.88 million there were 1.12 million and 0.51 million people in the equivalent cohorts. The famine-induced demographic damage in Hebei province accords roughly with the average for the country as a whole.

CONCLUSION

China in 1958–61 suffered in stage two of its demographic transition the type of trauma normally confined to the pre-transitional stage of the model, when the death rate temporarily exceeded the birth rate and China's population went into decline. Similar incidents of major demographic disasters during stage two of the demographic transition have occurred elsewhere in the world. The Danish example of 1831 is well documented (Andersen, 1980). What makes China's case particulary noteworthy is the scale of the disaster, its apparently nationwide extent and the fact that for almost a quarter of a century very few people outside China were aware of the existence, let alone the dimensions, of the disaster. In fact the worldwide encyclopaedia of famines (Nash, 1976) makes no mention of China's 1959–61 disaster and the contemporary view of the London *Times* (2 June 1962) was that while there was malnutrition in China it nowhere amounted to famine. A similar viewpoint is regularly encountered in the academic literature. Perkins (1969), an authority on China's agriculture, in reviewing the poor harvests of 1959–61, concluded that in the past they

> would have meant millions of deaths in the areas most severely affected. Tight control, particularly an effective system of rationing, together with the development of the railroads, meant that few if any starved outright. Instead the nutritional levels of the whole country were maintained . . . As a result the regime averted a major disaster.

Nowadays, as the foregoing text has shown, we come to a very different conclusion and rank China's 1958–61 disaster as one of the most devastating the world has ever seen. To reach such a conclusion one needed the data-enriched sources of the 1980s, and the Chinese are to be congratulated for making available, in the post-Mao era, such a wide range of economic and demographic material.

The available demographic data appear to show that China's population disaster was nationwide rather than localized, and if the famine was similarly distributed, then we may have to conclude that policy failures rather than weather problems were the primary cause of the disaster. Weather-induced harvest failures within China normally have a localized impact, with some areas devastated while others are virtually unaffected. Disasters arising from national policy may well have a nationwide effect. However, the possibility exists that the food distribution system within China may have ensured some degree of equality in food availability across the entire country. In this case regional production problems, in drought-affected areas, may have been transmitted into consumption problems across the entire country. A definitive analysis of the regional impact of the disaster must await the publication of demographic data for all of the provinces of China.

Past demographic problems are not entirely divorced from present-day population policies in China. The rapid and massive fluctuation of fertility in the late 1950s and the early 1960s generated successive large and small cohorts of population and over time these massively varying cohorts have had a very disruptive impact on the provision of socio-economic services such as education and employment. Normally the echo effect of these peaks and troughs is transmitted via the age structure to future generations and thus past demographic problems are sustained into the future. The baby boom of 1963 reached the age of marriage and childbearing in the mid-1980s and the realization of this large inbuilt momentum for population growth was one of the factors that led the Chinese government to initiate its one-child policy. The generation born of the baby boom in the early 1960s are being required to limit their fertility severely in an attempt to restrain the rate of population growth and to contain the size of China's population within the 1,200 million targeted for the year 2000.

Those familiar with the Soviet famine and associated demographic disaster of the early 1930s (Dalrymple, 1964) will see many similarities with China's disaster of 1958–61. Such an outcome is particularly ironic, for the Great Leap Forward, which may well have precipitated China's famine, was Mao's attempt to break away from the Soviet-style of development and launch a model of development that was distinctively Chinese.

Societies which are famine-prone are, by definition, high-risk environments, and it is generally assumed (Bongaarts and Cain, 1982) that such environments create a disincentive to limit fertility. Children are produced as an insurance against disaster and thus the longer-term demographic response to famine is seen as the persistence of high fertility. Such beliefs find no support whatsoever in China's demographic experience in the 25 years after the famine. Over the past quarter of a century China has experienced a spectacular decline of fertility (Jowett, 1986) and in spite of the demographic disaster of 1958–61 China now enjoys advanced levels of demographic transition at a very early stage of economic development.

REFERENCES

Abbreviations

FBIS-CHI-81-067	Foreign Broadcast Information Service, Daily Report, China, 1981, no. 67.
JPRS-CPS-85-028	Joint Publication Research Service. China Report: Political, Sociological and Military Affairs, 1985, no. 28.
JPRS-CEA-81-128	Joint Publication Research Service. China Report: Economic Affairs, 1981, no. 128.

156 A. J. Jowett

Aird, J. S. (1969) Population Growth, in Eckstein, A. et al., *Economic Trends in Communist China*:183–328.

Alsop, J. (1962) On China's Descending Spiral, *China Quarterly*, 11:21–37.

Andersen, O. (1980) A Malaria Epidemic in Denmark, in Charbonneau, H. and Larose, A. *The Great Mortalities: Methodological Studies of Demographic Crises in the Past*:33–49.

Ashton, B. et al. (1984) Famine in China, 1958–61, *Population and Development Review*, 10, 4:613 –45.

Banister, J. (1984) An Analysis of Recent Data on the Population of China, *Population and Development Review*, 10, 2:241–71.

Bernstein, T. P. (1983) Starving to Death in China, *The New York Review of Books*, 16 June:36–8.

Bernstein, T. P. (1984) Stalinism, Famine and Chinese Peasants, *Theory and Society*, 13, 339–77.

Bongaarts, J. and Cain, M. (1982) Demographic Responses to Famine, in Cahill, K. M. (ed.) *Famine*, Orbis, Maryknoll, N.Y., 44–59.

Bongaarts, J. and Delgado, H. (1981) Effects of Nutritional Status on Fertility in Rural Guatemala, in Leridon, H. and Menken, J. (eds), *Natural Fertility*, Ordina, Liege: 109–33.

Coale, A. J. (1984) *Rapid Population Change in China, 1952–1982*, National Academy Press, Washington D C.

Dalrymple, D. G. (1964) The Soviet Famine of 1932–34, *Soviet Studies*, 15:250–84.

Domes, J. (1985) *The Government and Politics of the PRC*, Westview Press, Boulder.

FAO (Food and Agriculture Organization) (1984) *Production Yearbook*, 38.

Gong, H. (1985) An Analysis of the Size and Structure of Households in Beijing. *Renkou yu Jingji (Population and the Economy)*, 1 (25 February), 44–50. Translated in JPRS-CPS-85-060 (20 June), 86–97.

Gopalan, C. and Naidu, A. N. (1972) Nutrition and Fertility, *The Lancet*, 18 November, 1077–9.

Hill, K. (1985) *Demographic Trends in China 1953–1982*, Population Health and Nutrition Department, World Bank, PHN Technical Note, 85, 4.

Jowett, A. J. (1985) China's Foodgrains: Production and Performance 1949–81, *GeoJournal*, 10, 4, 373–88.

Jowett, A. J. (1986) China: Population Change and Population Control, *GeoJournal*, 12, 4, 349–63.

Keys, A. B., Brozek, J., Henschel, A., Maickelsen, O. and Taylor, H. L. (1950) *The Biology of Human Starvation*, 2 vols, University of Minnesota Press, Minneapolis.

Kincannon, L. and Banister, J. (1984) Perspectives on China's 1982

Census, paper presented at the international seminar on China's 1982 census, Beijing, China, 26–31 March.

Lavely, W. R. (1984) The Rural Chinese Fertility Transition: A Report from Shifang Xian, Sichuan, *Population Studies*, 38:365-84.

Le Roy Ladurie, E. (1975) Famine Amenorrhea, in Forster, R. and Ranum, O., *Biology of Man in History*, 163–78.

Lin, R. and Chen, D. (1983) *Population Geography of Henan* (in Chinese).

Liu Shaoqi (1969) Selected Edition on Liu Shao-chi's (Liu Shaoqi's) Counter-revolutionary Revisionist Crimes. Translated in *Selections from China Mainland Magazines*, 652.

London, M. and London, I. D. (1976) The Other China: Hunger, *Worldview*, 19, 5:4–11.

Luo, G. (1981) An Analysis of the Formation and Development of China's Planned Economy, *Jingji Yanjiu (Economic Research)*, 2:37–45. Translated in JPRS-CEA-81-128 (9 April), 1–13.

MacFarquhar, R. (1983) *The Origins of the Cultural Revolution*, vol. 2, *The Great Leap Forward, 1958-1960*, Oxford University Press, Oxford.

Mallory, W. H. (1928) *China: Land of Famine*, American Geographical Society, New York.

Nash, J. R. (1976) *Darkest Hours: A Narrative Encyclopaedia of World-Wide Disasters*, Nelson-Hall, Chicago.

Perkins, D. H. (1969) *Agricultural Development in China, 1368–1968*, Edinburgh University Press, Edinburgh.

Piazza, A. (1983) *Trends in Food and Nutrient Availability in China, 1950–81*, World Bank Staff Working Paper 607.

Population Census Office (1982) *Major Figures from the Third National Census of Population* (in Chinese).

Population Census Office (1985) *1982 Population Census of China* (results of computer tabulation), State Statistical Bureau, Beijing (in Chinese).

Renkou yu Jingji (1983) *An Analysis of the National One-per-Thousand Fertility Survey*, special issue, *Renkou yu Jingji (Population and the Economy)*, Beijing (in Chinese).

Shanghai Municipal Statistical Bureau (1984) *Shanghai Tongji Nianjian (Shanghai Statistical Yearbook)* 1983. Partial translation in JPRS-CPS-85-003, 44-66.

Smil, V. (1985) China's Food, *Scientific American*, 253, 6:104–12.

Smil, V. (1986) Food Production and Quality of Diet in China, *Population and Development Review*, 12, 1:25–45.

State Statistical Bureau (1981-) *Statistical Yearbooks of China*, 1981–1985.

Stein, Z., Susser, M., Saenger, E. and Marolla, F. (1975) *Famine and Human Development* (The Dutch Hunger Winter of 1944–45), Oxford University Press, New York.

Stein, Z. and Susser, M. (1978) Famine and Fertility, in Mosley, W. H.

(ed.), *Nutrition and Human Reproduction*, Plenum, New York.

Sun Yefang (1981) Consolidate Statistical Work and Reform the Statistical System, *Jingji Guanli (Economic Management)*, 2 (15 February) 3-5. Translated in FBIS-CHI-81-058, L4-9.

Wang, W. (1984) A Preliminary Analysis of China's Mortality Rate, *Renkou Yanjiu* (Population Research), 5 (29 September) 25–31. Translated in JPRS-CPS-85-028 (22 March 1985), 8–21.

Wang, X.C. and Lou, J. (1983) An Outline of the Population Geography of Jiangsu Province, *GeoJournal* 7, 1:53–8.

W. K. (1961) Communist China's Agricultural Calamities, *China Quarterly*, 6:64-75.

World Bank (1984) *World Development Report.*

Xue Muqiao (1981) Adjust the National Economy and Promote Balanced Growth. *Jingji Yanjiu (Economic Research)*, 2 (20 February) 25–31. Translated in FBIS-CHI-81-067, K9-19.

11

Paradise Delayed: Epidemics of Infectious Disease in the Industrialized World

Peter Curson

THE REVOLUTION IN PUBLIC HEALTH

One of the most dramatic developments in health during the last century has been the largely successful conquest of infectious disease. Less than 70 years ago diseases like phthisis, typhoid, diphtheria, whooping cough, measles, pneumonia and various enteric infections constituted a major public health problem, particularly for young children, while epidemic outbreaks of diseases like plague, smallpox and influenza could at times paralyse whole cities and cause tremendous suffering. The first steps in the conquest of infectious disease depended upon a growing realization of the association of unsanitary environmental conditions and disease prevalence. The second phase occurred some decades later when rising standards of living, pharmacological innovations, modern anaesthetics, X-rays, sulphonamides, improved surgical techniques and, in the 1940s and early 1950s, the discovery of penicillin and other antibiotics combined to force down mortality rates and to lessen the threat of epidemic disease.

The advent of antibiotics radically changed the clinical picture of many infections. Pneumonia and bronchitis, for example, ceased to be killers of children and young adults and became a complication in the course of a chronic illness such as heart disease or emphysema. By the end of the first half of the twentieth century this revolution in public health had all but run its course. By the early

1950s most people living in the industrialized countries enjoyed high levels of sanitation, personal hygiene and nutrition and possessed high living standards as well as reasonable access to large and sophisticated medical care systems. Such changes, coupled with declining birth rates (pre-1940) transformed the age-composition of many industrialized nations.

While changes in the environment clearly played an important role in the decline of infectious disease there were also important changes in the host-disease-agent relationship. It seems more than likely that many infectious pathogens underwent a change in infectivity and virulence during the latter part of the nineteenth and the early twentieth century. In addition, changes in the human environment, particularly nutritional improvements, undoubtedly increased human resistance to many of the more common infections as well as increasing the incidence of many non-infectious diseases such as coronary heart disease and dental caries. Infectious disease, once primarily the scourge of young children, had by the 1950s become the domain of the elderly, the chronically ill and the immunologically compromised. Whatever the causative mechanisms involved, the industrialized world was said to have entered a new phase of demographic and epidemiologic development where mortality was very low particularly among the young, where explosive epidemics of infectious disease had become a thing of the past, and where ageing of the population had produced a dramatic transformation in the pattern of disease. In the relatively older populations of industrialized nations, infectious disease was substantially reduced in importance and replaced in significance by degenerative and societal diseases such as cardiovascular disease, stroke, cancer, accidents and suicide as the main causes of mortality and morbidity.

The Revolution in Public Health Reappraised

By the 1950s the broad changes that had taken place in industrial societies with respect to patterns of disease and the ageing of the population had directed public health attention away from the physical environment and infectious disease towards consideration of the relevance of the social environment for health – particularly the role of man-made toxicants, noxious social conditions and unhealthy life-styles. It remains paradoxical, however, that despite the biological, medical, socio-economic and demographic changes mentioned above, many infectious diseases have not disappeared but remain widespread in industrial societies and for particular social groups constitute an important threat to public health. To some extent the claim that outbreaks of infectious disease are no longer important in the epidemiological regime of industrialized nations is an oversimplified one. While it is true that the incidence of many common infections has declined significantly since the 1920s and that infectious disease causes few deaths today, the fact remains that infections are an important cause of morbidity and that despite the availability of effective treatment many remain inadequately controlled. Many 'older' infections have persisted in industrialized nations, particularly among the more disadvantaged sectors of the population. This is particularly the case with respect to infections like measles, diphtheria, meningitis, rheumatic fever and asthma, and clearly suggests that not all social groups in developed societies have participated equally in the general epidemiological changes of the last century. This, allied to the emergence of a series of 'new' viral infections over the last few decades means that infectious disease still plays a not unimportant role in the health situation of industrialized countries. The emergence and/or survival of many infectious agents in the latter part of the twentieth century has been facilitated by three broad factors. Firstly, many pathogens have undergone changes themselves. This is perhaps best seen with respect to influenza where antigenic changes in the virus have seen new strains of the disease emerge. There has also been the emergence of a series of drug-resistant strains of pathogens such as penicillin-resistent strains of gonorrhea. Finally, it would appear that some pathogens have undergone significant ecological change in so far as they have developed new multiple-host disease systems. In some cases the primary host may have even become largely immune to the disease itself and act more in the role of a vector. The pathogen responsible for salmonellosis is a good example of a multiple host system involving wild and domestic animals as well as humans.

In the second place, changes in human mobility (particularly the advent of air travel) and in living and working conditions have facilitated the transmission of many infections. Crowded living, working and travel conditions together with the maintenance of artificially controlled interior climates have undoubtedly facilitated the aerosol spread of many diseases.

Finally, changes in life-style and health behaviour have generally made it much easier for 'older' infections to persist and for 'new' viral infections to spread.

INFECTIOUS DISEASE IN INDUSTRIALIZED COUNTRIES

Four major categories of infectious disease continue to remain of importance in the industrial world.

1   The persistence or resurgence of 'older' infections localized in specific social groups.
2   The persistence or resurgence of 'older' infections which because of human attitudes and/or behaviour have either maintained a high prevalence despite the ready availability of treatment, as in the case of many of the sexually-transmitted diseases (STDs) or the salmonelloses, or have become epidemic from time to time.
3   The persistence of 'older' viral infections for which no specific treatment or cure is available and which continue to cause high morbidity but low mortality, e.g. influenza, infectious mononucleosis, chickenpox.
4   The emergence of 'new' viral infections, e.g. AIDS, legionnaires' disease.

The Persistence of 'Older' Infections in Particular Social Groups

The benefits of a controlled benign physical environment and equal access to health-care facilities have never been uniformly shared by all groups in industrialized countries. Particular sub-groups, particularly those of lower socio-economic status and 'visible' ethnic and racial groups, have often exhibited a higher than average risk of exposure to unhygienic and hazardous working and living conditions, possess limited access to health-care services and consistently expose their children to unacceptable health risks. For many such people the promise of controlling the physical environment and the avoidance of infectious disease hazards remains largely unfulfilled. In many cases current morbidity and mortality rates among such groups closely resembles rates of a third world country or of the industrial world a century ago. Epidemics of infectious disease, particularly childhood infections such as measles, whooping cough, diphtheria and meningitis, still play an important role among such groups as Indians, Negroes and Hispanics in the USA, Pacific islanders and Maoris in New Zealand, Aborigines and southeast Asian migrants in Australia, Pakistanis and Indians in the UK, north Africans in France and non-whites in South Africa, as well as other socially-disadvantaged sectors of modern societies such as Skid Row populations and the unemployed. Often the rates of infectious disease among these groups far exceed those prevailing in the white European populations. In the 1982 measles epidemic in New Zealand, for example, Maoris and Pacific islanders were eight and six times respectively more likely than European New Zealanders to be admitted to hospital and in the 1986–7 meningococcal meningitis epidemic Maoris were fifteen times and Pacific islanders twenty-two times more likely than Europeans to be hospitalized (Rudman, 1986). In some cases the rates of infectious disease among such groups may even exceed current rates in third world countries. Rheumatic fever rates among Maori children in South Auckland during 1986, for example, were of the order of 150 cases per 100,000 population (Rudman, 1986). Evidence from many industrial countries reveals the very strong social class gradient in health and mortality and the substantial differences in the health status and behaviour that exist between the advantaged and disadvantaged sectors of the population. In the USA, for example, whereas approximately 70 per cent of all white children aged 1–4 years were fully immunized against diphtheria, tetanus and whooping cough in 1983, only 48 per cent of non-white children were so protected. For polio immunization the figures were 62 per cent and 37 per cent respectively (US Department of Health, 1984). Such patterns also have a distinctive spatial arrangement, so called 'poverty areas' within cities traditionally possessing the lowest immunization rates.

The Persistence or Resurgence of 'Older' Infections because of Some Change in Human Behaviour

This second category includes on the one hand a number of 'older' infections which because of human behaviour have maintained a high prevalence despite the availability of effective treatment, and on the other a series of infections, formerly controlled by preventative measures such as vaccination, which have reappeared because of a change in human behaviour. Greater sexual freedom stemming from the sexual revolution of the late 1950s led to an increase in promiscuity and a related increase in sexually-transmitted diseases. Gonorrhea, for example, probably constitutes the most prevalent bacterial infection in the industrialized world today, despite the availability of effective treatment.

The whooping cough epidemics in the UK in 1978 and 1982 and the significant increase in epidemics of food poisoning in the post-1970 period are prime examples of the second type. The recent epidemics of whooping cough in the UK were largely the result of public controversy over the safety of the vaccine, which led to a decline in whooping cough vaccinations. The result was that the number of cases of whooping cough in 1978 was the highest recorded since 1957. Epidemics of food-borne infections are among the most significant in industrial nations today and probably account for more than a million cases and a thousand deaths from salmonellosis every year. Many such epidemics originate from the institutional preparation of food or in some cases from consumer demands for so-called 'pure unadulterated' foods. At least 60 epidemics of milk-borne salmonellosis in the UK in the period 1970–83 affecting probably more than 4,000 people with at least 12 deaths resulted from the sale of raw milk at the farm gate, in the fashionable belief that 'natural' foods were of higher quality (Dixon, 1986). The polio outbreak in the Netherlands in 1978 represents another example of human behaviour encouraging infectious disease. This epidemic occurred exclusively in those municipalities where, because of local objections to immunization on religious grounds, immunization coverage was less than 60 per cent (WHO, 1981).

With respect to this broad category of infectious disease, one of the most disturbing features is that over the past decade the proportion of children vaccinated in many industrialized countries against viral and bacterial infections has markedly declined.

The Persistence of 'Older' Viral Infections

Epidemics of many 'older' viral infections for which no specific cure exists remain common throughout the industrialized world although their severity is considerably less than in previous times.

Influenza remains the most important cause of morbidity and mortality in many countries. During the Asian flu pandemic of 1957–8, for example, it is estimated that 70 million of the USA's 180 million population contracted the disease over an eight-week period, an attack rate of 39 per cent (Westwood, 1980). Outbreaks of diseases such as chickenpox, mumps, rubella and mononucleosis remain commonplace in western societies. Currently there are of the order of 95–100 cases per 100,000 population of chickenpox every year in the USA, 2–4 of mumps and 6–8 of infectious mononucleosis (US Department of Health, 1980).

The Emergence of 'New' Viral Infections

The number of viral agents responsible for infections has steadily increased over the last 30 years. Many of these 'new' infections, such as the Marburg virus, legionnaires' disease, Lassa fever, toxic shock syndrome, genital herpes and AIDS have had a tremendous psychological impact on a generation long considered safe from dangerous epidemic diseases. Some, such as legionnaires' disease have produced short-lived epidemics, whereas others like genital herpes and AIDS have become much more widespread, and in the case of AIDS pose a long-term threat.

Recent Epidemics in Industrialized Countries

Table 11.1 records some of the more important epidemics of infectious disease to have occurred in industrialized countries since the late 1960s. This table is not intended to be all-inclusive but simply illustrative of the type and range of epidemics of infectious disease to have affected such countries in recent years. One of the basic problems encountered in attempting to construct a complete picture of epidemics is the generally low visibility of such infections. To a large extent this results from three factors:

1 In the case of epidemics such as food poisoning, a complete picture may only come to light if the outbreak occurs in flight, on a cruise or in an institution. Outside such situations, many cases of food poisoning may go unrecorded because victims have dispersed and/or may simply dismiss their symptoms as jet lag, travel weariness or an 'upset stomach' and rarely seek medical advice.

Table 11.1 Epidemics of infectious disease in industrialized countries, selected examples 1968–1987

Year	Disease	Specific population attacked	No. of cases	No. of deaths	Location
1968	Norwalk gastroenteritis (Norwalk virus)	School-age children	160	0	Norwalk, Ohio, USA
1968–9	Hong Kong 'flu	Most age groups	150,000,000[a]	140,000[a]	Worldwide
1969–70	Influenza	Adults, esp. elderly	8,000,000[a]	31,000[a]	England/Wales
1970	Smallpox	Adults	18	–	Meschede, West Germany
1972–5	Diphtheria	Skid Row adults	558	4	Seattle, USA
1972	Smallpox	Adults	174	35	Yugoslavia
1973–5	Diphtheria	American Indians	122	0	King County, Washington, USA
1976	Legionnaires' disease	US army veterans	218	29	Philadelphia, USA
1978	Polio	10–35 year olds	110	0	Netherlands
1978	Whooping cough	Young children, 2–5 years	65,975	12	UK
1979	Measles	Young children, 0–9 years	22,257	[b]	Canada
1979	Meningococcal cerebro-spinal meningitis	Children under 5 years	2,036	[b]	France
1980	Acute respiratory disease (Cocksackie A21)	Army personnel	107	0	Army Camp, Scotland
1980	Toxic shock syndrome	Females, 0–64 years	867	88	USA
1981	Measles	Young children, 0–9 years	50,000[a]	5	NSW, Australia

1981	Streptococcal pharyngitis	Adults	300	0	Portland, Oregon USA
1980–1	Q fever	Adults	12	[b]	Sth Ontario/Nova Scotia, Canada
1981	Salmonella	Adults/Children	260	1	Victoria/South Australia/ NSW, Australia
1982	Whooping cough	Young children, 2–5 years	65,810	14	UK
1982	Salmonella Napoli	Children under 15 years	272	0	UK
1983	Measles	Young children, 0–9 years	75,308	12[a]	UK
1983–	AIDS	Homosexuals, bisexuals, IV drug users, haemophiliacs, blood transfusion recipients(some heterosexuals in Africa and elsewhere)	More than 110,000[a] (5–8,000,000 infected with virus)	25,000[a]	Worldwide
1983–4	Hepatitis A	Children and young adults	313	0	Muskingum County, Ohio, USA
1984	Salmonella	British Airways passengers and crew	766	0	UK
1984	Food poisoning	Adults	400	0	Bradford, England
1986–7	Meningococcal meningitis	Young children: Maoris/ Pacific Islanders	100s[a]	[b]	New Zealand

[a] Author's estimate.
[b] No data available.

Sources: Australian Dept. of Health, 1983–86; Chen et al., 1985; Christopher et al., 1983; Dixon, 1986; Hopkins, 1983; Inglis, 1981; OPCS, 1984–85; Pedersen et al., 1977; U. S. Dept. of Health, 1975–83; WHO, 1980–87.

2   The localization of many epidemics of infectious disease in particular low-status social groups may contribute to the low visibility of the epidemic in the wider community.

3   Infections with a high prevalence but low mortality may be simply accepted as a normal life-cycle or life-style event and arouse little public concern.

Only where outbreaks of disease reach pandemic status and/or produce exceptional morbidity (e.g. influenza), where the nature of the disease agent engenders widespread fear and anxiety (e.g. smallpox, polio) or where the onset of a 'new' and lethal infection arouses public anxiety (e.g. legionnaires' disease, AIDS) do epidemics attain a high level of visibility in industrialized countries.

HUMAN BEHAVIOUR AND EPIDEMICS

People have always reacted with great emotion in the face of epidemic disease. Human attitudes and behaviour to epidemics reflect among other things how a society and individuals conceptualize death and disease in their overall scheme of things.

Attitudes towards disease develop largely as a result of past experience and such attitudes would appear to be acquired through parental and societal conditioning, through observing and being influenced by other people as well as being openly taught to hold particular attitudes. Until the early twentieth century epidemics of infectious disease were commonplace events in industrialized countries. Earlier generations were closely acquainted with diseases like measles, scarlet fever, diphtheria, whooping cough, smallpox, polio and plague. Attitudes towards epidemics are deeply embedded in the historical memory. As Langer argues, it seems more than plausible that children, having experienced the fear and hysteria of their parents and the panic of the community, would react to succeeding epidemics in a similar but even more exaggerated manner. 'Anxiety and fear being transmitted from one generation to another, constantly aggravated' (Langer, 1958:299–300). If this is true then it goes a long way towards explaining current attitudes and behaviour towards the AIDS epidemic.

Unlike most natural disasters, epidemics are not 'consensus crises in which core values are reinforced, altruistic norms of behaviour extended and social conflict minimized' (Rice, 1982:4). Rather, epidemics tend to magnify basic social divisions and conflicts and expose latent tensions and antagonisms within societies. Epidemics thus remain an acid test of human behaviour and constitute a unique laboratory for the study of individual and group behaviour during times of great stress. The way in which people react to epidemics reveals much about the way societies function and are structured. The psychological climate pertaining to epidemics, particularly the fear and anxiety and the way this is manifested in behaviour, tells us something about how particular groups manipulate such disasters for their own ends. There seems to be a particular socio-psychological sequence of human responses to epidemics. Figure 11.1, which is an attempt to view these responses within a broad temporal and epidemological framework, distinguishes between a so-called 'normal' response and a pathological response.

Initially there may be some apprehension expressed to reports of overseas cases which are seen by some people as 'cues' heralding the epidemic's arrival. The appearance of isolated local cases may give rise to a denial/disbelief reaction in which people tend to rationalize changing circumstances by adding qualifiers to the perceived threat, for example, the improbability of the disease striking *me* or *here*. Sometimes an increase in the number of local cases can produce a degree of shock and the perception of the epidemic as startling and crisis-provoking. It is, however, when the epidemic begins in earnest that human reaction is at its most intense leading to an escalation of emotional reactions including anger, anxiety, confusion and shock. In some cases there is the feeling of being emotionally swamped. At its peak the epidemic becomes all-intrusive and shock and confusion are linked in such a way as to heighten the fear and terror eventually compounding into a fear/bedlam stage of behaviour. Feedback during this stage reinforces the initial shock and in many leads to a crumbling away of their sense of invulnerability. It is during this stage of the epidemic that fear, anxiety and hysteria produce such behavioural responses as extreme avoidance of areas and people thought to be infected and aggression towards perceived carriers of disease. Social conflicts tend to be augmented and scapegoats sought, and some people seek recourse to penitential exercises and traditional explanations. All this is greatly augmented by media treatment of the epidemic and by

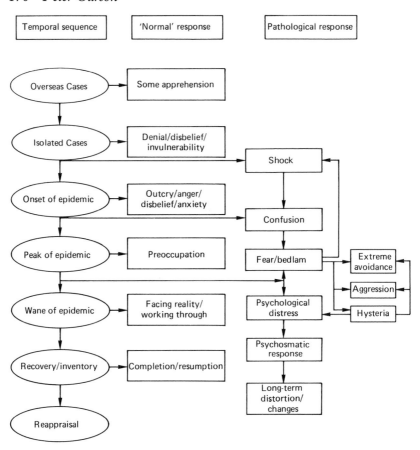

Figure 11.1   The social psychology of epidemics

official measures advanced to control its spread. In some individuals this may lead to a state of psychological distress including the belief that their world is no longer safe and that they are no longer worthy of that safety. It may also lead to extremes of denial, a general numbing of the senses, waves of uncontrollable emotion, a loss of ability to concentrate and the avoidance of topics even vaguely associated with the epidemic. In some cases this may lead to long-term changes, particularly in the ability to love or work, as well as psychosomatic illness.

ACQUIRED IMMUNE DEFICIENCY SYNDROME (AIDS): A CASE
STUDY

AIDS has in the last few years become recognized as a global health
problem of major dimensions. Cases have been reported in most
countries including more than 30,000 in the USA, 4,000 in Europe,
600 in Canada and 400 in Australia as well as many thousands in
Africa and Latin America. At the beginning of 1987 more than
42,400 cases of AIDS had been reported to the WHO, of which 73
per cent were in the USA alone. All in all five countries (USA,
France, Canada, the Federal Republic of Germany and the UK)
accounted for 82 per cent of all reported cases. The highest rates,
however, were found in the third world, particularly in a group of
central African countries (see table 11.2). In the industrial world
the disease remains primarily an urban–institutional epidemic with
the highest rates to be found in cities like New York, San Francisco
and Sydney as well as in correctional institutions within such cities.
In 1985, when the AIDS rate was 58 per 100,000 population in New
York City, the rate in New York prisons was of the order of 584

Table 11.2   AIDS cases and rates, selected countries, March 1987

Country	Cases	Rate per Million
USA	31,036	128.8
France	1,221	22.1
Canada	873	34.1
West Germany	959	15.8
Uganda	766[a]	50.4
Brazil	1,012	7.1
Zaire	759[a]	27.1
U.K.	686	12.1
Haiti	785	133.0
Tanzania	699	31.2
Australia	407	25.8
Italy	460	8.0
Congo	250[a]	138.9
Zambia	250[a]	35.2
Central African Republic	202[a]	74.8

[a] Figures from end of 1986 only.
Source: WHO figures, 11 March 1987.

cases per 100,000 (Rosenfeld, 1985). Possibly between three and five million people in the industrialized world have been infected by the virus, and 20–30 per cent of these could be reasonably expected to develop AIDS within the next five years. AIDS consequently now ranks as one of the most serious epidemics to have affected western countries in the past 50 years. More importantly perhaps, the disease has sparked off a wave of fear, hysteria and controversy unmatched in extent and intensity since the days of the polio outbreaks of the late 1940s and early 1950s. AIDS is in many ways typical of epidemics of infectious disease in industrialized countries. First, it is an urban-based epidemic. Secondly, its impact has fallen most heavily upon selected minority groups. Thirdly, it has provoked a wave of fear, hysteria and controversy out of all proportion to the actual number of cases and deaths, which has spread through society giving rise to practices of scapegoating, ostracism and discrimination. Finally, the media have played a crucial role in dictating the course of and reaction to the disease.

The US Public Health Service has postulated that by 1991 there will have been 270,000 cases of AIDS and 179,000 deaths from the disease in the USA. Today, possibly as many as two million Americans, 150,000 Britons and French, 100,000 West Germans and 80,000 Canadians and Australians have been infected by the virus. By 1984 AIDS had become a major cause of death among men in the USA and in New York and San Francisco it had become one of the five leading causes of death for males aged 30–39 years (Kristal, 1986). By 1985 it had become the major cause of premature mortality for males aged 15–64 years in New York City with rates slightly higher than those for suicide and homocide (Kristal, 1986).

The reported cases of AIDS, however, tell only part of the story. In the first place, a substantial number of cases may not be recognized or reported. Secondly, only those cases which meet the strict criteria of the US Centers for Disease Control are formally notified. Finally, many people who are infected by the virus may take years to develop the symptoms of AIDS. By consequence, as figure 11.2 shows, those people formally diagnosed as having AIDS represent only the tip of a huge iceberg of potential disease.

AIDS is in many ways an epidemiologist's dream – a slow viral disease, apparently fatal, that seems to affect very specific populations. AIDS meets the medical definition of a syndrome, that is, a

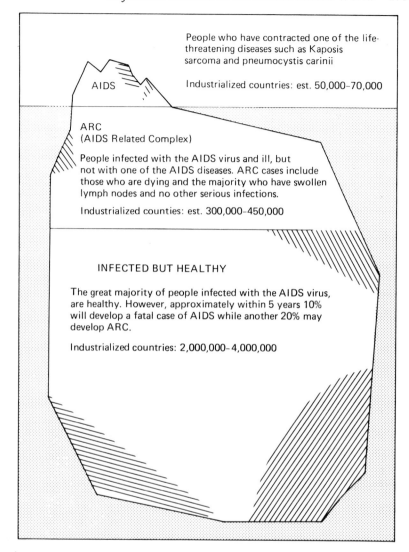

People who have contracted one of the life-threatening diseases such as Kaposis sarcoma and pneumocystis carinii

Industrialized countries: est. 50,000-70,000

AIDS

ARC
(AIDS Related Complex)

People infected with the AIDS virus and ill, but not with one of the AIDS diseases. ARC cases include those who are dying and the majority who have swollen lymph nodes and no other serious infections.

Industrialized counties: est. 300,000-450,000

INFECTED BUT HEALTHY

The great majority of people infected with the AIDS virus, are healthy. However, approximately within 5 years 10% will develop a fatal case of AIDS while another 20% may develop ARC.

Industrialized countries: 2,000,000-4,000,000

Figure 11.2   The AIDS iceberg

disease with a series of clinical manifestations that tend to run together. Primarily it is a disease of young, previously healthy people characterized by impairment of the body's cellular immune system. Clinically it is characterized by severe weight loss, fever, fatigue amd malaise, diarrhoea, enlarged lymph glands, increased incidence of opportunistic infections and certain tumours normally harmless to healthy people and abnormalities in the body's immune system. There is a high risk of death within two years of onset. Many sufferers develop an opportunistic tumor (Karposi's sarcoma) or an extremely rare form of pneumonia (pneumocystis carinii).

There is still considerable debate as to the origins and nature of AIDS. One argument is that AIDS is a multifactorial disease caused by several interrelated factors involving the specific life-style and pathogenic assaults experienced by particular social groups and not a specific syndrome or new infectious agent. Supporters of this view argue that anyone continually exposed to a wide variety of constant assaults on their immune system is likely to get AIDS. Given the exotic nature and multiplicity of infections and immunosuppressors to which homosexuals are repeatedly exposed, the obvious question was not why such people fell ill but rather why they remained well. AIDS was seen as a bedfellow of sexual promiscuity, 'the sexual tax paid by men who frequent baths and bars, where pickups were easy and hygiene was poor' (Black, 1985:52). Such a theory has obviously not found sympathy with many gay groups. The other basic theory of the nature of AIDS, widely supported by orthodox and conservative medical authorities, firmly supports the view that the disease is caused by a specific virus that hits like a 'bolt out of the blue' and that life-style and behaviour have little part to play in infection.

AIDS was first recognized in spring 1981 after a number of cases of pneumocystis carinii had presented in Los Angeles. In retrospect it would appear that the disease may have existed in the USA and Europe from the late 1970s. Possibly the disease has existed in central Africa for much longer. For example, 35 per cent of blood samples collected from healthy Kinshasa workers in 1970 revealed the presence of AIDS antibodies (Sattaur and Hamblin, 1985). The first western record of the disease (retrospectively diagnosed) was that of a Danish Surgeon who had been working in Zaire and who died of pneumocystis in 1976. Most evidence points to an African origin for the disease and it is possible that the virus may have survived as a zoonosis for decades, largely harmless to the human population, only to be transformed into a much more virulent infection when transported to a new urban environment with new sexual practices and poor hygiene. By 1984 it was evident that the disease was rampant in parts of central Africa and involved not only homosexual males, drug users and blood transfusion cases

Table 11.3.   AIDS – comparative risk groups 1985–1987, percentages

	USA[a]	Europe[b]	UK[c]	Australia[d]
Homosexual/bisexual	64.6	69.0	88.2	87.7
IV drug user	16.8	5.7	1.5	0.0
Haemophiliac	0.9	3.4	4.1	1.0
Homosexual/bisexual/IV drug user	7.7	1.5	1.0	0.7
Heterosexual	3.8	[e]	2.9	0.5
Blood transfusion recipient	[e]	[e]	1.6	5.6
Parent with AIDS (paediatric case)	1.4	[e]	0.5	[e]
Other/unknown	3.0	18.2	0.2	0.2
Total cases	28098	1573	610	407

[a] As at 12 Sept. 1986.
[b] As at 30 Sept. 1985.
[c] As at 31 Dec. 1986.
[d] As at 25 Feb. 1987.
[e] No data.
Source: Australian Department of Health, 1984–87.

but also sexually active heterosexual men and women. In Zaire, Rwanda, Zambia and Uganda the disease was also noted to be particularly prevalent among the higher socio-economic groups. How AIDS reached the industrialized world remains debatable. Possibly it was carried from Zaire to Haiti by returning labourers and later reached the USA with Haitian refugees or via sexual contact between US tourists and Haitian prostitutes. Possibly it arrived through consignments of infected blood imported from central African sources. The disease may have also reached Europe with the migration of central Africans to urban areas. It is clear, however, that once the disease became established amongst the homosexual community in a series of major US and European cities it quickly spread further afield.

In industrial societies the groups most at risk of catching AIDS are predominantly homosexual/bisexual males, intravenous drug users, haemophiliacs and blood transfusion recipients. Table 11.3 reveals how these categories account for between 82 and 98 per cent of all cases of AIDS diagnosed in the USA, Europe, Australia and UK. As yet the only evidence of second-generation spread outside these risk groups has been to children of infected parents and a small number of heterosexuals via the medium of a bisexual partner or contact with an infected prostitute. Within such groups the transmission of the disease occurs through one of four main mechanisms:

sexual contact;
exposure to blood-contaminated hypodermic needles;
contaminated blood products;
vertical transmission from infected mothers to their children.

All epidemics remain to some extent a source of fear and panic as well as a source of exploitation and discrimination. AIDS is no exception. The media have played a vital role in the epidemic. The instinct to play on people's fears has proved irresistible. Newspapers in particular have created widespread hysteria with their sensationalist assertions of a plague 'to rival the Black Death'. AIDS has undoubtedly turned out to be an excellent source of media copy and there is little doubt that the media exploited the epidemic simply to sell more newspapers. The sensational way in which AIDS has been presented to the public has undoubtedly fostered public hysteria and paranoia. Reports of a highly contagious and lethal disease spreading to the wider population by casual contact have not been substantiated. The upshot of this has been what the *New Republic* has called 'AFRAIDS' (Acute Fear Regarding AIDS), a sort of AIDS psychosis – a wave of hysteria and fear whose symptoms include avoidance, ostracism, discrimination, scapegoating and violence. Whereas AIDS has affected only a very small fraction of the industrial world's population, AFRAIDS may have affected more than 150,000,000 (*New Republic*, 1985). 'Plague fear' is of course one of the most basic of all human fears and fear of AIDS is no exception. The reaction to AIDS is a mixture of rational and irrational fears regarding contagion and disease generally together with irrational fears of sexuality and otherness (Altman, 1986:59).

In many circumstances, fear of the epidemic has given rise to blatant and often violent harassment of homosexuals. Many have been denied the right to lawful employment, refused entry to clubs and bars, evicted from their homes, refused insurance and physically attacked on the streets. The epidemic has also provided a classic moral dilemma for parents of children exposed to the virus, that is, whether to inform educational authorities or remain tight-lipped. In situations of disclosure, other parents have removed their children from school. What distinguishes epidemics like AIDS from the perils of life is not so much the danger of the disease itself as the often extraordinary and draconian measures advanced for its control. Such measures and the way in which they were applied have contributed to the upsurge of emotional reaction. Moreover, it is almost inevitable that such measures fall disproportionately upon disadvantaged minority groups. In the case of AIDS, legislation has been mooted to restrict the movement and forcibly detain AIDS sufferers. Men have been banned from giving blood, people with the disease have been threatened with fines if they have sexual intercourse without first informing their partners. Doctors treating AIDS have been required to notify the authorities of the name and address of their patients. In the USA all military recruits have been tested for AIDS since August 1985 and insurance companies have considered mandatory blood tests of applicants for large policies.

AIDS has also become big business and the race to discover a cure had led to episodes of stock market frenzy. AIDS blood-testing services and the manufacture of condoms have become profitable sectors of the business world and the promise of substantial profits have attracted many large multinationals.

CONCLUSIONS

The persistence of epidemics of infectious disease must be seen as one index of the failure of public health systems to come to terms with a series of basic problems inherent in industrialized societies. In the first place there is the problem of how to change deeply entrenched health attitudes and health behaviour and to appreciate fully that it is often people at highest risk who have the lowest regard for prevention and public health. The AIDS epidemic provides a good example of the serious failure of public health to control sexually-transmitted disease particularly among homosexuals. The resurgence of childhood infections among disadvantaged groups in countries like New Zealand is an example of what the lack of responsible health behaviour and parenting skills can lead to. Secondly, maintaining public health is a difficult undertaking at the best of times, requiring a skilful balancing act of two conflicting forces – individual rights and liberties on the one hand, and the overall well-being of the community on the other. In times of epidemic crisis the uneasy equilibrium between these two forces is easily upset. It remains a basic weakness of western public health that it has never resolved this basic conflict. Epidemics often force us to consider priorities and choices such as freedom versus coercion and social responsibility versus individual rights. They also pose the question of who is ultimately responsible for the community's health. In addition, many people in the industrialized world do not like rules, regulations and taxes even when imposed in the name of public health. The dilemma of infectious disease and public health in the industrial world remains unresolved.

REFERENCES

Australian Department of Health (1983–6) *Communicable Diseases Intelligence*, Canberra.

Altman, D. (1986) *Aids and the New Puritanism*, Pluto, London.

Black, D. (1985) The Plague Years, *Rolling Stone*, 444:52.

Brandt, A. M. (1985) *No Magic Bullet: A Social History of Venereal Disease in the United States since 1880*, Oxford University Press, New York.

Chen, R. T. et al. (1985) Diptheria in the United States, 1971–81, *American Journal of Public Health*, 75, 12:1395.

Christopher, P. J. et al. (1983) Measles in the 1980s, *Medical Journal of Australia*, 12 November: 419–88.

Dixon, B. (1986) Salmonella for Starters, *New Scientist*, 7 August:43–6.

Goleman, D. R. (1985) Disasters Leave Hidden Scars on the Mind, *New York Times*, reprinted in *Sydney Morning Herald*, 2 December:9.

Hopkins, D. R. (1983) *Princes and Peasants: Smallpox in History*, University of Chicago Press, Chicago.

Inglis, B. (1981) *The Diseases of Civilisation*, Hodder and Stoughton, London.

Kristal, A. R. (1986) The Impact of the Acquired Immunodeficiency Syndrome on Patterns of Premature Death in New York City, *Journal of the American Medical Association*, 255, 17:2306–10.

Langer, W. L. (1958) The Next Assignment, *American Historical Review*, 63, 2:299–300.

New Republic (1985) AFRAIDS, 14 October:7.

OPCS (Office of Population Censuses and Surveys) (1984, 1985) *Monitor: Infectious Diseases, December Quarter*, 4 September 1984 :3 December 1985, London.

OPCS (1985) *Monitor: Annual Review of Communicable Diseases 1982*, 15 January, London.

Pedersen, A. H. B. et al. (1977) Diptheria on Skid Road, Seattle, Washington, *Public Health Reports*, 92, 4:336–42.

Rice, G. W. (1982) The Armistice Epidemic: A Framework for Analysing the Social Impact of the 1919 Influenza Epidemic in New Zealand, unpublished paper presented at the Australian Historical Association Conference, Sydney.

Rosenfeld, S. (1985) AIDS behind Bars, *San Francisco Examiner*, 29 September:A20.

Rudman, B. (1986) Our Third World Child Health Care, *New Zealand Listener*, 27 September:15–18.

San Francisco Chronicle (1985) the AIDS Iceberg, 6 September.

Sattaur, O. and Hamblin, T. (1985) Second Virus linked to AIDS Cancer, *New Scientist*, 11 April:8.

US Department of Health and Human Services (1975–83) Morbidity and Mortality Weekly, Centers for Disease Control, Atlanta.

US Department of Health and Human Sevices (1984) *Health United States 1984*, National Center of Health Statistics, Maryland.

Westwood, J. C. N. (1980) *The Hazard from Dangerous Exotic Diseases*, Macmillan, London:6.

WHO (World Health Organisation) (1980–7) *Weekly Epidemiological Record*, WHO Geneva.

12

Disasters and Diseases as they Affect the Growth and Distribution of the Population of Uganda

Hans K. Hecklau

DISASTERS AND DISEASES IN THE SECOND HALF OF THE NINETEENTH CENTURY

Uganda, called by the explorer H. M. Stanley 'the Pearl of Africa', was not a peaceful country during the nineteenth century. Stanley was impressed by the well organized kingdom of Buganda, which was only a small part of the territory which became the British Protectorate of Uganda at the turn of the last century, comprising a population which consisted of many peoples at different levels of social and economic development speaking about 20 languages. The kingdom of Buganda came into being some centuries ago at roughly the same time as the kingdoms of Bunyoro, Ankole, Toro and others which were either smaller or less centralized than these. In other parts of Uganda the population was organized on a clan level, lacking a centralized power. Man-made disasters, like internecine wars of succession, for instance in Buganda and Bunyoro, warfare between the kingdoms and repeated slave raids in many parts of Uganda, disturbed the natural growth of the population. Natural disasters like famines or epidemic diseases – sometimes in a complex combination with man-made disasters – repeatedly caused heavy population losses.

Langlands (1971:32) has thoroughly elaborated the numerous

contemporary records and publications in order to investigate the growth and distribution of the population in Uganda district by district since the second half of the last century. He demonstrates that natural and man-made disasters had a strong impact on population growth and distribution. Although facts and figures on historical population development may not be reliable, one has to keep in mind that undisturbed population growth over a long time would have populated all the regions of Uganda suited to cultivation or herding up to their full capacity, resulting at least in the destruction of the environment, as one has been able to observe in so many African landscapes recently. In Uganda, however, there are still today regions which are underpopulated.

TRYPANOSOMIASIS AND POPULATION DISTRIBUTION

In Foster's (1970:93) view, which can be generally accepted, sleeping sickness is the most important disease that has ever afflicted Uganda. According to Onyango (1975:54), it is reliably estimated that between a quarter to a third of a million people died from sleeping sickness during the epidemic of 1900–20 which killed roughly a third of the population in the affected areas at that time. Langlands (1967:37), who investigated in great detail the outbreak and spread of the epidemic, came to the following conclusions:

> Demographically the loss of even 300,000 persons would long since have been replaced, for many of those who died would have been beyond a child-bearing age anyway, and the number of young females as the potential progenitors of the next generation who died may have been relatively few. But the replacement of the population has not taken place in those same areas from which the people died. One may detect parts of Uganda which are still 'depopulated' as compared with their population densities of the late nineteenth century. Bunya county of south Busoga, Buvuma, Sese and other island groups of Lake Victoria have fewer people now than they had in 1900 – though other factors such as famine may have contributed to their depletion. With the sole exception of the Samia coast of south Bukedi, the surviving populations of all the lake shore areas of Victoria, Edward, George and Albert lakes moved and these areas still

remain unpopulated or, in the case of Buvuma and Sese, still have fewer people in 1967 than those who moved in 1911. Thus all these areas may be regarded as being uninhabited or under-populated because of the sleeping sickness regulations which required the removal of the people, not because of the sleeping sickness per se.

Could a sleeping sickness epidemic happen again today, claiming many thousands of victims? Sleeping sickness outbreaks have occurred again and again in several places and are well documented by various publications. Onyango (1975) has published a map of the main foci of sleeping sickness in Uganda. It is said that there are new cases of sleeping sickness at present in Uganda, and the tsetse flies are spreading again due to bush encroachment on badly neglected areas where the peasant population was decimated by violence or was forced to leave its homes, though a mass epidemic is unlikely because modern medicine can cure the illness and prevent the spread. Tsetse flies, however, do not only transmit trypano-somes among humans, infecting them with trypanosomiasis, they also infest wild animals and cattle causing a cattle disease called *nagana*. Of much greater economic importance than human sleep-ing sickness, it is among other factors responsible for the limited pace and extent of rural development in Africa (Jordan, 1986).

Robertson (1961) states in the annual report of the tsetse control department of Uganda:

During the 1930s and early 1940s the cattle industry of Uganda was very seriously threatened by a series of widespread and rapid advances of the savannah tsetse, *G. morsitans* and *G. pallidipes*. These advances occurred mainly in central and northern Uganda, in the Buganda and Northern Provinces. In all they spread over and hence denied to cattle more than 8,000 sq miles (20,800 sq km) of the best grazing lands in the country.

The tsetse control department took action against the spreading tsetse fly infestation by various means, such as clearing tsetse-in-fested bush, shooting game as potential vectors of trypanosomes, and since 1955 spraying insecticides like DDT and later Dieldrin to kill the flies. According to Robertson (1963:31), about 7,000 sq miles (10,800 sq km) of country were reclaimed successfully from the savannah tsetse between the Second World War and the start of Uganda's independence; but he admits that Uganda at that time was still faced with difficult residual problems in completing effective consolidation in much of the newly reclaimed country. One can easily imagine that after the outbreak of civil war in Uganda no action was taken to deal with reclaiming tsetse-infected land; on the contrary, bush encroachment on deserted farmland gave rise to further infestation of large portions of land.

DISEASE AND POPULATION GROWTH

A wide range of illnesses have occurred in Uganda, some of them fatal infectious diseases which kept population densities down, before the government medical service could be built up by the administration of the Uganda Protectorate. Disease occurences in Uganda are examined in detail in the *Uganda Atlas of Disease Distribution* (Hall and Langlands, 1975), and Foster (1970) gives an interesting overview of the early history of scientific medicine in Uganda. After independence the government medical service developed into one of the most of efficient in Africa. During the first decade of independence the number of medical doctors had doubled, and the number of nurses had roughly tripled (see table 12.1).

Cole and Wiebe (1985:1) summarize the development of Uganda's health service:

At independence in 1962 and in the early 1970s, Uganda had one of the most highly developed health service delivery systems in

Table 12.1 Registered medical practitioners, dentists, pharmacists, midwives and nurses in Uganda, 1952–1971

	Doctors	Dentists	Midwives	Nurses	Pharmacists
1952	249	9	755	a	12
1962	552	28	1156	1354	72
1971	1171	53	3013	3680	66
1981	611	17	a	a	a

a not known.
Source: Uganda Government (1964), table UQ.1 and Republic of Uganda (1973) table Q.1. Laenderbericht Uganda 1988.

Africa. The services provided in smaller health units in outlying villages and towns were integrated with the services provided in the large, regionally located hospitals. The country's network of hospitals, health centres and dispensary and maternity units was well staffed by trained health workers at all levels. Referral systems were well organized. Follow-up care was routinely encouraged. Few patients in 1972 had to travel more than ten kilometres to their nearest health post. Then came the troubles associated with the Idi Amin years, the subsequent war of liberation and the aftermath of the war . . . In 1974, with the economy deteriorating and the security situation worsening, many Ugandan doctors and other professionals left to take up positions outside the country . . . Buildings, roads and other physical infrastructure had deteriorated badly or been destroyed. Spare parts were in short supply or unavailable. Access to clean water and basic sanitation facilities, once possible for a large proportion of the population, had been thoroughly disrupted. Facilities and equipment in most hospitals and other service institutions had been destroyed or looted . . .

With the deteriorating health service the immunization programmes againsts tuberculosis, poliomyelitis, measles, diphtheria, pertussis (whooping cough) and tetanus came to an end. Therefore infectious diseases which had been brought under control in the past were spreading again. Alnwick, Stirling and Kyeyune (1985:83) were confirmed in their view 'that a relatively small number of infectious and parasitic diseases, representing approximately a third of reported hospital morbidity and over two-thirds of hospital deaths, are the greatest causes of morbidity and mortality in Ugandan hospitals' (see table 12.2).

Venereal diseases are not included in table 12.2. Infections by gonococcus rose from 141, 319 cases in 1973 to 331,992 cases in 1974, not to mention syphilis which is not reported in the public statistics (Laenderbericht Uganda, 1986:22). Of all illnesses, venereal diseases had the most important impact on population growth in Uganda, not by mortality but by reducing the birth rate due to the infertility of the infected women. According to Foster (1970:78) venereal diseases used to be very common in Uganda, and all varieties were seen. The Baganda blamed the Arabs for their introduction but that is an open question, and it can be taken for

Table 12.2   Out–patient attendances for selected diseases at government
and voluntary hospitals, Uganda, 1970–1971 and 1981–1982

Disease	1970–1		1980–2	
	Cases	% of total	Cases	% of total
Pneumonic and respiratory infections	190,995	12.1	805,543	18.1
Other fever	103,110	6.5	483,867	10.9
Malaria	72,891	4.6	264,093	5.9
Measles	36,692	2.3	68,384	1.5
Gastroenteritis	32,339	2.0	128,603	2.9
Hookworm	15,608	1.0	98,615	2.2
Ascariasis	12,659	0.8	83,448	1.9
Anaemia	12,269	0.8	23,650	0.5
Whooping cough	10,445	0.7	23,157	0.5
Dysentery	9,600	0.6	36,211	0.8
Kwashiorkor	3,153	0.2	21,681	0.5
Tuberculosis	2,388	0.2	6,143	0.1
Vitamin deficiency	1,803	0.1	9,033	0.2
Schistosomiasis	1,669	0.1	8,199	0.2
Diptheria	828	0.1	360	
Guinea worm	419		997	
Meningitis	331		643	
Poliomyelitis	1,279	0.1	748	
Total above	508,478	32.2	2,603,375	46.3
Total all others	1,070,113	67.8	2,390,200	53.7
Grand total	1,578,591	100.0	4,453,575	100.0

Source: Alnwick, Stirling and Kyeyune (1985:82).

granted that the sexual behaviour of the population is responsible
for at least the spread of venereal diseases. Langlands (1971:45)
emphasized that 'by 1920 a good deal of alarm concerning the high
incidence of venereal diseases was being expressed, for Bunyoro as
much as for Buganda', and he quoted the HMSO *Report of the East
African Commission* (1925:54), which stated: 'In the district of
Bunyoro, for example, practically the whole population is syphili-
tic, and in 1923 the death rate per thousand was stated as 25.67 as
against a birth rate of 16.81. The percentage of still births was 36'.
According to Bennett (1975:64) gonorrhoea, which also causes female
sterility, has been the most prevalent venereal disease in Uganda.

Table 12.3 Population growth in Uganda, 1931–1984

Years	Total population
1931	3,500,000
1948	4,900,000
1959	6,449,558
1969	9,456,466
1980	12,630,000
1987	16,858,000

Source: Uganda censuses of 1948, 1959, 1969, 1984: Laenderbericht Uganda, 1988.

Gallo (1987) supposes that the newest and most dangerous disease, the Acquired Immune Deficiency Syndrome (AIDS) has its origin somewhere in central Africa. AIDS, in Uganda called slim disease, has hit the population in the central south-western parts of the country badly. In Uganda the number of AIDS victims is doubling every four to six months. Dr Samuel Okware, the Ministry of Health official in charge of Uganda's AIDS prevention programme, has stated that in the year 2000, one in every two sexually active adults will be infected. 'Researchers believe promiscuity combined with higher incidence of venereal disease among Africans has accelerated the spread of the AIDS virus. Last November the nonprofit-making London-based Panos Institute reported that the rate of gonorrhoea per 100,000 people is 10,000 in Kampala, Uganda . . . compared with about 975 in New York City and 310 in London' (*Time* 16 February 1987).

Disasters and diseases certainly used to be 'population checks' in the Malthusian sense, preventing the country from overpopulation in past centuries. In general the birth rate was sometimes higher than the death rate and vice versa. The establishment of law and order in the twentieth century and the development of the health service in Uganda resulted in a decline of the death rate but continuing high birth rates as in most developing countries, resulting in a more rapid population growth (see table 12.3).

Despite the breakdown of the health service, the menace of a wide range of dangerous infectious diseases and the lowering of the crude birth rate due to venereal diseases, the population of Uganda doubled in the 21 years between census years of 1969 and 1980. Notwithstanding all the natural and man-made mishaps, the natural growth of Uganda's population is unbroken. The birth rate was still high enough to surpass by far the death rate including the casualties of the turmoil.

MIGRATION INTO UGANDA CAUSED BY REGIONAL DISPARITIES AND VIOLENCE OUTSIDE UGANDA

According to Articles 15–18 of the Uganda Agreement of 1900 – which refers to the former kingdom of Buganda only – between the British government and the Kabaka of Buganda, private ownership of land came into existence for the first time in the history of Buganda. About 50,000 sq km of land was divided between the Kabaka, members of his family, various chiefs of different ranks, the British Crown, the mission societies and others. At the same time cash crops, mainly cotton and coffee, were introduced into the subsistence economy of Uganda, giving rise to a very successful economic development under the 'pax Britanica' which lasted about 60 years (Hecklau, 1978:106–9). The development of market-orientated agricultural production, not only on the relatively few plantations which came into being, but also on a broad scale on peasant farms, was possible only with the employment of paid labour. The labourers immigrated with and without their families from overcrowded regions of east Africa, where young families found it extremely difficult to make their living on their own farmsteads due to shortage of land. In 1959 roughly a tenth of Uganda's population originated from outside Uganda (see table 12.4). Shortly after independence internecine conflicts between the ruling Tutsi and the suppressed Hutu broke out in Rwanda as well as in Burundi and forced many Tutsi out of Rwanda and many Hutu out of Burundi. Many Tutsi families immigrated into Uganda, and many managed to bring their cattle with them. In Zaire several years of civil war and the resulting economic chaos caused many people to flee their country, more than 100,000 of them finding shelter in Uganda. In southern Sudan, the resistance of the Christian and animistic population to Islamization by the central government and the widespread feeling that they are economically neglected have led many people to join the guerilla groups who are fighting fiercely against domination by the Khartoum government. It has also resulted in some tens of thousand of refugees crossing the border to

Table 12.4 Population of non-Ugandan origin in Uganda, 1959 and 1969

Country of origin	1959 (1) Total	% of Uganda's population	1969 (2) Total	% of Uganda's population
	African population originating outside Uganda		African population by country of birth	
All African countries	681,914	10.6	751,259	7.9
Rwanda	378,656	5.9	253,154	2.7
Burundi	138,749	2.2	78,523	0.8
Kenya	81,517	1.3	154,096	1.6
Tanganyika/Tanzania	33,570	0.5	51,876	0.5
Congo/Zaire	24,296	0.4	155,392	1.6
Sudan	23,339	0.4	56,156	0.6
	Non-African population		Non-African population	
India inc. Goa/Pakistan	71,933	1.12	74,308	0.78
Arabian countries	1,946	0.03	3,238	
European countries	10,866	0.17	9,533	0.10

Source: 1 Uganda census 1959: African population, table IV; non-African population, table II; 2 Uganda census 1969, vol. III, tables 4, 9, 17, 25.

Uganda and founding new homes, mainly in the former districts of West Nile, Madi and Acholi (today Arua, Moyo, Gulu and Kitgum).

Kabera (1986:2) describes the issue of refugees in Uganda as follows:

Efforts were made to repatriate the Sudanese and Zaire refugees the majority of whom were repatriated in 1974. The number of refugees reported to be still in resettlements in Uganda by 1983 was 109,000 of whom about 85 per cent were Banyarwanda (Tutsi refugees from Rwanda). There had been some restrictions of labour movements into Uganda and by 1969 many economic migrants doing unskilled jobs in Uganda were beginning to go back to their homes. Towards the end of 1982, a move to force the Banyarwanda refugees out of south-west Uganda was started. Within three months an estimated 50,000 Banyarwanda who had otherwise lived in a fairly settled manner, given circumstances of time, had fled Uganda. Some thirty to forty thousand managed to cross the border to Rwanda while ten thousand went to Tanzania. Many of these returned at the time Museveni's forces had cut western Uganda off from the administration in Kampala during the second half of 1985. The issue of the Banyarwanda refugees has not been finalized but assurances were made by both President Museveni of Uganda and Habyalimana of Rwanda in October 1986, that some solution to the problem will be reached soon.

MIGRATION CAUSED BY VIOLENCE INSIDE UGANDA

After a promising start with independence on 9 October 1962 the people of Uganda were soon faced with grave economic and ethno-political problems. On 25 January 1971 the elected president Milton Obote was ousted by Idi Amin who led the country into a political disaster which is still not settled. Idi Amin was pushed out of the country in April 1979 by Tanzanian and Ugandan troops, and Yussef Lule took office, to be replaced two months later by Godfrey Binaisa, who made the statement that reports claiming that no less than 500,000 people lost their lives during Amin's rule were not exaggerated.

In 1972, Amin expelled the Asian community, which consisted of about 75,000 persons who had either immigrated to Uganda from the Indian sub-continent or were descendants of these immigrants, accusing them of sabotaging the national economy of Uganda. At that time he might have been right to a certain degree; the Asians, who held key positions in the national economy, felt unsafe in Uganda and therefore tried to smuggle as much of their wealth as possible out of the country. After the exodus of the Asians the monetary economy suffered heavy losses, and foreign trade dwindled. Amin wanted to make Uganda black and ordered the Ugandanization of the Asian assets, valued at about US$400 million invested in about 3,500 companies, including many retail shops in towns and villages. But there were not enough African businessmen prepared to run companies. Very soon the shops closed and the companies ceased operating. As the security situation worsened most Europeans left Uganda too. This was the beginning of the breakdown of the health services of the country, because the majority of the medical doctors were Europeans and Asians. Many African employees lost their jobs and returned to their rural homes.

Halbach (1973) has compiled and commented on reports of the expulsion of the Asian community published in the daily *Uganda Argus*, which was renamed *Voice of Uganda* after nationalization. The conditions of life in many towns worsened after the economic collapse caused by fighting and looting. The well developed central place system now no longer functioned. 'Many towns are still in existence on maps only' was one of the headlines in the German Berlin daily *Tagesspiegel* of January 1987. Groups of people not only fled the towns in badly affected areas but also migrated from unsafe rural areas to safer rural areas or were forced to leave their homes by the army which tried to pacify the country. A heartbreaking example is the 22,000 sq km area of the Luwero triangle. Johnston (1985) reports on the gloomy situation of the many thousands of displaced persons in this region. Because of the lack of precise data it seems impossible to locate and quantify the rural–rural migrations properly. It is also unknown how many Ugandans have fled the country since Idi Amin seized power in 1971.

Kabera (1986), as an eye witness of the horrible events in his country, describes the population movements caused by the retreat of Idi Amin's followers and by the struggle for power between Obote, Okello and Museveni. Many people of Uganda hope that Museveni will be able to restore law and order so that uncounted thousands of displaced persons can settle down and make a new start. The foreign observer cannot avoid the impression that the present-day violence in Uganda has a background in the tribal conflicts of pre-colonial times. Uganda is in many parts a beautiful and fertile country, still rich enough to support all her different peoples if they keep peace among themselves.

REFERENCES

Alnwick, D. J., Stirling, M. R. and Kyeyune, G. (1985) Morbidity and Mortality in Selected Uganda Hospitals, 1981–1982, in Dodge, C. P. and Wiebe, P. D. (eds), *Crisis in Uganda: The Breakdown of Health Services*, Pergamon, Oxford.

Bennett, F. J. (1975) Venereal Diseases and Other Spirochaetical Diseases, in Hall, S. A. and Langlands, B. W. (eds) *Uganda Atlas of Disease Distribution*, Nairobi.

Cole, C. D. and Wiebe, P. D. (1985) Introduction, in Dodge C. P., and Wiebe, P. D. (eds) *Crisis in Uganda: The Breakdown of Health Services*, Pergamon, Oxford.

Foster, W. D. (1970) (reprinted 1980) *The Early History of Scientific Medicine in Uganda*, Uganda Literature Bureau, Kampala.

Gallo, R.S. (1987) Das Aids-Virus, *Spektrum der Wissenschaft*, 3:83–93 (*Scientific American*: Internationale Ausgabe in Deutscher Sprache).

Halbach, J. H. (1973) *Die Ausweisung der Asiaten aus Uganda*. Sieben Monate Amin'scher Politik in Dokumenten, ifo-Forschungsberichte der Afrika-Studienstelle, 39, Weltform Verlag, Muenchen.

Hall, S. A. and Langlands, B. W. (eds) (1975) *Uganda Atlas of Disease Distribution*, Nairobi.

Harrell-Bond, B. E. (1986) *Imposing Aid*, Oxford University Press, Oxford.

Hecklau, H. K. (1978) *Agrargeographie Ostafrika: Afrika-Kartenwek*, Beiheft zu Blatt 11, Borntraeger Berlin Stuttgart.

HMSO (1985) *Report of the East African Commission*, (C2385) Colonial Office, London.

Johnston, A. (1985) The Luwero Triangle: Emergency Operations in Luwero, Mubende and Mpigi Districts, in Dodge, C. P. and Wiebe, P. D. (eds), *Crisis in Uganda: The Breakdown of Health Services*, Pergamon, Oxford: 97–106.

Jordan, A. M. (1986) *Trypanosomiasis Control and African Rural Development*, Longman, London.

Kabera, J. B. (1983) Rural Population Redistribution in Uganda since

1900, in Clarke, J. I. and Kosinski, L. A. (eds), *Redistribution of Population in Africa*, Heinemann, London: 192–201.

Kabera, J. B. (1986) Population Movement in and out of Uganda since Amin's Rule, 1971, unpublished manuscript, Kampala.

Laenderbericht Uganda (1986–8) *Statistik des Auslandes*, ed. Statistisches Bundesamt Wiesbaden. Kohlhammer Stuttgart, Mainz.

Langlands, B. W. (1967) *Sleeping Sickness in Uganda 1900–1920*, Department of Geography, Makerere University, Kampala, Occasional Paper 1.

Langlands, B. W. (1971) *The Population Geography of Bunyoro District*, Department of Geography, Makerere University, Kampala, Occasional Paper 35.

Onyango, R. J. (1975) African Human Trypanosomiasis (Sleeping Sickness), in Hall, S. A. and Langlands, B. W. (eds), *Uganda Atlas of Disease Distribution*, Nairobi.

Robertson, A. G. (1961) Foreword, in *Annual Report of Tsetse Control Department*, Government Printer, Entebbe.

Robertson, A. G. (1963) Tsetse Control in Uganda, *The East African Geographical Review*, 1:21–32.

Uganda Government *Statistical Abstract 1964*.

Republic of Uganda *Statistical Abstract 1973*.

13

The Disaster Life Cycle and Human Adjustments: Lessons from Three Mile Island and Chernobyl

Chris C. Park

INTRODUCTION

Environmental hazards and natural disasters have been much studied since the pioneering work of Burton and Kates (1964). Most of our present understanding comes from studies of natural disasters (e.g. floods, droughts, earthquakes and volcanic eruptions), and from some types of technological disasters (such as Love Canal in New York, Seveso in Italy and Bhopal in India). Despite widespread concern about and opposition to nuclear power, the relative lack of serious nuclear accidents has (thankfully) made it difficult to assess to what extent human behaviour in reality might differ from theory or expectations.

A convenient way of viewing human reactions to any type of disaster is via the 'disaster life-cycle' model. This chapter will introduce the basic model, and evaluate its utility in the light of experience of coping with nuclear accidents of Three Mile Island in the USA (1979) and at Chernobyl in Russia (1986).

THREE MILE ISLAND AND CHERNOBYL IN CONTEXT

The nuclear industry has a shaky track record. Between 1971 and 1985 there were 151 known nuclear accidents in 14 different countries

(Petrosyants, 1986). Not all were of disaster proportions, and some are better reported than others.

Amongst the worst was the huge underground explosion at a nuclear waste site near Kyshtym, east of the Ural Mountains in Russia, in 1957 (Medvedev, 1976). Many hundreds are believed to have died from radiation sickness, a large area of farmland was contaminated and at least 30 villages were abandoned and deleted from the Russian maps. The 1957 graphite fire at Windscale (now Sellafield) in north-west England also released radioactive material over a wide area, which might have contributed to the above-normal incidence of cancer (especially leukaemia) in the area (Taylor, 1981). It is worrying that the full extent of both disasters was only to emerge many years afterwards; both governments played down the risk and restricted the availability of information at the time.

Three Mile Island

The worst nuclear accident in the USA occurred in March 1979 at the Three Mile Island (TMI) plant near Harrisburg, Pennsylvania. It started in the Unit Two generating plant, at 4.00 am on 28 March: 'superheated, pressurized steam began to shoot out of a safety valve; three minutes later one of the steam generators was out of commision; five minutes later, the reactor core was beginning to boil dry' (Nagaraja, 1982:64). Plant operators quickly realized that a core meltdown was imminent; if that happened it would cause violent explosions and widespread pollution of air and groundwater which would seriously affect the surrounding area for decades.

The history of the event is well recorded by local observers (e.g. Martin, 1980) and in the official 'Kemeny Report' (President's Commission, 1979). The feared melt-down was averted, and very little radioactive material was released outside the plant. Most was trapped within the steel and concrete containment building over the damaged reactor.

Chernobyl

The disaster at the Chernobyl nuclear power complex in the Ukraine (USSR) in April 1986 is down on record as the world's worst nuclear accident. It started at 1.23 a.m. on 26 April, and was a result of serious operator errors and misjudgements which disabled the automatic cooling and emergency systems during an unauthorized test on the unit's turbo-generators (Lewis, 1986). Reactor overheating caused a massive power surge, followed instantly by two violent explosions which ripped the top off the reactor and the reactor building (which had no containment facilities).

Highly radioactive fission products poured out into the atmosphere for over ten days, and they were blown and deposited over much of Europe during the first few weeks in May. A fuller description of the accident is given in the formal Soviet report (USSR State Committee, 1986), and its wider consequences are explored elsewhere (Park, 1989).

Contrasts

There are interesting contrasts between Three Mile Island (TMI) and Chernobyl. The latter was a much bigger event, in all senses. Chernobyl released massive amounts of radioactive materials (over 10 million times as much as TMI). There were many more casualties – over 24 dead (mostly from radiation poisoning), and more than 100,000 evacuated (likely to be for decades, if not permanently). Nobody died because of or was injured by TMI, and people returned to the area within weeks at the longest.

The radiation cloud from Chernobyl contaminated a vast area, covering most of Europe and Scandinavia, whereas it was difficult to detect above-normal radiation levels more than a few kilometres away from TMI. The timescale of damage also differs. TMI poses few lasting problems, other than cleaning up the damaged plant, re-starting Unit One and rebuilding people's confidence in nuclear energy. Chernobyl cast a long shadow which will last a long time. Doctors expect high rates of leukaemia to emerge over the next five years among people within 100 km of Chernobyl at the time of the accident, and increased rates of cancer over the next few decades. Most of the Ukraine – the Soviet Union's traditional 'bread basket' – will be seriously contaminated for decades.

Superimposed on these scale differences are obvious institutional differences. Centralized Soviet decision-making, tight control on information and restrictions on the movement of people (mainly local residents and western reporters) strongly influenced reactions to the Chernobyl accident – inside and outside the Soviet Union. They were more delayed, more frustrated and less well informed than reactions to TMI.

THE DISASTER LIFE-CYCLE

Experience of natural disasters involves a range of activities which are inter-related, may overlap in time and cover different time periods (depending on the type, scale and character of the disaster). The disaster 'life-cycle' has four main phases (Park, 1983): pre-disaster, relief, rehabilitation and reconstruction. Inevitably the period of time occupied by each phase, and the specific details of activities carried out, will vary from one type and scale of disaster to another.

Pre-disaster

Before a disaster occurs, it is very much 'business as usual' in the area. Social and economic activity continue as routine, and quality of life for locals is normal. With nuclear accidents this phase is marked by public anxiety over the prospect of something going wrong. This is fuelled by many factors. Nuclear physics and engineering are largely unintelligible to the layman, and the terms and measuring units used are generally unfamiliar and incomprehensible. Radiation is widely known to be linked with cancer, and both are regarded as modern-day evils. Assumed links between civil and military nuclear operations compound the issue. Moreover, unlike most other physical threats, radiation is insidious – we cannot see, hear, smell, taste, feel or otherwise sense it. Finally, there is often widespread concern over the suitability and workability of disaster contingency plans – will theory translate neatly into practice?

Anti-nuclear feelings were probably higher around TMI than around Chernobyl (where information was tightly controlled), but in neither place was the disaster really anticipated. Most disasters (especially technological ones) strike without warning, and the disaster itself is generally short-lived (even if its consequences are not). This initial phase is suddenly terminated by the disaster itself.

Relief

As soon as any disaster strikes, all social and economic activities are disrupted, and an emergency period follows. Search and rescue operations, burying the dead and caring for affected people (the injured, orphaned, shelterless) take top priority. The emphasis is on speed and efficiency – no time must be wasted if lives are to be saved and repaired. Within hours or days efforts are normally made to provide food, water, clothing, shelter and medical care to survivors, and to stop continued loss and disruption related to the event (such as spread of fire or infectious disease, collapse of damaged buildings and structures).

At TMI the relief phase was short-lived. The only damage to property was within the containment building. Local emergency services (fire, ambulances, hospitals) were mobilized but not used. No-one died or was injured in the accident, and evacuation of local people was advised but not ordered. Governor Thornburg recommended that pregnant women and pre-school children within five miles of the plant should evacuate, and that all residents within ten miles should stay inside with doors and windows closed.

Evacuation behaviour at TMI has been examined in a number of studies (Cutter and Barnes, 1982; Zeigler and Johnson, 1984). Only 39 per cent of the 650,000 or so people at risk within 32 km of the plant chose to evacuate themselves (mainly as a result of the Governor's advisory statement). Most (74 per cent) of those stayed with friends and relatives within 100 km – no-one used the officially designated evacuation reception areas (18 km from the plant). Half returned home within a week; 98 per cent had returned within three weeks.

There is no evidence of widespread public panic around TMI, but many were anxious. Much of the information made available in the first few days was ambiguous if not contradictory. Scientists and policy-makers found it difficult to agree on the best course of action and the Governor eventually (on 1 April) designated the Nuclear Regulatory Commission (NRC) as the sole source of technical information on the status of the reactor. The NRC also extended the voluntary evacuation zone from 8 km to 16 km, and later to 32 km, which caused some confusion and anxiety (and increased the number of potential evacuees from 27,000 to nearly 700,000 within hours).

Chernobyl presented quite different problems during the relief phase. Knowledge of what had happened at the power station was only to emerge two days after the accident, after Swedish radiation monitoring equipment had picked up above-normal levels in the air, and Moscow reluctantly conceded that an accident had occurred. The most pressing problems were to extinguish the raging fires (30 had broken out around the reactor after it exploded) and to seal the damaged reactor (from which fission products were spilling out uncontrollably into the atmosphere). Until these were taken care of, the disaster itself would continue and relief as such would be impossible.

Teams of firemen were drafted in from nearby Pripyat and Chernobyl. They worked in dangerous conditions – immense heat, high radiation, twisted and unstable structures – with apparently little concern for their own safety. The fires were out within about 15 hours, but it took 12 days to seal the reactor, by dropping 5,000 tonnes of sand, lead, boron and clay on to it from military helicopters. Again, personnel put their own lives and health at risk to complete the task.

Relief as such began with the controlled evacuation of local people. A decision was made on the evening of the accident that all people within 10 km should be moved to safety. Unspecified organizational problems delayed this by 36 hours (during which radiation levels were dangerously high, and health risks were increasing by the hour). Around 25,000 people were eventually taken to safety in Kiev (130 km away). A few days later the evacuation zone was extended to 30 km, to include Pripyat and Chernobyl. Nearly 84,000 people were evacuated (six days after the accident), initially to Kiev, in a convoy of 1,100 commandeered buses.

The Chernobyl evacuation differed from that at TMI in several obvious ways. It was enforced, rather than voluntary. It involved many more people over a much wider area. They had no choice over where and when they left their homes and farms. They were given no advice about when (or even if) they might expect to be able to return.

Relief at Chernobyl was also an international concern. Many countries hurriedly made plans to repatriate nationals who had been in the area (including most of the Ukraine) during or after the accident. British students staying in Kiev and Minsk (about 300 km away), Austrian steel specialists at Shlobin (150 km away) and Finnish construction workers from Kiev were flown home. Many countries advised people not to travel to the western Soviet Union unless they absolutely had to. It later emerged that many Russian mothers and children also fled from Kiev (mainly by train to Moscow), initially on their own initiative but later with official guidance.

While this vast human exodus was under way, 200 plant workers and firemen were in hospital receiving urgent medical attention. The worst 139 cases had been flown straight to Moscow, where many were to receive bone-marrow transplants (the only way of treating those who have been exposed to dangerously high radiation levels).

Further afield, the relief phase diffused around Europe as the radiation cloud drifted first northwards over Scandinavia and later south-west over central and southern Europe and eventually over Britain. Many countries banned the import of foodstuffs (fruit, vegetables, milk, fresh meat, animals for slaughter, game and freshwater fish) from countries within 1,000 km of Chernobyl, to reduce the health hazard from consuming contaminated food and drink. Some countries banned the sale of milk and dairy products from sheep and cattle which grazed fresh (contaminated) grass. While anxiety was heightened throughout Europe during the first week in May, only in Poland was the radiation situation so bad that stable iodine was issued as a prophylactic (preventive medicine) to an estimated ten million children and young people.

In sum, relief at TMI meant anxiety and inconvenience for local residents, but none died or was injured and many decided to stay in the area. At Chernobyl the relief operation was more urgent (it was a matter of international as well as local concern) and it affected many more people directly and indirectly. The relief phase comes to an end when the immediate priorities – search and rescue, taking care of the dead and injured, dealing with unstable and damaged structures and buildings, and so on – have been addressed. There is no precise day on which this happens, but it gives way progressively to the longer rehabilitation phase.

Rehabilitation

Here the actions are designed to restore community cohesion and the physical fabric of the disaster area, to allow a progressive return to normality. In many disasters temporary housing replaces mass shelters, the injured are moved from field hospitals to regular hospitals, and money and resources are made available to the unemployed and the homeless.

The lack of physical damage and direct casualties at TMI meant that no formal rehabilitation programme was necessary there. But there is evidence of need for some form of psychological rehabilitation. Many locals interviewed after the accident (Goldstein and Schorr, 1982) felt that the lack of visible evidence contributed to their continued sense of uncertainty about how the accident might affect their health in the long term. Some doctors report more fear, anxiety, demoralization and signs of stress in locals since the accident. Many locals also have a continued feeling of vulnerability to future unseen problems at the plant: the 'silent enemy' could strike again, they feel, and they might not even be aware of it. Locals also have less trust than before the accident of public officials; their perceived credibility appears to have been badly eroded by their handling of the evacuation and information programme.

Rehabilitation at Chernobyl will be a much longer term and more broadly based affair. There are a large number of areas where 'repair' work will be required.

Some are essentially medical problems. Those who were injured in the explosion and fires on site, and who have not already died from radiation poisoning, will have to be cared for and their families supported. Those who develop cancer and leukaemias from radiation poisoning will have to be diagnosed and treated.

The Soviet authorities have established a register of all 135,000 people who were within 30 km of the plant at the time of the accident. Their exposure to radiation was checked (by mid-summer), and their health was being monitored by doctors. The official estimate given in the formal Soviet report (USSR State Committee, 1986) is that a few hundred from this population are likely to die over the next 70 years from cancers related to the accident. This compares with an expected death toll from cancer from natural causes of around 14,000 for the same period.

An estimated 100 million people throughout Europe and the western Soviet Union received some exposure to low levels of radiation (especially to iodine-131 and caesium-137). The official Soviet estimate is that around 15 million of these are likely to contract some form of cancer in the next 70 years. Order-of-magnitude estimates of the number likely to contract cancer as a result of Chernobyl are in the 1,000–2,000 range (Lewis, 1986). Some estimates are as high as 24,000.

There are other, social and economic problems. The 100,000 or so evacuees will pay much of the human toll for Chernobyl. Many of them will be on the long-term casualty list, and are likely to develop various forms of cancer because they were exposed to high radiation levels for several days or longer before they were evacuated. Many are being resettled in new flats and houses in Kiev, with furniture paid for by the state. But this will be little compensation for what they left behind. They left with nothing but the clothes they had on; they took few belongings with them (there was neither time nor space, and they would be heavily contaminated in any case); they had no immediate source of income and no jobs to go to. Many did not know where their families and friends had gone.

A public appeal was launched for funds to help the evacuees, and within six months around £500 million had been collected by voluntary donations. This, coupled with state help and support, will go some way towards compensating the displaced families for their immediate financial and material losses. But the overall cost in terms of human inconvenience and suffering is likely to be high. These will be the forgotten victims of Chernobyl.

There is also a group of practical problems. In the area around Chernobyl the priorities are containment and decontamination. As soon as the damaged reactor had been sealed, work began on building a giant concrete tomb around the reactor building. Three concrete factories were commissioned, and within months the entire building housing damaged reactor number three (as tall as a 20-storey block) was encased in concrete to prevent any further contamination of the surrounding area with radiation.

Surrounding areas, including the nearby towns of Chernobyl and Pripyat and many farms, will have to be cleaned up and decontaminated before they can be safely used again. Within months of the accident large areas of soil, farmland and forest around the plant were being treated to reduce radiation levels. Experimental work in decontaminating large areas continues. Buildings and streets in Pripyat (then deserted save for the work teams) were washed down to remove radioactive dust and particles. Concrete barriers were built along the banks of local rivers to prevent contaminated water from entering the Dneiper River, which supplies half of Kiev's drinking water. New artesian wells were sunk in case uncontaminated water supplies should begin to run short.

One goal of the immediate rehabilitation programme was to get the two undamaged reactors back into operation as soon as possible. Before the accident Chernobyl was providing 15 per cent of the country's nuclear electricity, and this was sorely missed. By September 1986 (five months after the accident) numbers one and two reactors were back on stream. Efforts on-site were greatly boosted by the completion in the autumn of a new village for the shift teams, 50 km from the plant. The facilities and home comforts were a welcome relief after many months living in caravans!

While the most pressing problems are those in and around Chernobyl, the accident has also left a legacy of problems in countries downwind who received high fallout from the radiation cloud which drifted across Scandinavia and Europe. The list is a long one. It includes the very survival of 15,000 Lapp nomads in central Sweden whose reindeer have unacceptably high radiation levels through eating contaminated berries, fish and lichens. It also includes sheep farmers in Wales, western Scotland and Cumbria who were prevented from bringing their sheep to market for at least a year because they had eaten contaminated grass and continue to have high body levels of radiation.

The financial cost is also high. The British National Farmers' Union estimates that by late summer 1986 Chernobyl had already cost British farmers over $14 million. The bill for ruined food in Sweden is put at around $144 million. Despite some promises that the Soviet Union would provide adequate compensation to its neighbours for damage caused by Chernobyl, it has been left to individual governments to foot the bill and decide on their own schemes of compensation payments.

Reconstruction

The aim during long-term reconstruction is to restore the quality of life and economic stability to at least the pre-disaster level. After most types of disaster, permanent roads, utilities and buildings are provided where necessary; productive economic activity is re-started; communities are encouraged to re-focus their attention on the future and on long-term stability. The overall programme is designed to reduce vulnerability to further disasters, to increase self-reliance, and to restore normality to the area as quickly as possible.

There are few reconstruction tasks at TMI outside the reactor building. Three years after the accident the undamaged Unit One had still not been re-started, and no decision had been made on how to dispose of the 600,000 gallons of contaminated water in the containment building of Unit Two (Nagaraja, 1982); neither was there any agreement over who would pay the estimated $1 billion clean-up bill (President's Commission, 1979).

While the accident did not directly damage local industry, it did so indirectly via the 256,000 man-days which were lost during the voluntary evacuation. Nelkin (1981) estimates that this cost the local manufacturing industry between $5.7 million and $8.2 million, and the non-manufacturing sector between $2.8 million and $3.8 million. Lost revenue from tourism cost up to an extra $8 million, and agriculture lost around $1 million.

But the wider issue of flagging public confidence in nuclear power generation must be addressed. There is no doubt that US confidence in nuclear energy was badly shaken by the TMI accident. Since then, few if any new nuclear power stations have been ordered, and options on others have not all been taken up. It will take some time before the credibility of the nuclear industry is fully repaired – if indeed it ever is.

Reconstruction after Chernobyl will be an altogether different problem. The full extent of damage to farmland and industry in the Ukraine is not yet clear – but it is bound to be long-lasting and wide-ranging. Vast areas remain to be decontaminated. Large numbers remain in temporary exile after evacuation. The Soviet authorities, after giving consideration to design improvements in the RBMK-type reactor (as installed at Chernobyl), announced in summer 1986 that it would press ahead with its planned programme of expanding nuclear energy production. This would double nuclear power's share of electricity production to around 21 per cent by 1990.

CONCLUSIONS

The disaster 'life-cycle' is a convenient if simple model for sum-marizing human reactions to any type of disaster. It allows the activities and priorities at different stages in coping with a disaster to be examined in context, and it provides a useful vehicle for monitoring human adjustments at different time-scales.

But it is no more than a simple model, and as such has clear limitations. It does, however, encourage the whole spectrum of human adjustments to be considered in their proper time context. In this sense it has some value in contingency planning, because it provides a framework for making both immediate and longer-term decisions about how best to cope with disaster.

Few disasters occur in isolation. Most, regrettably, are repeat performances of disasters which have happened somewhere before. Many technological disasters – like nuclear accidents – can be avoided by careful planning, design and construction, provided that we are prepared to pay the cost. Disaster contingency planning and preparedness studies are now becoming more common. But the lessons from Three Mile Island and Chernobyl reveal that more research is required into how people perceive hazard risk, how they make decisions about coping with a disaster once it has happened, how reliable information can be made available at the time it is required, and how the broader socio-economic costs of disaster can be compensated for.

REFERENCES

Burton, I. and Kates, R. W. (1964) The Perception of Natural Hazards in Resource Management, *Natural Resources Journal*, 3:412–41.
Cutter, S. L. and Barnes, K. (1982) Evacuation Behaviour and Three Mile Island, *Disasters*, 6:116–24.
Goldstein, R. and Schorr, J. K. (1982) The Long-Term Impact of a Man-Made Disaster: An Examination of a Small Town in the Aftermath of the Three Mile Island Nuclear Reactor Accident, *Disasters*, 6:50–9.
Lewis, H. W. (1986) The Accident at the Chernobyl Nuclear Power Plant and its Consequences, *Environment*, 28:25–7.
Martin, D. (1980) *Three Mile Island; Prologue or Epilogue?* Ballinger, Cambridge, Mass.

Medvedev, Z. (1976) Two Decades of Dissidence, *New Scientist*, 72:264–7.

Nagaraja, K. J. (1982) The Legacy of Three Mile Island, *Disasters*, 6:64–6.

Nelkin, D. (1981) Some Social and Political Dimensions of Nuclear Power: Examples from Three Mile Island, *American Political Science Review*, 75:132–42.

Park, C. C. (1983) *Environmental Hazards*, Macmillan, London.

Park, C. C. (1989) *Chernobyl – The Long Shadow*, Routledge, London.

Petrosyants, A. (1986) The Soviet Union and the Development of Nuclear Power, *IAEA Bulletin International Atomic Energy Agency*, Autumn: 5–8.

President's Commission on the Accident at Three Mile Island (1979) *The Need for Change: the Legacy of Three Mile Island*, US Government Printing Office, Washington DC.

Taylor, P. (1981) *The Windscale Fire, 1957*, Political Ecology Research Group, Oxford.

USSR State Committee on the Utilization of Atomic Energy (1986) *The Accident at the Chernobyl Nuclear Power Plant and its Consequences.* Report to IAEA Experts' Meeting, Vienna (August).

Zeigler, D. J. and Johnson, J. H. (1984) Evacuation Behaviour in Response to Nuclear Power Plant Accidents, *Professional Geographer*, 36:207–15.

14

The Bhopal Disaster

S. L. Kayastha and Prithvish Nag

Bhopal, the capital of Madhya Pradesh (see figure 14.1) has witnessed more rapid growth than the other urban centres of the state; its population recorded a decennial growth of 72.62 per cent in 1961–71 and 74.35 per cent in 1971–81, to reach 671,000 (Dubey, 1984). Both planned and non-planned housing developed rapidly. The factors responsible for the rapid development of the city's population include establishment of new administrative functions and socio-economic institutions, and industrial development, especially the setting up of Bharat Heavy Electricals Plant and the Union Carbide Plant. The new industrial units were added as part of a conscious policy to help the growth of employment and prosperity.

Scientific, technological and industrial development is considered to be important for economic growth and for improvement in the living standards of the people. However, this development has to be judiciously considered in relation to processes, practices and impacts, especially in view of the increasing technological and industrial hazards that are associated with such development. In the developing countries, there is a greater likelihood of introducing hazardous technologies either because of restricted choice of opportunities for industrial development, or because of inadequate perception and assessment with respect to suitability and safety at the time industrial plants are established. There is an evident lack of policy and planning. Haphazard growth of technology and industry is a hazard rather than a panacea for economic ill-health, so the careful selection of technology and planning of industry are vital. This, however, does not obviate the necessity for emergency or

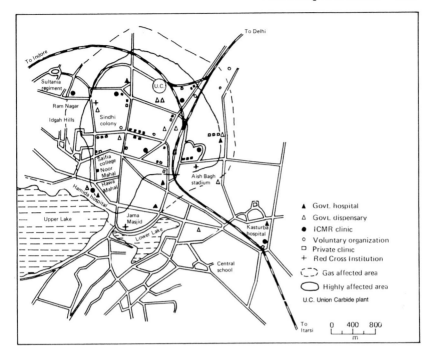

To Delhi

To Indore

Sultania
regiment

Ram Nagar

Idgah Hills

Sindhi
colony

U.C.

Saifia
college

Noor
Mahal

Hawa
Mahal

Hamida hospital

Aish Bagh
stadium

Upper Lake

Jama
Masjid

Lower Lake

Kasturba
hospital

Central
school

To
Itarsi

▲ Govt. hospital
△ Govt. dispensary
● ICMR clinic
○ Voluntary organization
□ Private clinic
+ Red Cross Institution

Gas affected area

Highly affected area

U.C. Union Carbide plant

0   400   800
m

Figure 14.1   The Bhopal disaster

disaster preparedness and management measures. White (1986:8) has pointed out this challenge, which is to design and carry out measures that will alleviate human distress and which include both warning systems to alert people in the path of destruction, and evacuation procedures that can guide them to safety. The crises resulting from industrial disasters are now becoming more frequent and having a greater impact on population and environment. The disasters at Bhopal, Chernobyl, Love Canal, and the Tylenol poisonings, are striking examples. It seems likely that by the turn of the century such disasters and crises will increase in frequency as a result of the proliferation of new technologies in developed countries, and the rapid entry into developing countries of more hazardous technologies. The causes include technological, organizational, human and social factors that make industrial plants and products hazardous. The impacts include immediate loss of life and health, social and cultural disruption, and even political unrest or changes. All these facets were vividly brought into focus and analyzed in the Bhopal disaster.

GENESIS

The Bhopal disaster, which occurred on 2–3 December 1984 due to the calamitous leakage of methyl isocyanate (MIC) from Union Carbide's pesticide plant in Bhopal, is possibly the world's biggest chemical disaster to date (Kayastha, 1986). The causes are many but the main one is considered to be the lack or inadequacy of safety measures at the plant. This study of the disaster is based on newspaper reports since December 1984, certain government publications made available to the public, magazine articles, and some books.

The citizens of Bhopal cannot forget the night of 2 December and the morning of 3 December 1984, which witnessed the death of more than 2,500 innocent persons, leaving no fewer than 200,000 affected for the rest of their lives. The MIC killer-gas leakage forced people to flee their homes in the middle of a winter night. The so-called 'fail-safe system' of the Union Carbide plant was a failure. Leaking valves in the filter cleaning system were said to be the initiating cause. This leakage was not the first; there had been one in 1981 on a restricted scale, and it is surprising that greater care was not taken subsequently. It is stated that besides numerous design deficiencies, the Bhopal plant had been characterized by many signs of ill-health including sustained erosion of good maintenance practices and an indiscriminate economy drive. All these factors combined to cause the multiple failures that underlay the calamitous accident (*Times of India*, 1985). Earlier, in the middle of 1984, a report (released in mid-December 1984) prepared by the three American experts who had studied the Bhopal plant's safety measures, had expressed that 'the plant represented either a higher potential for serious accident, or more serious consequences if an accident should occur' (Khandekar and Dubey, 1984). It is therefore highly regrettable that in spite of this warning by the American experts, especially when such a lethal gas as MIC was involved in the process, all possible measures were not taken by the Union Carbide Company and its management. The Indian unit lacked the computerized early warning and fail-safe system used in the company's US factory, where it is obligatory that any factory using MIC and phosgene should be located at least 50 km away from human habitation, agricultural activity, railway line or airport. This safeguard was not undertaken in Bhopal. Union Carbide had first intended to put up this plant in Canada but the Canadian government had turned it down.

Union Carbide (India) Ltd set up a formulation plant in May, 1969 to manufacture pesticides in Bhopal, and new facilities for manufacturing pesticides were added so that the plant spread over 36 ha. Stored in the plant were 43 tonnes of liquified MIC, in complete disregard of the safety measures required for its storage. The refrigeration unit was shut down, and the pipelines that connected the MIC tank to the vent-gas scrubbers and the flare tower were stated to have been dismantled for maintenance. Thus, design faults apart, the management ignored even the limited safety devices provided in the plant. MIC has to be stored under refrigeration at below 15°C, valves have to function properly, vent scrubbers have to be kept ready to neutralize any leakage, a flare has to be kept ready to burn and neutralize any leakage of gas, and a water curtain around the plant has to be maintained to dissolve any escaping MIC. These devices were not fully functional, some not even partly, to counter the gas leak that caused the disaster. It is remarked in a government publication (Department of Information and Publicity, 1986), that 'even if all these safety devices had functioned as designed, they could not have completely neutralized the run-away gases which escaped from the storage tank that fateful night. Such devices to meet such a situation were just not built into the Indian facility'. The Bhopal disaster occurred because nothing could be done, while there was still time, to keep the plant in good shape and sound health with proper safety provisions, in order to stop the leakage of lethal gas.

THE DISASTER

The people of Bhopal had no premonition of the disaster on the evening of 2 December, 1984. They went to bed as usual, without knowing that a chemical time-bomb was ticking away. The leakage of MIC had started by midnight. If the warning system of the Union Carbide Plant had been set off immediately, many people could have escaped death and disability. People started to feel the effects, resulting in a violent cough and burning sensation in the eyes, around 12.30–1.00 a.m. There was general panic and people fled in confusion in all directions.

The deadly gas spread on the wind, its asphyxiating effect felt in ward after ward of the city claiming hundreds of casualties, both human and animal. Hundreds lay dead on roads and in their houses. Many rushed to overflowing hospitals to doctors who did not know of any specific treatment. The carcasses of dead animals littered roads and residential areas. Both human and animal corpses had to be removed and disposed of speedily to remove any fear of the outbreak of epidemic disease. In the work of evacuation and disposal, the army rendered very valuable help, rescuing people, moving them to hospitals and removing dead bodies with great efficiency and responsibility.

The disaster had a lingering effect, and continued to take a toll of human lives several days afterwards. Dead bodies were so numerous that morgues were set up for their identification, which presented a spectre worse than that seen in wartime. Fresh cases of MIC poisoning continued to arrive day after day. The government closed the slaughter houses for fear of consumption of poisoned meat. The number of dead persons is difficult to state exactly on account of wide variations in government figures and unofficial estimates. According to government figures, over 2,500 persons died and over 200,000 were affected, 75 per cent of whom were slum dwellers. As always, it is the poor who suffered most.

On the seventh day after the disaster, there was a new source of panic. It was revealed that 15 tonnes of lethal MIC still remained to be disposed of. In spite of all assurances of a safe operation, panic continued to grip the population. All schools and colleges were closed after 10 December for 12 days. By evening of 13 December, over 100,000 persons had left the city, many patients fleeing their hospital beds. By 14 December, a quarter of the city's population had fled, and there was a crisis of confidence. Nearly 24 tonnes of gas had to be disposed of or converted, which was more than the estimated amount. Such was the state of affairs that the management of the plant did not even know how much gas it had in store.

As the antidote to poisoning by MIC gas was not known, people continued to suffer from the ill effects. So extensive was the damage that the entire area affected by the poison gas covered 36 wards of the city with a population of about 500,000.

The disaster impaired the health of many thousands, who were rendered incapable of carrying on their occupations to earn their livelihood. All normal activity stopped for a while, and trade, commerce and industrial activity were greatly disrupted. The environmental situation in the slum areas affected by the gas deteriorated rapidly. A large number of casualties were suffered and there were fears of spread of epidemic disease as a result of the widespread death and decay. According to a survey, vegetation in an area of 3.5 sq km around the factory was severely affected, 10.5 sq km were badly affected and 5 sq km were mildly affected. Interestingly, some species of plants were unharmed when found growing near the lakes, which probably shows that water had a diluting effect (Agarwal and Narain, 1986:221).

The affected people felt breathless and weak. They faced a shattered economy with shattered health. Sometimes, routine medical treatment with antibiotics, etc., showed more harmful side-effects than benefits. Thus the poor and affected wage-earners found themselves injured, weak and helpless. The government was quite responsive, but it simply was not prepared for an emergency of such proportions. It lacked the infrastructure which high-risk industrialization renders imperative for reducing appalling loss of life and suffering. This suffering was compounded because the Union Carbide Company had given no advice on the poison gas, and the type of effective treatment for poison gas sufferers. According to a reported survey of 2,000 families by the Indian Council of Medical Research (ICMR) in February/March 1985, 1,600 persons were found to be suffering from lung problems, 1,425 from eye problems and 5,067 from both. A British expert observed that a highly reactive agent like MIC, which can react with DNA and protein in the body's cells, could lead to cancer. According to Capersson (1981), environmental pollution from leakage and mobility of radiation and chemicals, including pesticides, has serious effects on plants, animal and human life and may even cause genetic damage. The ICMR has stressed the need for careful follow-up studies to monitor such delayed effects as may occur. Autopsies on the poison gas victims in the Bhopal disaster have revealed a cherry-red colour of the blood, similar to that found in cyanide poisoning, in this case possibly hydrogen cyanide. In addition to physical injury, many suffered from panic and anxiety which required psychiatric treatment.

RELIEF AND REHABILITATION

No known toxicological literature was available, generally or from the company, on antidotes to the effects of MIC. The effects on the nervous system, musculo-skeletal system and the endocrinal system have yet to be specifically identified. The patients therefore did not necessarily respond to symptomatic treatment. The numbers of those who needed treatment, food, funds and care ran into thousands. They had to be treated by more than a thousand doctors, nurses, paramedics, and others from the voluntary organizations. A large number of patients were treated for eye ailments, chest and lung effects, gastro-intestinal disorders and psychiatric problems. Food, milk and other items of nourishment were provided to patients by government agencies and voluntary organizations. It was realized at the outset that an exclusive administrative machinery was needed to deal with the aftermath, which led to the creation of a Department of Gas Relief and Rehabilitation in order to reduce substantially the response time for various requirements.

After meeting the immediate need of emergency treatment, the main problem was to feed those who were rendered jobless and destitute. Free rations, comprising food-grains, sugar and edible oil were provided by the government. In addition, free milk was given to children and nursing mothers. The expenditure incurred in one year (December 1984–December 1985) on food-grains alone amounted to Rs 200 million. Some 212 centres disrtributed rations on 130,000 ration cards. An ex-gratia payment of Rs 10,000 was made for each death to the next-of-kin, Rs 2,000 to each person seriously injured, and Rs 1,000 to each of those who suffered minor injuries. Efforts were made to identify such cases for on-the-spot payment. Deaths due to poison-gas effects are still taking place, and efforts are made to identify these for grant of ex-gratia aid. Surveys in the affected area showed that apart from financial help in cases of death and injury, there were many families who had no resources to meet their immediate needs; 88,000 such families in 36 affected wards were offered financial assistance of Rs 1,500 each, almost all of whom benefited from this timely help. Further, 302 widows are getting pensions of Rs 200 per month, and 1,482 destitute persons are being given a pension of Rs 60 per month. Compensatory assistance has also been paid for 2,135 dead livestock (Rs 3,500 for a buffalo and Rs 20 for poultry), and 28,000 injured animals have been treated in veterinary hospitals.

Medical relief had to be organized on a vast scale for the gas-affected patients. Local, regional and national medical institutions, and official and voluntary organizations came forward to provide medical treatment. Existing medical and health facilities had to be expanded and new ones organized for this purpose. At present 18 medical institutions are working in the affected area, treating a daily average of 3,500–4,000 patients. The MIC Cell documents all the treatment provided to the affected patients. The long-term effects are not yet fully comprehended, and fears still persist about them. The Bhopal Gas Disaster Research Centre of ICMR is extensively and deeply involved in the research effort, and in addition 26 ICMR research projects on this aspect have been entrusted to the local medical institutions, and to scientists from other parts of the country. Thirteen affected localities are being studied in three groups of severely, moderately and mildly affected persons, the population in each group being 30,843, 38,600 and 20,934. A separate 'control group' for comparison comprises unaffected localities and has a population of 16,902. An assessment of their health status, including morbidity, is being made. The main areas of research interest are epidemiological and long-term morbidity, mortality, pulmonary involvements, eye ailments, pathological disorders, clinical and forensic toxicological studies, and cancer. Those who were mildly affected have responded better to treatment than those severely affected, who suffered permanent impairment of health and quality of life and loss of earning capacity.

Many cases of pulmonary tuberculosis found in the disaster area, although having recovered from tuberculosis after treatment, are still suffering effects of the poison gas. Some patients who had symptoms of burns in their air passages, still experience difficulty in breathing and get exhausted after even slight exertion. Patients suffering from pulmonary fibrosis also experience breathlessness. The medical studies conducted in the disaster area have revealed that those suffering from pulmonary diseases have experienced further deterioration in health, symptomatically as well as functionally. Exposure to poison gas is found to have caused chemical burns in the upper gastro-intestinal tract, resulting in flatulence, pain in the abdomen and loss of appetite. Patients having eye ailments, breathlessness and gastro-intestinal troubles still continue to suffer. Another survey showed that about 13 per cent of the population in the affected area suffered from mental problems such as anxiety, neurosis, depression and loss of will to work and live usefully.

Among 2,566 expectant mothers, there were 355 spontaneous abortions (13.8 per cent of pregnancies), whereas the normal rate is usually only 2 per cent, 88 stillbirths and 33 babies born suffering congenital malformation. Moreover, most of the babies born were underweight and experienced below-average physical and mental growth. Children affected by the poison gas suffer from respiratory troubles, coughs and breathlessness, and are more prone to infections. At a tender age, they have psychiatric problems, mostly disturbed sleep, irritability and neurosis.

Although the less-affected and better-off section of the population could make valiant efforts for their socio-economic rehabilitation, the majority, particularly the poor who suffered most, needed support to restore them to a socially desirable and economically remunerative life. Social rehabilitation demanded efforts in improving the quality of life in the affected areas, and in looking after the welfare of women and children. A socio-economic survey underlined the need for programmes that would help improve the living environment and contribute to the welfare of the affected population, which was socially deprived and economically ruined. For this purpose 633 centres had to be established for the care of infants and children and nursing and expectant mothers, providing them with a package of services that included supplementary nutrition, medical services, non-formal education, health-check and immunization facilities. The centres are also meant to be community centres offering meeting and other facilities. About Rs 10 million have been spent on provision of supplementary nutrition alone. A 4 ha SOS village was established to house the orphans and destitutes of the gas-affected area.

Environmental improvement was considered essential to provide qualitatively acceptable conditions for living. A number of schemes have been initiated for the provision of drinking water, roads, drains, toilets and street lighting, improvement of shelters, development of open spaces, reclamation of low-lying areas, solid-waste disposal, and development of housing sites. Several government departments are involved in the task of environmental improvement of the affected area at an estimated cost of over Rs 17 million during 1985–7. Besides these agencies, several voluntary organizations have rendered very valuable assistance in the fields of rehabilitation, medical care, education and training programmes.

A socio-economic survey of January – December 1985 helped to develop a realistic employment profile of the affected population. Nearly 25,000 families were found to have suffered either a total loss of income or considerable reduction in their physical earning capacity. This target group is planned to be covered in a period of two years. The strategy adopted for assistance is two-pronged. The first and primary thrust consists of provision of loans to help in self-employment under a special training and employment programme for the urban poor ('STEP UP') as a continuing scheme; 25,000 families are being financed with such loans of up to Rs 12,000 each. The second thrust aims at permanent upgrading for income-earning skills. About 5,000 persons will be trained within the two-year period. It is gratifying to note a resurgence of economic activity in the affected area and to see that people are developing hope for a new and a fruitful life (Department of Information and Publicity, 1985). Various departments of the government and certain export enterprises have shown interest in purchasing articles from the production centres run by the disaster-affected people. However, in order to foster greater self-reliance, the interest of the production centres has shifted from dependence on government orders to service-sector trades, such as automobile mechanics, plumbing, electrical wiring and welding; moreover, 580 worksheds are being allotted to small-scale industries such as hosiery, handloom woollens, ready-made garments and other manufactures, and nearly 3,600 persons, including trained personnel, will find employment in them. With self-help and assistance by government and other organizations, the deprived and disabled are trying to reestablish the social and economic ways and means for a worthwhile and reasonably assured socio-economic pattern of life.

The Bhopal disaster not only killed and disabled thousands of people, but it also caused disruption and loss to work and employment, trade and industry, and civic and social life in Bhopal. The losses were enormous in terms of life, assets and occupational work. So far, 518,771 claims have been received by the state government's Directorate of Claims. The claimants have received little in terms of the value of their losses. The government and voluntary agencies have provided only token relief to the affected people to help sustain them through the emergency and also towards rehabilitation. Claimants have not received any compensation for their losses. Even two years after the disaster, the claims remained unsettled and therefore the people became pessimistic about achieving redress, although it means so much to them. In fairness, it may be observed that the city's people have risen virtually from the ashes or ruins; from another Hiroshima. The people have now turned, a little apprehensively, to new activities and to a new life with hopes and dreams for a better destiny.

ISSUES AFTER THE BHOPAL DISASTER

The Bhopal disaster brings into focus several issues related to industrial safety, siting of hazardous plants, pollution, environmental damage and provision of adequate health and safety laws; all must be addressed if occurrence of another disaster is to be prevented. The destructive capacity of such disasters is so immense that society cannot afford to let them happen. The general public who are exposed to grave danger from such events is not involved in policy matters; they are not even informed of the possible hazards of the operation of such factories or plants. In their study of 'Technological hazards in the third world', which includes a systematic analysis of perceptual responses in the case of the Bhopal catastrophe, Karan, Bladen and Wilson (1986) observe that most slum dwellers near the plant were not aware of the hazards of living adjacent to a producer of toxic chemicals. The government of India must examine carefully the wisdom of importing foreign technologies, especially those unsuited to local conditions. Catastrophic accidents like the Bhopal disaster are highly visible and cannot be concealed; but pollution, which leads to slow deaths and crippling disabilities and environmental damages is not so visible to all concerned.

Some of those belonging to the scientific and technological community feel that it is imperative to have an independent national organization that can put pressure on the government and industries to reduce environmental abuses and risks of human injury. Such an organization should inform and involve people in developing industrial safety and a clean and safe environment, for example, it would be desirable to have green belts around the hazardous factories to keep them away from built-up areas. Other aspects needing serious consideration are the import of banned and restricted chemicals, transportation and handling of toxic chemicals and pesticides, and ensuring that only safe and suitable technology is imported. The factories tend to become centres of rapid population growth; unplanned settlement, mostly slums, developed around the Bhopal plant on land owned by the government, which made no serious effort to remove them. A zoning policy can work only if the government plans ahead with an overall policy for planned housing and regulatory measures to obviate the possibility of the growth of slums and unplanned settlements.

In all policy matters, citizens must be informed and involved if the policy objectives are to be served. Well-informed and involved community efforts are assets to policy implementation. If there is one lesson to be drawn from the Bhopal disaster, it is that public perception of risk is as important a factor in planning as the actual risk. The government has also to develop a national policy on industrial disaster mitigation and relief measures. It is imperative particularly for developing countries like India to have such an emergency response system for the increasingly risky industrial environment. The International Chemical and Energy Workers Federation has formulated a code which specifically mentions obligatory provision of full information on certain aspects as a safety measure; these include notification of accidents and risks, preparation of safety analysis, emergency planning, plant design, transport of hazardous materials, and the duty of multinationals to ensure high safety standards in all countries and not to export substances banned in their own countries (*The Statesman*, 1985). It is now realized that there is great potential for improvement of post-crisis responses, particularly in the area of communication with the media and the public, compensation for claims and safety improvements. It is desirable that to avoid such catastrophes, more scientists, technologists and social groups should work for technological solutions and risk management systems.

POSTCRIPT

After a long legal battle and more than four years after the disaster in Bhopal, the Supreme Court of India has finally given its verdict on 15 February 1989 and ordered the Union Carbide Co. Ltd. to pay 470 million dollars or about 7050 million rupees as compensation to the gas victims. Both the Government of India and the Union Carbide have accepted this verdict, and the amount. The gas victims had asked for a much larger sum, and are not satisfied with this settlement.

From a report in Hindustan Times
15.2.88. p.1.

REFERENCES

Agarwal, Anil and Narain, Samita (1986) *The State of India's Environment 1984–85*, New Delhi.

Capersson, T. (1981) Recent Biophysical Methods of Analysis of Genetic Damage in Man Caused by Environmental Agents, in Sharma, A. K. et al. (eds), *Impact of Development of Science and Technology on Environment*, Indian Science Congress Association, Calcutta: 95–106.

Department of Information and Publicity (1985) *We Shall Overcome*, Government of Madhya Pradesh, Bhopal: 1–32.

Department of Information and Publicity (1986) *Bhopal Disaster and its Aftermath*, Government of Madhya Pradesh, Bhopal: 1–21.

Dubey, K. C. (1984) General Population Tables, Series II, *Madhya Pradesh, Part II-A, Census of India*, Delhi: 118–274.

Karan, P. P., Bladen, W. A. and Wilson, J. R. (1986) Technological Hazards in the Third World, *Geographical Review*, 70, 2: 195–208.

Kayastha, S. L. (1986) Environmental Policies in India, in C. C. Park (ed.), *Environmental Policies: An International Review*, Croom Helm, London: 223–58.

Khandekar, S. and Dubey, S. (1984) Bhopal, City of Death, *India Today*, New Delhi, 31: 4–24.

The Statesman (1986) New Delhi, 24 November: 4.

Times of India (1985) New Delhi, 21 January.

White, G. F. (1986) *Nature on the Rampage*, National Geographical Society, Washington DC.

15

Wars – Mortality – Poverty

Stanislaw Otok

Peace and security on the one hand and socio-economic development on the other are closely related and interdependent. All that
can be annihilated by war, along with all efforts to promote social
progress and peace. According to various sources, the six years of
the Second World War cost the lives of 35 million people; others
estimate 50 million or sometimes even 60 million victims of both
military actions and accompanying terror. It was a great collapse of
social order and a disaster hard to comprehend. The war created a
general, deep desire to safeguard the world's security and an outcry
for human rights, social justice, decent standards of living, and the
abolition of all forms of colonialism. Some of these aims were
achieved to a certain extent during the post-war period, with
progress particularly conspicuous in the process of social change.

The post-war period, however, was not devoid of local or regional conflicts or unrest. There have been 150 more or less serious
conflicts since the end of the 1939–45 war, which have claimed
16–20 million lives, not only of soldiers but also of civilians. Table
15.1 presents the location of conflicts and the loss of lives; the data
do not, however, include the victims of civil wars. Moreover, the
total loss of lives in all identified conflicts is only approximate – the
real figure is greater than the numbers of civilians and soldiers
killed.

The majority of the wars mentioned in table 15.1 were caused by
old, unsolved conflicts. Detailed information concerning the data
collected in the table shows that from among the 103 war conflicts
during the period 1954–83, as many as 40 larger or smaller military
conflicts broke out in 1983 alone, involving 75 countries and about

Table 15.1   Estimated number of conflicts and loss of lives, 1945–1983

Location of conflicts	Number of conflicts	Loss of lives (thousands)		
		Civilians	Soldiers	Total
Far East	27	4,501	3,406	9,185
Africa	30	1,970	1,388	3,552
South Asia	10	1,874	574	2,449
Middle East	17	264	132	547
Latin America	16	305	133	451
Europe	3			175
Total	103	8,914	5,643	16,358

Source: Sivard (1983).

4 million soldiers, among whom soldiers from eight countries were fighting in foreign territories. After 1945 most of the conflicts occurred in the poor countries of Asia, Africa and Latin America. Although some industrial countries were involved to a certain extent in many of the conflicts, it was the territories where military actions were taking place that were directly affected.

Apart from the listed wars and the number of victims, there were internal conflicts resulting from political differences. These conflicts often resulted in a substantial loss of life, as estimated from press documentation (table 15.2).

These figures show that over 22 million persons were killed in the period 1945–83 as a result of wars and internal political conflicts accompanied by military encounters. These are estimates calculated on the basis of press information and publications by Peace Institutes. Disregarding the numerous reasons for the conflicts, it should be stressed that each of them resulted in social unrest and deterioration as well as delays in improvement, or even the reversal, of the population's material situation, and the waste of previous social achievements on both sides of the conflict. In 1983 there were approximately 29 million persons on active military service all over the world (IISS, 1984), excluding reserves or personnel of paramilitary organizations or services. During the two decades to 1981 the total number of regular military personnel grew by one-third. In the developed countries as a whole there was a slight drop in the total number serving in the armed forces in relation to the

Table 15.2   Loss of lives in internal political conflicts, 1945–1983

Location of conflicts	Number of victims (thousands)
Far East	150
South Asia	3,150
Middle East	85
Africa	2,500
Latin America	125
North America	0.5
West and south Europe	40
East Europe and USSR	42
Australasia	0.2
Total	6,092.7

total population; the number serving in the armed forces decreased from 11 persons per 1,000 inhabitants to 9. During the same period however, there was an absolute growth of the armed forces of developing countries.

The geographical distribution of armed forces is completely different from the present geographical location of war conflicts. In the enormous armed forces in the world in 1983, the joint forces of the two main military groups, NATO and WTO, constituted two-fifths of the total number of 29 million regular military personnel (IISS, 1984). One-third of the world's armoured units and air forces are located in Europe. With reference to nuclear weapons, the concentration within the two military treaties is almost complete; they have over 95 per cent of the weapons. Global military expenditure in the particular countries is enormous, but it is exceedingly difficult to present in figures.

In 1984, the UN Secretariat experts on 'All aspects of the conventional arms race and on disarmament' reported on this problem as follows:

The calculation of the world military expenditure is of necessity imprecise due to such variables as differences in exchange rates, secrecy of information, problems on deciding how to allow for differences in the system and costing of military production and difficulties in how to allow for price changes in the civilian and military sections or the economy. (UN General Assembly Resolution A/39/348:69)

Helpful information in this respect comes from the Stockholm International Peace Research Institute *Yearbook* 1984, which estimates total military expenditure in 1983 at US$750–800 billion (SIPRI, 1984). In 1984 it was more than US$800 billiion, 80 per cent being spent on conventional arms and forces; this means $130 for every single person in the world, this representing more than the average annual personal income in many developing countries.

In developed countries military expenditure in the 1980s was higher than that on health services; in developing countries it was ten times the amount spent on health and three times the amount spent on education. A particular example here is the fact that the cost of a new nuclear submarine equals the total expenditure on education in 23 developing countries with 160 million schoolchildren (SIPRI, 1984).

Most of the world's total military expenditure is concentrated in six countries: the five permanent members of the UN Security Council plus the Federal Republic of Germany. The developing countries contributed 25 per cent of the world's total expenditure in 1984, and of this sum south-east Asia contributed 45 per cent, the Middle East and Egypt 35 per cent, Latin America 12 per cent and Africa (excluding Egypt) 8 per cent. An important element in the escalation of military expenditure was the high cost of weapons and technology; this reduced finance for social and economic programmes, but the burden is different in the particular countries.

A study outlining the world's social situation (Otok, 1984) divided all countries into four groups with varied social situations (see figure 15.1) according to five criteria: (1) the amount of protein consumed; (2) average life expectancy; (3) number of hospital beds per 10,000 inhabitants; (4) percentage of children with access to education; and (5) number of radio sets per 1,000 inhabitants. This study is complemented here with the data (for each group) on the average percentage of national product spent on armaments (Sivard, 1982), and table 15.3 contains the mean values of the classification indices for the four groups of countries and for the whole world.

As shown by detailed data illustrating the problem of the social situation in particular countries, military expenditures in relation to social expenditures (represented here by health service expenditures) are glaringly disproportionate. It may be assumed that requirements for health services in some countries are very low

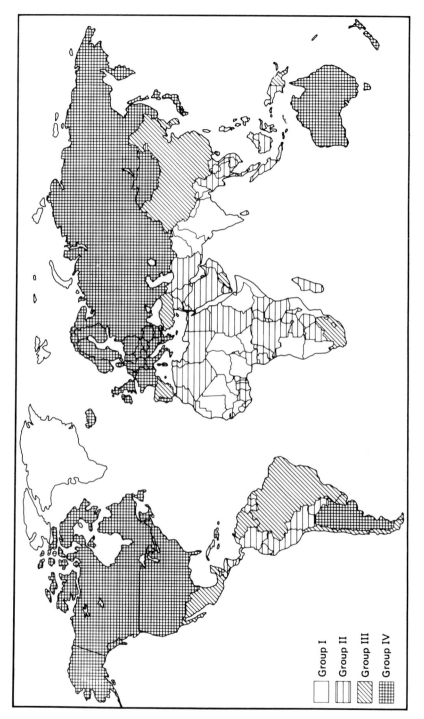

Figure 15.1 Regional differentiation of four groups of countries according to their social situation

Group I
Group II
Group III
Group IV

Table 15.3 Mean values of classification indices of the world social situation

Groups of countries	Amount of protein consumed, g	Average life length, years	No. of hospitals beds per 10,000 inhabitants	% of children with access to education	No. of radio sets per 1,000 inhabitants	% of GNP allocated to armaments
World average	69.82	55.52	41.70	64.69	195.99	4.0
Group I	55.84	40.30	10.50	28.04	35.24	3.5
Group II	56.36	48.53	20.85	60.78	91.14	4.3
Group III	70.78	62.41	33.97	79.05	198.05	4.3
Group IV	96.48	70.48	94.96	87.63	504.84	4.0

Source: Otok (1984).

because the population is healthy, but this is contradicted by the facts of how life expectancy and a high infant and child mortality rate, the latter being recognized by the UN as a verified index of socio-economic development.

Indices referring to the social situation of the countries included in group I are usually below the world average. The lowest life expectancy is recorded in Burkina Faso (31.6 years); Afghanistan has the lowest index in health service (1.7 hospital beds per 10,000 inhabitants); and Burkina Faso has the lowest percentage of children with access to general education (9 per cent). Although the percentage of the national income earmarked for military purposes is only 3.5 per cent in group I as a whole (against a world average of 4.0 per cent) in Mauritania it was 14.3 per cent, in the Republic of Yemen 10.5 per cent, in Ethiopia 8.9 per cent, in Chad 7.2 per cent and in Pakistan 5.1 per cent, while in the other countries from group I it was from 0.8 per cent to 3.1 per cent.

The countries making up group II have indices of their social situation similar to the world average, excluding the indices of hospital beds and radio sets which are only half the world averages. The highest levels of military expenditure are noted in the following countries: Saudi Arabia (22.4 per cent of national income), Jordan (14.3 per cent), Vietnam (10.6 per cent), Egypt (9.9 per cent) and Zambia (9.5 per cent). In the other countries in group II the share of military expenditure in national income is between 0.8 per cent and 8.0 per cent.

The countries making up group III have indices characterizing their social situation equal or almost equal to world average values, although in most of these countries the level of medical care is unsatisfactory and the number of hospital beds per 10,000 inhabitants below the world average. Military expenditure is high in Syria (20.1 per cent of national income), Albania (8.0 per cent), China (6.7 per cent) and South Korea (5.5 per cent), while in the other countries in the group spending on armaments consumes from 0.8 per cent to 5.0 per cent of national income.

Countries in group IV have all the indices referring to their social situation above the world average. These are highly developed countries with a good social situation. Military expenditure constitutes in Israel 29.8 per cent of national income, in the USSR 10.7 per cent, in Mongolia 10.2 per cent, in Greece 6.1 per cent, in the USA 5.2 per cent, in Great Britain 4.8 per cent and in the other countries of the group between 0.9 per cent and 4.0 per cent.

Detailed analysis of the social situation in particular groups of countries leads to the conclusion that although many countries are poor and underdeveloped, huge sums of money are allocated for military purposes there, but not for eliminating poverty.

How is this situation to be reversed? There is no simple means. Although the relationship between disarmament and development appears close, there is no international institution that would automatically transfer funds from armaments to the social and economic needs of the population. Many proposals of this kind have nevertheless been discussed in the international forum. In 1973 a resolution calling for a single, 10 per cent reduction of military budgets by all the permanent members of the Security Council was passed by the United Nations. Money saved in this way was to be allocated for social and economic development in developing countries. The resolution also appealed to other countries with high military and economic potential to join this project. A number of other proposals were registered at the 10th special General Assembly session on disarmament in 1978, most concerned with taxation of military budgets and allocating the sums thus acquired to the United Nations to be used for promoting development, mainly in those countries where the income per inhabitant was less than US$200. After a detailed discussion of various proposals and a study on 'the relationship between disarmament and development', the General Assembly authorized (resolution No. 37/48, dated 9 December 1982) the UN Institute for Disarmament Research to analyse in co-operation with other international institutions the possibilities of implementing the concept of an international disarmament fund for promoting development. Not all the UN members approved of the resolution. Although there was no consensus as to the way of raising disarmament funds, the discussion on disarmament and development during the session of the Disarmament Commission in 1984 was generally considered significant. It was also generally agreed to accumulate disarmament funds and to use them for peaceful purposes.

Summing up, it is worth stressing that the extent of total militarization is tremendous. At the beginning of the 1980s it was valued at about 6 per cent of total world gross product and nearly 50 million people were employed in military industry and services directly or indirectly connected with it. Moreover, half a million research workers and engineers, i.e. about 20 per cent of the world's total employment in this industry, were engaged in military research and the development of military technology. For how many human lives is annihilation being prepared?

REFERENCES

Freedman, L. (1985) *Atlas of Global Strategy*, Macmillan, London. IISS (International Institute for Strategic Studies), (1984) *The Military Balance 1983–1984*, London.

Otok, S. (1984) Regional Differentiation of the World's Social Situation, *Miscellanea Geographica*, Warsaw.

SIPRI (Stockholm International Peace Research Institute) (1984) *Yearbook 1984*, London:117–22.

Sivard, R. L. (1983) *World Military Expenditures*, Washington D. C.

16

Was the Spanish Civil War, 1936–1939, a Demographic Disaster?

Maria Carmen Faus Pujol

To study the impact on the population of such a crucial event as the Spanish Civil War of 1936–9 is a formidable task for several reasons. First is the unreliability of the statistics available, because the course of events of the war influenced the precision and accuracy of registration of the demographic incidents of those years. Consequently, all the data available should be considered with reserve and caution. Secondly, the special characteristics of the setting of the war also make this study difficult. It is worth remembering that Spain was divided into two ideologically different areas known as *zona roja* (red zone) and *zona nacional* (national zone) whose limits fluctuated during the course of the war. The data from each zone do not always correspond to the same geographical environment nor to the same group of population. In keeping with the rate at which the war fronts changed, a significant exodus of population took place.

Accordingly, conclusions on the demographic repercussions of the last civil war in Spain will never be completely accurate. Moreover, it must be remembered that the censuses published by the INE (Spanish Statistics Institute) are decennial, so that data relating to the years of the war were masked within the total figures for the population of the decade. In spite of this, using as a source of information the annual publications of the INE and comparing this information with the pre- and post-war data, an approximate

Table 16.1   Evolution of births and population in Spain, 1926–1940

Years	Births, thousands	Population, millions	Birth rate
1926	636		
1927	633	23.0[a]	27.52
1928	666		
1929	653		
1930	660	23.6	27.97
1931	649	23.8	27.27
1932	670	24.2	27.69
1933	667	24.4	27.34
1934	637	24.6	25.77
1935	631	24.9	25.34
1936	602	24.7	24.37
1937	536	25.1	22.59
1938	453	25.2	20.02
1939	417	25.1	16.45
1940	611	26.0	24.37

[a] Average value of population 1926–29
Source: Villar Salinas, (1942); INE; author's findings.

assessment of the impact of the war on the Spanish population can be deduced.

The purpose of this study was two-fold: first, to examine the short-term and future repercussions of the war on the trend in population and the way in which the basic demographic phenomena, i.e. fertility and mortality, evolved; and secondly, to analyse the changes which resulted in the structure of the population.

FERTILITY

The Spanish Civil War had important consequences on fertility. However, it is necessary to analyse briefly the birth rate figures and their trend during the pre-war years in order to obtain a more realistic interpretation of the situation.

During the decade prior to the outbreak of the war, the annual figures for births were well above 600,000 (see table 16.1); for a total population count which varied between 22 million in 1926 and 24 million in 1936 this gave birth rates of 25– 30 per thousand: 29.2 in 1926–30 and 27.3 in 1931–5.

Although these figures may appear high, they were not so high for a society which in the words of de Miguel (1982) was still traditional. Compared to figures for the beginning of the century (about 35 per thousand), they were ten points lower, and Spain was approaching rapidly the characteristic norms of demographic behaviour in western Europe.

The Civil War played a catalytic role in the decline of births in Spain. According to the statistical predictions, the average annual number of births during the five years between 1936 and 1940 should have been 655,000. As early as the first complete year of war, the total amount of births had decreased by 65,000. However, if we accept that the numbers of births in 1936 and 1937 were 8 per cent and 18 per cent less than predicted, this means 52,000 fewer births than expected in 1936 and 118,000 fewer in 1937. This decline became more acute at the end of the war: in 1939 there were only 417,000 births as opposed to over 600,000 births in the year before the war. For a population of 25 million the birth rate had lowered to 16 per thousand, which is to say that a figure typical of most developed countries at that time had been reached, but due to very different circumstances. After the war, the birth rate increased and Spain was not to reach these figures again until 1979.

It had taken the period 1900–36 for the birth rate to decrease by ten points, but a similar decline occurred during the three years of the war. Taking into account the existing total figures for the population, and assuming that it had maintained the demographic structure of the pre-war years, more than half a million possible lives can be calculated to have been lost in the period 1936–9; in other words, the relative number of births decreased by 23 per cent.

From the information analysed by Villar Salinas (1942), it can be deduced that there was not the same relative decrease in the amount of births in both the regions at war; in the *zona roja* the birth rate underwent a 22.2 per cent decline while in the *zona nacional* the decline was only 13.7 per cent. It is not easy to interpret the reasons for this difference, but explanations such as that the population in the *zona roja* was made up of elderly people, or that the economic situation was more difficult on one side than the other, or that birth control was practised, are not acceptable. What is known of those years shows that there were no substantial differences of this kind between one zone and the other. Migration might have been higher in the republican zone (*zona roja*) and this would affect the birth rate; if this were the case it would have occurred at the end of the war. It is more logical to think that records were not kept with the same accuracy on both sides. However this argument is not totally valid, since there are not such great differences in the other types of demographic records, such as the sex of those born, or the number of those born alive in relation to those stillborn before and during the war. It would be very strange that errors were made with some records and not others. The likely explanation is in the predominance of towns which the *zona roja* held up to nearly the end of the war, and which gave a differential pattern of behaviour between rural and urban populations in relation to fertility.

In conclusion, it can be affirmed that the war accelerated the decrease in the birth rate which had been taking place since the beginning of the century. The physical separation of men and women, the decrease in marriages, the difficulties of a society in war and migration are reasons which explain the lower birth figures in those years.

The decrease in the birth rate bears a certain relation to the general fertility of women between the ages of 15 and 49 years and above all to the specific fertility of married women, especially when it concerns 'traditional' societies in which the majority of births are within wedlock, i.e. there is a clear predominance of legitimate births. This was the case in the Spanish society in those years, which leads us to consider the impact of the war on marriage.

The Impact of the War on Marriage

From the figures published by the Spanish Statistics Institute, Villar Salinas (1942) calculated the average annual figures of marriages for the decade prior to the war at 161,406, that is 7.3 per thousand. This figure was reduced to 6 per thousand precisely for the five years which include the war, during which it was reduced further, so that it could be estimated to be at 5.36 per thousand.

A direct correlation between the number of marriages and the number of births in the following year can be observed, if the number of marriages which took place in those years is related to the number of births (see figure 16.1).

In general, the total numbers of marriages were always lower than predicted for the years of the war. Weddings celebrated were 138,000 fewer than had been expected between 1936 and 1939. As a

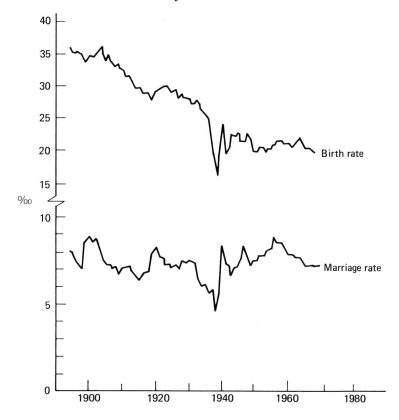

Figure 16.1   Birth and marriage rates of the population of Spain, 1890s–1960s

result of the war, 21.4 per cent of weddings were postponed temporarily, but these delays are usually cancelled out once the reason for the decline disappears; hence the number of marriages which took place in the five years between 1941 and 1945 are well above those for the five years of the war. On the other hand, the possible births from the marriages that were not celebrated were not totally made up due to the advanced ages of the couples.

Before the war the average age of marriage of women was about 24.3 years. Due to the postponement of weddings in the following years, the predominant age of women getting married was 30 or more, and the reduced reproductive period of married women was negative from a demographic point of view.

MORTALITY

From the social and psychological points of view, the most out-standing effect of a war is usually the loss of life. A lot has been written about the number of deaths which occurred during the Spanish Civil War, but in spite of the controversy which this has caused, there is no consensus concerning the mortality rate. More-over, it is difficult to calculate just how many victims of the war there were. Sometimes, individuals thought to be dead had only disappeared, and reappeared after a lapse in time; on some oc-casions those who had died were not registered as dead even though the families of the deceased had proof of their deaths. Quite a number of those who died on the battlefield had no identification, and finally, not all the deaths which occurred were in direct consequence of the war.

Certain mortality figures for those years of war are known from the Spanish Statistics Institute's data, but these are not equivalent to the real numbers of deaths for the reasons stated above; they merely correspond to deaths accompanied by death certificates. According to more reliable estimates, the number of deaths be-tween 1936 and 1940 was well above 1,744,000, which was the number of registered deaths.

In accordance with the trend of registered deaths during the decade before the war, and assuming that this trend had been maintained, the figures of registered deaths mean an increase of 17 per cent over deaths expected if there had been no war. However, the unregistered deaths must be added to those registered, bringing the 17 per cent up to 18 per cent. Counting only the registered deaths, more than 250,000 persons lost their lives as a result of the war.

The male population suffered more from the effects of the war than the female population: 55 per cent of those who died during the war were men. The most critical periods, judging from the mortality rate for men, were in 1937 with 250,000 male deaths and 1939 when the number of male deaths exceeded 260,000. Accord-ing to Villar Salinas (1942), the difference between deaths with death certificates and those expected was 26.8 per cent.

The female mortality rate remained below the male mortality rate from before the war, with an annual average of 195,000 deaths from

1926 to 1935 and 193,000 during the war – which seems a strange occurrence for a period of war. The female mortality rate was lower than the male, as in all European countries, but plausible reasons cannot be found to explain the decrease of the female mortality rate during those years. One of the most likely reasons could be errors due to registration of deaths, as has already been mentioned. Nonetheless, it must be noted that the total figures are hidden within the real trend. If the real figures for the mortality rate for women are compared to those estimated for the same period of war, female mortality also increased relatively, although only by 5.8 per cent, which is still far below the relative increase for males.

In analysing the impact of the war in relation to loss of population, it is necessary to take into account that not all deaths which occurred within this period were direct consequences of the fighting. It is necessary to differentiate between the deaths by violence, natural deaths and those that occurred due to the appalling conditions prevailing in the country.

The direct victims of the war are divided approximately equally between the two zones in conflict with an average of about 65,000 deaths per year, amounting to total of nearly 300,000 violent deaths in action. As the total of deaths which occurred during the war increased to more than 1,744,000, four-fifths of the deaths may be deduced to have been due directly to war. To this figure one must add at least another 5 per cent of deaths related to the war, such as those resulting from appalling sanitary conditions and executions by firing squad.

Pre-war sanitary conditions were good, as the general reduction of the mortality rate shows. During the war, while the point of widespread outbreaks of epidemics may not actually have been reached, many infections and parasitic illnesses became general which previously had been eradicated. In some provinces deaths caused by illnesses exceeded those caused by the war, although hunger, which is usually one of the consequences of war, did not seem to play an important role in the mortality rate.

Executions by firing squad were carried out on both sides but there is no unanimity about the number of victims who died because of their ideology. Salas Larrazabal (1977), who has managed to gain access to the existing archives and other documents, estimates that there were about 129,200 victims of repression in both zones.

Table 16.2   Evolution of the mortality rate in Spain, 1930–1950

Years	Mortality per thousand	Infant mortality per thousand
1930	16.8	11.7
1931	17.3	11.6
1932	16.3	11.2
1933	16.4	11.2
1934	16.0	11.3
1935	15.6	10.0
1936	16.9	10.9
1937	18.8	13.0
1938	19.2	12.0
1939	18.4	13.5
1940	16.5	10.9
1945	12.2	8.5

Source: Spanish Statistics Institute; author's findings.

With all the necessary reservations, estimates of excess mortality in the war vary between 246,000 and 346,000, 47 per cent of which were due to violent deaths. But if we add 220,000 violent deaths after the war, between 1940 and 1943, plus 25,000 deaths registered later and also 25,000 deaths of foreigners, the real excess of mortality comes to more than 600,000 persons (see table 16.2).

THE INFLUENCE OF THE WAR ON POPULATION AND
DEMOGRAPHIC STRUCTURE

Once the war had ended, the population in Spain was lower than would have been expected in normal circumstances. The war had a great influence on the rate of population growth, which had already been falling, especially since 1932.

The 18.5 million people who formed the Spanish population in 1900 increased to 23.5 million in 1930 and approached 26 million in 1940, immediately after the war. Given the loss of life during the war, these results appear somewhat surprising. However, the demographic repercussions of the conflict can be seen from the decrease in intercensal growth. The increase in population between 1920 and 1930 was reduced by nearly half during 1930–40. From that moment onwards the demographic recovery was slow, and the intercensal increase of 1920–30 was not recovered until the period of Spanish economic development in the 1960s.

The impact of the war on the total population was without doubt greater than the statistics show. The census of population taken in 1940 is very unreliable; an excess of 490,000 inscriptions are supposed to be contained in this census. This is the only explanation for the fact that at the end of such a hard war as the Spanish Civil War there was a much higher population figure than when it started.

The reasons for these irregularities in the census are easily understood, because during the year in which the census was carried out there were still many displaced persons and it was difficult to take a satisfactory count. Moreover, in addition to the technical problems involved, there were other circumstances which led to overcounting. Rationing, which was introduced during the war and which lasted until 1953, encouraged irregularities. All kinds of deceptions were resorted to in order to obtain extra rationing coupons. Many deaths went unregistered, people who had emigrated still figured on the registers of their places of origin, and a great number of town dwellers also registered in villages in order to take advantage of the facilities which the farmers enjoyed when providing themselves with food. It was not until 1960 that the census of 1940 was brought into some semblance of order by incorporating these factors. This explains why the age pyramid for 1950 is so unrepresentative (see figure 16.2).

The Spanish Civil War also provoked a large-scale displacement of population. Migration, first to Europe and then to Latin America, was high. Although some returned, it is calculated that about 300,000 people left Spain for ever. The emigrants were supported by already established emigrants. Annual departures at the beginning of the century exceeded 100,000 persons; although emigration was reduced by approximately a third with the outbreak of the First World War, when many returned to Spain, and reduced again from 1931 to 1935 due to the economic crisis and the restrictive laws of immigration in Latin America (Puyol, 1979; Rodriguez Osuna, 1985), the aid of those emigrants in foreign countries, above all in Latin America, helped to facilitate the exodus of political and ideological emigrants.

Adding the approximate numbers of emigrants as a result of the

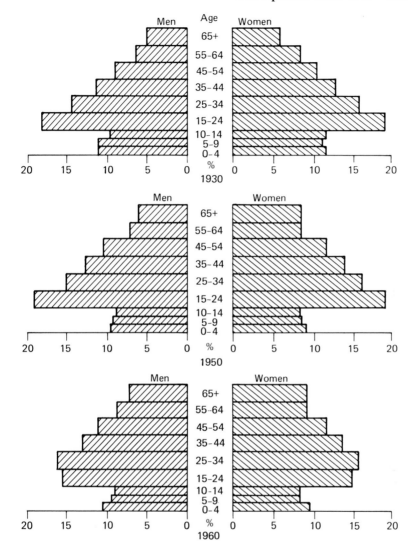

Figure 16.2   Age pyramids of Spanish population, 1930, 1950 and 1960

Civil War to the minimum 800,000 deficit between the estimated increase and the real increase, and the loss of lives during the war, the decrease in population in relation to that calculated is about 1,200,000 persons.

Because of irregularities in the census, the age pyramid does not reflect the true impact of the war. However, that impact can be clearly appreciated in the pyramid for 1960, once the irregularities in the census had been corrected (see figure 16.2).

CONCLUSION

The conclusion that can be drawn from this analysis of the demographic consequences of the Spanish Civil War of 1936–9 is that the war had very negative consequences for population, as can be seen from the following eight points:

1   The war had a very unfavourable influence on the basic demographic phenomena, by considerably decreasing the birth rate and increasing the mortality rate, especially among the young male population.
2   The reduction of the birth rate which had been taking place from the beginning of the century was accelerated to give similar figures to those of more developed western European countries at that time.
3   The war acted as a catalyst to the demographic transition which had started at the beginning of the century, thus explaining the peculiarities of Spanish demographic behaviour from 1950.
4   The natural growth of the Spanish population during the years of the war was 76 per cent lower than was expected, had the predicted trends of the 1930s been maintained.
5   The loss of lives during the war is estimated at 1,744,000, if only those deaths which were registered are taken into account, but it is known that there were about at least another 55–60,000 victims whose deaths were not registered.
6   Another 300,000 persons, who abandoned Spain for ever after the end of the war, must also be added to the figures of those who lost their lives as a direct result of the war in arriving at total population losses.
7   The general demographic structure was severely affected. The number of males in Spanish society was reduced and the sex-ratio became unbalanced at the same time as an acute ageing of the population became apparent.
8   These irregularities were not detected in the census taken in 1940 because of the deceptions practised by the Spanish

population, which were attributed to the socio-economic conditions of the war, thereby making this census very unreliable. The effect of the war on the demographic structure of the population can only be observed from the 1960 census onwards.

REFERENCES

Alonso Gil, A. (1982) España 1940–60: Crecimiento Económico (Spain 1940–60: Economic Growth), *Revista de Estudios Agrosociales*, 121, Instituto de Relaciones Agrarias, Madrid: 81–125.

Del Campo, S. (1957) Componentes del Crecimiento de la Población de España, 1940–1950 (Components of the Growth of Population of Spain, 1940–1950), *Revista de Estudios Políticos*, 95, Oct–Dec.

Del Campo, S. (1975) *Anàlisis de la Población de España* (*Analysis of the Population of Spain*), Ariel Quincenal, Barcelona.

Del Campo, S. and Navarro Lopez, M. (1987) *Nuevo Analisis de la Población Española* (*New Analysis of the Spanish Population*), Ariel Sociología, Barcelona.

De Miguel, A. (1982) *Diez Errores Sobre la Población Española* (*Ten Mistakes about the Spanish Population*), Tecnos Madrid.

Diez Nicolas, J. (1969) Estructura por Sexo y Edades de la Población Española, 1900–1960 (Structure by Age and Sex of the Spanish Population, 1900–1960), *Bol. del Centro de Estudios Sociales*, 9, 3.

Diez Nicolas, J. (1971) La Trancisión Demográfica en España (Demographic Transition in Spain), *Revista de Estudios Sociales*, 1, April–June.

Ferrer, M. (1972) *El Proceso de Superpoblación Urbana* (*The Process of Urban Overpopulation*), Confederacion Española de Cajas de Ahorro, Madrid.

Ferrer, M. (1975) *La Población entre la Vida y la Muerte* (*Population between Life and Death*), Prensa Española-Magisterio Español, Madrid.

Fundacion Foessa (1970) *Informe Sociológico sobre la Situación Social de España* (*Sociological Information about the Social Situation of Spain*), Madrid.

Garcia Fernandez, J. (1965) *La Emigracion Exterior de España* (*Emigration from Spain*), Ariel, Barcelona.

Higueras Arnal, A. (1967) *La Emigración Interior en España* (*Internal Migration in Spain*), Mundo del Trabajo, Madrid.

Instituto Nacional de Estadistica (INE) *Anuarios Estadísticos de España* (*Statistical Yearbooks of Spain*).

Leguina, J. (1975) *Fundamentos de Demografía: Siglo Veintiuno de España* (*Fundamentals of Demography: Spain in the 21st Century*), SA, Madrid.

Nadal, J. (1976) *La Población Española siglos XVI a XX* (*The Spanish Population from the 16th to 20th Centuries*), Ariel Quincenal, Barcelona.

Puyol, R. (1979) *Emigración y Desigualdades Regionales en España* (*Migration and Regional Inequality in Spain*), Biblioteca Universitaria EMESA, Madrid.

Rodriguez Osuna, J. (1985) *Población y Territorio en España siglos XIX y XX* (*Population and Territory in Spain in the 19th and 20th Centuries*), Espasa Calpe, Madrid.

Salas Larrazabal, R. (1977) *Perdidas de la Guerra* (*Losses of the War*) Planeta, Barcelona.

Villar Salinas, J. (1942) *Repercusiones Demográficas de la Ultima Guerra Civil Española* (*Demographic Consequences of the Last Spanish Civil War*), Premio Conde de Toreno de la Real Academia de Ciencias Morales y Políticas, Madrid.

17

Population, War and Politics: A Case Study of the Gaza Strip

Ahmed Said Dahlan

INTRODUCTION

During the British Mandate of Palestine (1920 to May 1948), the area which in 1948 became the long narrow rectangle known as the Gaza Strip was a part of the Gaza sub-district. In 1922, the area had only 28,708 inhabitants (Barron, 1922:6–8); in 1945 it had 64,970 (Hadawi, 1970:45–6); and on the eve of the first Israeli–Arab war of 1948 the population was estimated to be about 80,000.

As a consequence of that war, some 200,000 Palestinian refugees crowded into the Strip, raising the total population immediately to 280,000 (Dahlan, 1987:26). A large proportion of the refugees were housed in the eight refugee camps built by UNRWA in the early 1950s (see figure 17.1). By 1984, this small Strip, situated in the south-west of occupied Palestine (now Israel), with an area of only 364 sq. km, had a population of 509,900, making it one of the most densely populated and overcrowded areas in the world: a disaster of war and politics.

POPULATION CHANGES 1948–1984

During the period of Egyptian administration (1948–67), the population of the Gaza Strip grew from 280,000 in 1948 to 454,900 in 1966 (see table 17.1), with an annual growth rate of 2.7 per cent. During this time a movement of Gazans (mainly the indigenous Gazans) towards the Gulf states reduced the population of the Strip

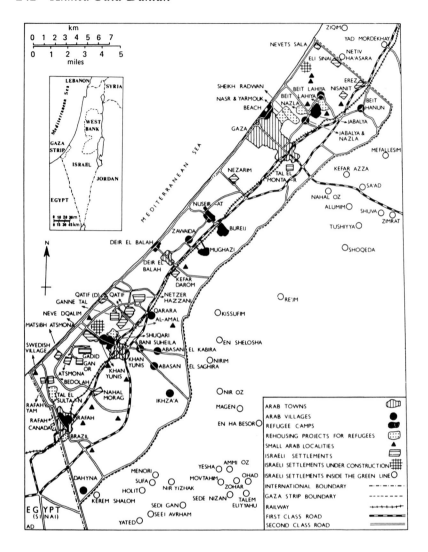

Figure 17.1 Location of Palestinian towns, villages, refugee camps and Israeli settlements in the Gaza Strip, 1985

by 1.64 per cent in 1959, but it was generally sustained by a high natural increase, averaging 3.0 per cent during 1950–64.

In September 1967, the Israeli army held the first ever census in the Gaza Strip, giving a total population of 356,261, approximately 100,000 lower than the 1966 Egyptian estimate. To reduce the population density in the teeming Gaza Strip, which in 1966 was

Table 17.1 Population change in the Gaza Strip, 1945–1984 [a]

Egyptian data (1)				Israeli data (2)			
End of period	Population, thousands	End of period	Population thousands	End of period	Population, thousands	End of period	Population thousands
1948	280.0	1958	357.5	1967(Sept)	356.3	1976	401.5
1950	288.1	1959	351.7	1968	326.0	1977	414.3
1951	294.9	1960	360.5	1969	332.7	1978	425.9
1952	299.3	1961	370.2	1970	338.2	1979	437.9
1953	306.3	1962	382.1	1971	346.1	1980	449.6
1954	312.8	1963	397.1	1972	354.1	1981	462.0
1955	318.7	1964	412.4	1973	367.9	1982	476.3
1956	336.0	1965	427.9	1974	379.6	1983	493.7
1957	345.8	1966	454.9	1975	390.5	1984	509.9

[a] Figures up to 1966 were collected from several sources and have been rounded to the nearest hundred. Israeli figures from 1968 until 1982 included the population of the Egyptian North Sinai which was occupied by Israel until the full withdrawal under the Camp David Accords. Therefore, appropriate deductions have been made and rounded to the nearest hundred to arrive at a figure for the Gaza Strip (see Dahlan, 1987).

Sources: 1 Egyptian period: data calculated from Abu El-Hajaj (1966:210); Issa (1979:55); and Khlousi (1967:51–3). 2 Israeli period: data from Central Bureau of Statistics (1969:633), (1983:758) and (1985:703).

1,250 persons per sq km, the Israeli authorities encouraged Gazan people to leave the area for Jordan, even providing bus fares to Amman. However, in July 1968, the Jordanian authorities began turning back these refugees (Kanovsky, 1970:181).

The Strip's population dropped by 128,900 between 1966 and 1968 (see table 17.1), declining by 33.3 per cent from the initial figure. Harris (1980:16) estimates that some 70,000 people emigrated from the Strip between June and December 1967. Furthermore, at the time of the 1967 war, 27,697 persons were trapped abroad (Central Bureau of Statistics, 1968:64): students, soldiers, merchants, visitors and employees in the Gulf states, who were not included in the 1967 census and were prevented from returning.

The 1967 exodus, which resulted from the war, reflected the widespread fear that the Israeli army would perpetrate a massacre against the Strip's inhabitants, as happened in 1956 when they occupied the Strip and 930 young men were massacred with a further 215 reported missing (Palestine Liberation Organization, 1983:169). In a field study carried out by Harris in 1976 in Baqa'a camp, the largest East Bank (Jordan) camp for 1967 refugees, 99.4 per cent of his sample emigrated under the fear of maltreatment from the Israeli invaders (Harris, 1978:406).

Similar outcomes were derived from the fieldwork of Dodd and Barakat (1968:45–7), which was conducted in September 1967 in Zeezya camp (Jordan). The refugees described their flight as temporary to protect their families, including the honour of their womenfolk. The sample shows that 75 per cent of the refugees wanted to return to their homes regardless of the circumstances, 18 per cent wished to return conditionally (if Israeli occupation came to an end) and 7 per cent did not wish to return. So far the Israeli government has refused to permit the displaced refugees to return to their homes.

Since 1969, migration of individuals from the Gaza Strip has continued, prompted by economic, political, educational and familial considerations; they numbered 53,210 persons during 1969–84. Between 1968 and 1984, the Strip's population grew from 326,000 to 509,900, an annual growth rate of only 2.8 per cent, despite an average natural increase of 3.41 per cent; obviously net migration has offset the natural increase by 0.61 per cent per annum. In fact, the Strip is distinguished by very high crude birth rates and low crude death rates; for instance, the CBR was 48.3 per thousand in 1984, compared with only 8 per thousand for the CDR.

However, for the inhabitants of the Gaza Strip, the high birth rates are not attributable solely to socio-economic and socio-religious factors; political considerations have also a great influence. Based on a survey conducted in 1985 by the author, 42.5 per cent of the sample considered the demographic factor as one of the most important pillars of their continuing struggle against the Israeli occupation and for the achievement of an independent Palestinian state.

THE DEMOGRAPHIC CONSEQUENCES OF THE 1967 WAR

Since the 1967 exodus was characterized by the selective movement of both families and individuals, the age–sex structure of the population was distorted, particularly in the adult age group (15–64 years).

The age structure of the Gaza Strip population is very youthful (see figure 17.2). In 1967, 50.6 per cent of the total Gazan population were young people (0–14 years), 44.6 per cent adults, and only 4.8 per cent aged people (65+). This distribution had altered by 1984 to 47.7 per cent, 49.6 per cent and 2.7 per cent respectively, while about 87.5 per cent were aged below 45 years and 35.5 per cent below 10 years. These trends indicate that the population structure is moving towards a more normal distribution after the decline of the role of migration.

Moreover, the impact of the 1967 displacement on the sex ratio is conspicuous. Table 17.2 shows that in 1967 the Gaza Strip had more females – 938 males per 1,000 females – but the sex ratio was as low as 770 in the 15–64 age group, and 469 in the 25–9 age-group. This imbalance in the sex ratio was influenced by socio-political factors after the 1967 war. The majority of displaced Gazans who fled from the Strip emigrated either to join the heads of their families abroad or from the fear of the occupation, or were expelled by the Israelis who ejected several thousand Palestinian youths to Egypt.

In comparison, in 1984 the overall sex ratio was more balanced (997), but males outnumbered females in all age groups up to 29, while females outnumbered males in the age groups of 35 and over (see table 17.2). This finding is the direct result of the 1967

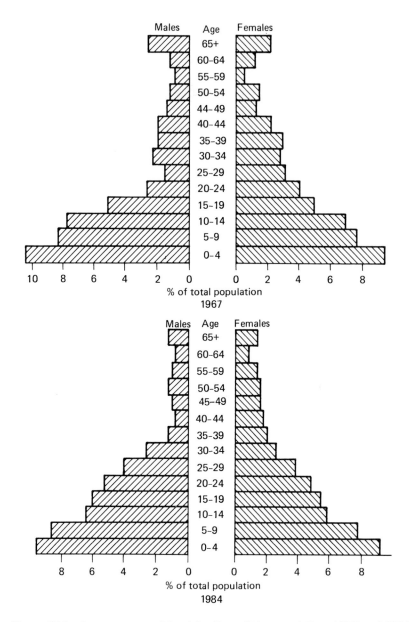

Figure 17.2 Age–sex pyramids of the Gaza Strip population, 1967 and 1984

Table 17.2 Age – sex composition of the population of the Gaza Strip, 1967 and 1984

Age group	September 1967 Census [a]				1984			
	Number of inhabitants			Sex ratio: Males per 1,000 females	Number of inhabitants			Sex ratio: Males per 1,000 females
	Males	Females	Total		Males	Females	Total	
0–4	36,796	33,430	70,226	1,100	50,100	47,100	97,200	1,064
5–9	29,421	27,318	56,739	1,077	44,000	39,800	83,800	1,106
10–14	27,298	24,579	51,877	1,111	32,800	29,600	62,400	1,108
15–19	17,914	17,610	35,524	1,017	30,500	27,600	58,100	1,105
20–24	9,161	14,440	23,601	634	26,500	24,500	51,000	1,082
25–29	5,350	11,418	16,768	469	20,400	19,400	39,800	1,052
30–34	7,703	10,361	18,064	743	13,200	13,200	26,400	1,000
35–39	6,688	10,533	17,221	635	6,000	10,200	16,200	588
40–44	6,620	8,322	14,942	795	4,100	9,200	13,300	446
45–49	4,591	4,592	9,183	1,000	5,100	8,200	13,300	622
50–54	3,828	5,215	9,043	734	6,100	8,200	14,300	744
55–59	2,772	2,152	4,924	1,288	5,100	7,100	12,200	718
60–64	3,982	4,520	8,502	881	4,000	4,100	8,100	976
65+	8,999	8,004	17,003	1,124	6,600	7,200	13,800	917
Total	171,123	182,494	353,617	938	254,500	255,400	509,900	997

[a] In 1967 2,644 persons were classified as age group unknown.
Source: Central Bureau of Statistics (1969:633) and (1985:705).

emigration which led to females outnumbering males in the age groups 20–44 years in 1967, and 17 years later in the age groups 35–64 years.

Viewed from another demographic aspect, the exodus increased the economic load upon the economically active population. In 1967 there were 124 dependants for every 100 persons in the productive age group (15–64 years); 113 of these were children and youths, and 11 were in the old age category. In comparison, in 1984 there were 102 dependants for every 100 persons in the productive ages; 96 under 15 years, and 6 over 65 years. In a nutshell, the overall dependency ratio of the Gaza Strip is very high, resulting from its very youthful population structure.

CHANGING SETTLEMENT PATTERNS

Since 1948, patterns of settlement in the Gaza Strip have altered greatly. Prior to 1948, there were only two types of settlement in the Strip, namely towns and villages. As a consequence of the 1948 flight from Palestine, a new type of settlement emerged when eight refugee camps were established and directed by UNRWA during 1952–5 as temporary shelters for Palestinian refugees, replacing the pre-existing nine tent camps. By 30 June 1966, there were 307,245 refugees registered with UNRWA in the Strip, of whom 200,637 (65.3 per cent) were living in camps (UNRWA, 1966).

As a result of the fighting between the Israeli and Egyptian armies in 1967, 1,020 rooms housing 485 families were destroyed in Gazan refugee camps, but data for the Strip as a whole are not available. During 1967–72, the Palestinian guerillas initiated military resistance operations against the Israeli troops across the Strip, but as the guerillas established their bases, primarily in the poor and overcrowded refugee camps, several measures were taken by the Israeli government to stamp out the resistance, varying from carving wide security roads in the camps, to initiating large resettlement schemes and implanting more Jewish settlements in the Strip.

The refugees' shelters in the camps have become the target of systematic destruction by the Israeli military authorities. In 1971, the shelters of 3,941 families were bulldozed in the eight refugee camps to make way for road networks to enable Israeli troops to suppress the military resistance. The evacuated refugees were either resettled in small accommodation projects built by UNRWA in Nuseirat, Bureij, Mughazi and Khan Yunis refugee camps, or in the vacant UNRWA shelters. Many were also resettled in the government-built dwelling projects named Shuqari, Brazil and Canada. In addition, a large number of refugees were rehoused with their relatives or found their own shelters, while another group was driven out to live in the occupied West Bank or in El-Arish in Northern Sinai, though after the Israeli withdrawal from El-Arish in 1979 those refugees vacated their accommodation and were re-housed again in the Al-Amal dwelling project near Khan Yunis. In December 1971, the UN General Assembly called upon Israel to desist from the destruction and the removal of refugees from their homes and to return them to their old camps (United Nations, 1972:14), but Israel rejected the request. In total, the 1971 security roads plan led to the evacuation of some 12 per cent of the total camp population.

The demolition of houses is a punitive measure actively applied inside the Gaza Strip. According to this measure, the homes of security offenders are either destroyed or sealed, leaving the families of those individuals with nowhere to live and with no right of compensation (Roy, 1986:126). Up to November 1985, the shelters of 248 families were destroyed punitively in Gaza's refugee camps alone (see table 17.3) The Israelis consider this measure, which violates the Fourth Geneva Convention of 1949 for protecting civilians in time of war, to be a necessary step for security purposes and to deter others from being involved in military resistance. Moreover, the shelters of 47 families were destroyed under Israeli claims that the constructions were outside the camp's boundaries, on state-owned land. Similarly, town planning is reported to have been responsible for destroying 1,060 rooms which sheltered 497 families and 2,609 persons. In the re-establishment of the border-line between Egypt and the occupied Gaza Strip in 1982, the shelters of 299 families from Rafah camp were swept away under the pretext of creating a security zone. Additionally, the 5,000 inhabitants in Canada camp, which lies on the Egyptian side of the border, are still waiting to be resettled inside the Gaza Strip because they are not Egyptian citizens.

Table 17.3   Demolition of rooms, and affected families and individuals, in the eight refugee camps of the Gaza Strip, as at 30 November 1985

Cause of demolition	Total no. of rooms	Total no. of affected families	Total no. of affected persons
Demolished by the 1967 war	1,020	485	3,435
Demolished in 1971 under the security roads plan	10,794	3,941	24,067
Punitive cases	642	248	1,659
Contravention	87	47	291
Town planning	1,060	497	2,609
Border line	893	299	1,905
Voluntary	6,547	3,802	23,157
Total	21,043	9,319	57,123

Source: UNRWA Accommodation Office of Gaza (1985).

REFUGEE RESETTLEMENT SCHEMES

Alongside the policy of thinning the camps, resettlement schemes began in 1974. So far, there are eight dwelling projects in the Strip twinning camps and projects (see figure 17.1). Because refugee camps are UNRWA's property, it has stressed to the Israeli authorities its policy that any movement of refugees should be voluntary (UNRWA, 1984:3); unfortunately a significant number were resettled by fear and pressure.

By late November 1985, 6,547 rooms accommodating 23,157 persons had been voluntarily demolished by refugees as a quid pro quo for government accommodation (see table 17.3). At the same time, registrations by UNRWA Accommodation Office of Gaza (UNRWA, 1985) show that the cumulative number of resettled refugees had amounted to 37,023, and therefore 13,866 or 37.5 per cent of the total were compulsorily rehoused. A similar result was derived from a second survey conducted by the author in Al-Amal project in Khan Yunis, indicating that 30.7 per cent of the sample were resettled forcibly (Dahlan, 1987:305).

In the early stage of the resettlement scheme, two-room houses built on 250 sq m plots were offered on 99-year leases, but in 1978 the policy changed, and refugees were offered 125 sq m plots on which they could build their own homes (Locke and Stewart, 1985:60).

Frequently, the Israeli authorities publicize that the aims of the resettlement scheme are purely humanitarian, aiming to improve the quality of life of the refugees, but it is seen by those who are the target of the plan as overtly political. By destroying the camps the evidence and status of Palestinian refugees will disappear, and this will enable the Israeli government to claim that the refugees are resettled in permanent homes. Israeli Defence Minister Moshe Dayan said in 1973: 'as long as the refugees remain in their camps . . . their children will say they come from Jaffa or Haifa; if they move out of the camps, the hope is they will feel an attachment to their new land' (National Lawyers Guild, 1978:27). Indeed, in a survey conducted by the author in Khan Yunis refugee camp in 1985, 79.2 per cent of the sample emphasized the political goals of the resettlement schemes, and added that their refugee identity would be in danger if they moved to the dwelling projects (Dahlan, 1987:335).

For the refugees, their repatriation is clearly the ideal solution. In the Khan Yunis camp sample, 95 per cent of the refugees surveyed emphasized the demand for a return to their homes in Palestine. Similar results were achieved earlier from a sample survey conducted for the Shiloah Centre of Tel Aviv University during 1967–9 in Jalazun camp near Ramallah in the occupied West Bank. Despite the refugees' fear and suspicion, 88.7 per cent of the sample demanded repatriation as the best solution to their problem (Shamir, 1974:61).

Although the Israeli authorities had evacuated 57,123 refugees from their camps over the years up to late 1985, the refugee population grew to 427,892 by 30 June 1985, of whom 236,486 (55.3 per cent) were living in camps (UNRWA, 1985). In conclusion, the proportion of those refugees living in camps has fallen compared with that for 1966.

The latest programme of resettlement was unveiled by ex-Minister Mordachai Ben Porat in 1983: a plan costing $1.5 billion to resettle all the refugees in camps within five years (Viorst, 1984:50). This plan has been frozen, but not abandoned, because of Israel's chronic economic problem.

ISRAELI SETTLEMENT

Until 1978 the Gaza Strip had only low priority in the Israeli settlement drive. Only five outposts were placed within the Strip, which were all paramilitary 'nahalim' (forts), lacking economic roots and stable populations (Lesch, 1985:49). Later, when the Israeli settlements in Northern Sinai were removed according to the Camp David Accords of September 1978, eliminating the buffer zone surrounding the Strip, a new settlement strategy was adopted by the Israeli government to plant more settlements inside the Strip instead. Consequently, 16 new settlements were established, of which two sites are under construction, giving a total of 21 (see figure 17.1).

The Israeli settlements were designed to break the territorial continuity of Palestinian settlements and to create a new buffer zone with the Egyptian Sinai in the south. Three blocks of Jewish settlements can be identified, one in the north, small clusters in the centre, and a large block in the south and west. According to Roy (1986:139), these settlements occupy a known figure of 22,250 dunums (22.25 sq km) of land and are populated by 2,150 settlers.

Moreover, the Israelis are trying to achieve a demographic transformation in the Strip for their benefit. The World Zionist Organization estimated that the Gaza Strip's Jewish population will reach 10,000 in 1990, and 20,000 in the year 2000. Projections show that the Palestinian population, in contrast, will be 625,290 in 1990 and about 878,500 in the year 2000 (Dahlan, 1987:127). Hence, the Jewish settlers will never have a demographic majority in the Strip. To deal with this discrepancy, some Israeli officials believe that the Palestinian population must somehow be reduced, and it has been alleged that the former Defence Minister Ariel Sharon hopes to evict all Palestinians (about 1.3 million) from the West Bank and Gaza and drive them into Jordan (Chomsky, 1983:49).

SUMMARY

The processes set in motion by the disastrous wars of 1948 and 1967 have substantially affected the subsequent geography of population and settlement in the Gaza Strip. In 1948, the Strip experienced heavy population gains as a consequence of the influx of Palestine refugees into the area; while after the 1967 war, massive population losses were reported, distorting temporarily the age–sex structure, though seventeen years later the prevailing high natural increase had smoothed out much of the distortion. Similarly, Gaza's geography of settlement has been transformed by refugee camps, refugee resettlement projects and Israeli settlements, all of which have been added since 1948.

To deal with the symbolic meaning of the refugee camps, the Israeli authorities, since the early stage of their occupation, have applied a clear policy of systematic destruction of refugees' shelters and initiation of resettlement schemes in order to erase the refugee camps from the Strip, as they represent a reminder of the Palestine tragedy. The Israelis admit to a hope that better living conditions can divert the Palestinian refugees from their nationalist goal of an independent Palestinian state.

Moreover, the Israeli settlements have been designed to surround the existing Palestinian settlements, and to ghettoize not only the inhabitants of refugee camps but also the population of the Gaza Strip as a whole. In addition, it would both isolate the Palestinian towns from each other and make it more difficult to build a Palestinian state in the future.

REFERENCES

Abu El-Hajaj, Y. (1966) *Buhuth fil-Alam Al-Arabi. Qita Ghazza: Dhurufu Al-Jughrafiyya wal-Iqtisadiyya (Research in the Arab World. Gaza Strip: its Geographical and Economic Conditions)*, Cairo (in Arabic).

Barron, J. B. (1922) *Report and General Abstracts of the Census of Palestine, 1922*, Greek Convent Press, Jerusalem.

Central Bureau of Statistics (1968) *Demographic Characteristics of the Population in the Administered Areas, data from Sample Enumeration.* Publication 3 of the Census of Population 1967, Jerusalem.

Central Bureau of Statistics (1969) *Statistical Abstract of Israel 20*, Jerusalem.

Central Bureau of Statistics (1983) *Statistical Abstract of Israel 34*, Jerusalem.

Central Bureau of Statistics (1985) *Statistical Abstract of Israel 36*, Jerusalem.

Chomsky, N. (1983) *The Fateful Triangle: The United States, Israel and the Palestinians*, Pluto, London Sydney.

Dahlan, A. S. (1987) *Population Characteristics and Settlement Changes in the Gaza Strip*, PhD thesis, Dept of Geography, University of Durham.

Dodd, P. and Barakat, H. (1968) *River Without Bridges: A Study of the Exodus of the 1967 Palestinian Arab Refugees*, Institute for Palestine Studies, Beirut.

Hadawi, S. (ed.) (1970) *Village Statistics 1945: A Classification of Land and Area Ownership in Palestine*, Palestine Research Centre, PLO, Beirut.

Harris, W. W. (1978) *Refugees and Settlers: Geographical Implication of the Arab–Israeli Conflict, 1967–1978*, Vol.2, PhD thesis, Dept of Geography, University of Durham.

Harris, W. W. (1980) *Taking Root: Israeli Settlement in the West Bank, The Golan and Gaza–Sinai, 1967–1980*, Research Studies Press, Chichester.

Issa, N. (1979) *Situation Démographique du Peuple Palestinien*, Commission Economique Pur L'Asie Occidentale, Beirut.

Kanovsky, E. (1970) *The Economic Impact of the Six-Day War. Israel, the Occupied Territories, Egypt, Jordan*, Praeger, New York.

Khlousi, M. A. (1967) *Al-Tanmiyya Al-Iqtisadiyyo fi Qita Ghazza 1948–1966 (Economic Development in the Gaza Strip 1948–1966)* Al-Matbaa Al-Tijariyya Al-Mataheda, Cairo (in Arabic).

Lesch, A. M. (1985) Gaza – Forgotten Corners of Palestine, *Journal of Palestine Studies*, 15, 1, Issue 57. Institute for Palestine Studies and Kuwait University, Washington DC.

Locke, R. and Stewart, A. (1985) *Bantustan Gaza*, Zed, London.

National Lawyers Guild (1978) *Treatment of Palestinians in Israeli-Occupied West Bank and Gaza*, Report of the National Lawyers Guild 1977 Middle East Delegation, New York.

Palestine Liberation Organization (1983) *Majzaret Qita Ghazza (The Gaza Strip Massacre)*, Department of Information, Dar al-Jahedh lil-Tiba'a, Damascus. Reprinted from the official copy published in 1957 by the Arab League (in Arabic).

Roy, S. (1986) *The Gaza Strip: A Demographic, Economic, Social and Legal Survey*, West Bank Data Base Project, Jerusalem.

Shamir, S. (1974) *Communications and Political Attitudes in West Bank Refugee Camps*, Shiloah Centre for Middle Eastern and African Studies, Tel Aviv University, Israel.

United Nations (1972) *Report of the Commisioner-General of the United Nations Relief and Works Agency for Palestine Refugees in the Near East: 1 July 1971–30 June 1972*, General Assembly Official Records: Twenty-Seventh Session, Supplement 13 (A/8713), New York.

UNRWA (1966) *Registration Statistical Bulletin for the Second Quarter 1966*, 2/66, Relief Services Division, UNRWA-Liaison Office, Geneva.

UNRWA (1984) *Palestine Refugees Today*, UNRWA Newsletter 108, UNRWA, Vienna.

UNRWA (1985) *Registration Statistical Bulletin for the Second Quarter 1985*, 2/85, Relief Services Division, UNRWA, Vienna.

UNRWA Accommodation Office of Gaza (1985) *Unpublished Documents and Statistical Registration from UNRWA, including Eligibility, Registration, Distribution and Accommodation Division*, UNRWA, Gaza, personal contact.

Viorst, M. (1984) *UNRWA and Peace in the Middle East*, Special Study 4, The Middle East Institute, Washington DC.

18

The Disaster of Apartheid Forced Removals

C. M. Rogerson

THE DISASTER

Brutal dispossession of land and forcible removal are pervasive themes which have fashioned the apartheid landscape. Seemingly, the South African state has an extraordinary and almost limitless capacity to uproot homes and families on a massive scale, to destroy established communities and to relocate, or more correctly, to dump people in remote and barren slums. Overall, it has been estimated that the apartheid state's vicious programme of mass population removals has touched, if not devastated, the lives of up to 7 million people since its inception in 1984 (Surplus People Project, 1983; Platzky and Walker, 1983, 1985). However, the scale of suffering and alienation, 'the labyrinth of broken communities, broken families and broken lives', remains beyond numerical calculation. This massive exercise in social engineering and the manipulation of space in South Africa must be appreciated as one of the essential cornerstones of apartheid ideology (Cohen, 1986). The people who are removed are almost entirely Black and are being relocated from what is deemed ostensibly as 'White' South African space into small, impoverished and fragmented areas of 'Black' space, the ten rural Bantustans and segregated townships or 'locations' in urban areas (Baldwin, 1975; Surplus People Project, 1983; Freund, 1984; Platzky and Walker, 1985; Christopher, 1986; Cohen, 1986).

Over the past decade, South Africa's relocation programme has come under the harsh academic spotlight and justifiably has become a target of international opprobrium. Researchers have exposed the programme of forced population removals as cruel, inhuman and shocking, exploding the state's carefully nurtured propaganda myth of resettlement being linked to economic development (Murray, 1981; Platzky, 1984; Platzky and Walker, 1985; Rogerson and Letsoalo, 1985). Moreover, the appalling conditions endured by resettled communities at several 'hidden' locations in the South African periphery have been chillingly described and documented (Nash, 1980; Tutu, 1980; Walker, 1980; Rogerson and Letsoalo, 1981; Surplus People Project, 1983; Platzky and Walker, 1985; Henderson, 1986). Through a mass of case studies the Surplus People Project (1983) recounts, with frightening consistency, a story of lack of consultation, lack of understanding, the arrival of unknown officials in the feared GG vehicles, who like angels of death mark and count houses, fields, stock, even graves; long waits, uncertainties and rumours, lack of recourse to advice and legal assistance; then dogs, bulldozers and government lorries.

It is crucial to appreciate that, as Platzky argues, 'the desperate conditions to be found in South Africa's relocation areas are not a result of some tragic natural disaster, but of carefully considered legislation intended to divide and control the people in an attempt to maintain economic and political power in the hands of the white minority' (Platzky, 1986:396). An increasing volume of material attests to the pain, anger and suffering which are the essential human consequences of forced removal through the shattering of formerly self-sufficient rural communities and their transformation to complete economic dependence upon migration and wage labour. Finally, recent studies have unmasked the trauma of removal as revealed graphically by the songs of resettled communities who invariably sing of a stark contrast of their lives before and after resettlement (Harries, 1987); whereas the former is a 'golden age', the latter is a time of 'death and suffering' (Harries, 1987:129).

In view of the cost of human devastation wrought by apartheid forced removals, it is highly apposite, with Nash (1980), to describe and categorize the whole programme as a 'disaster'. The task in the balance of this paper is to highlight certain facets of the continuing disaster of apartheid removals. More specifically, two themes will be addressed. First, the persistence of forced removals in the 1980s

Figure 18.1   The political division of South African space

will be interrogated through a debunking of two of the South African state's deceitful myths regarding removals, viz., the myths of 'voluntarism' and of 'suspension'. It is argued that during the 1980s the apartheid regime has learned something from the embarassments of foreign television coverage, shifting its methods of removal from the brute force of the shock troops in their GG trucks to the deployment of more subtle, yet equally insidious, tactics. Against this backdrop, in the second section the focus moves away from the plight of the victims of removal to examine what might be stylized as the 'vultures' of disaster. In particular, attention is drawn to the growing trend for manufacturing capital to take advantage of the reservoirs of cheap and 'super-exploitable' labour power which have been precipitated by the march of forced removals across the South African landscape (see figure 18:1).

THE PERSISTENCE OF FORCED REMOVALS IN SOUTH AFRICA

In the face of sharp international criticism and protest against forced removals, the apartheid state has sought to shroud the continuing disaster through a fog of a new bureaucratic language. Words such as 'development', 'consultation' or 'co-operation' are co-opted and used by officials involved in the removal process, changing their meaning (Platzky, 1986). Specifically, in the current news-speak of Botha reformism, the only kind of population removals occurring in South Africa are those of a supposedly 'voluntary' nature (Claassens, 1984). Moreover, as of 1 February 1985, government spokesmen announced the complete 'suspension' of forced removals (Platzky and Walker, 1985).

The era of 'voluntary' as opposed to forced removals was ushered in as an integral facet of the state's reform strategy which aims to refurbish South Africa's tarnished international image (Claassens, 1984). Nevertheless, it remains that the notion of 'voluntary' removals is a deceptive myth concealing the fact that 'the South African government has not renounced its policy of forced removals but is merely pursuing this policy in a more sophisticated way' (Morris, 1986:46).

Currently, the key influences upon the apartheid state's dealings with communities under threat of removal are two-fold: the extent to which communities are organized to resist removal and the degree to which fractures exist within communities allowing the state room for manipulative manoeuvring (Platzky, 1986, 1987). Regarding the so-called process of 'persuading' communities to move in a 'voluntary' manner, there emerges a fairly distinct pattern characterized by the growing escalation in the use of force (Claassens, 1984). The initial stages of negotiation or consultation revolve around a divide-and-rule stratagem towards the threatened community. More specifically, the state will endeavour to establish a machinery of consultation, albeit concentrating only upon friendly partners. In those cases where local leaders refuse to co-operate in removal, the state either bides its time until weaknesses appear in the community or occasionally may appoint an alternative 'leader' who will be offered a lucrative package of perks to secure co-operation in 'voluntary' removal. Generally speaking, this tactic of dividing communities, by setting up, bribing and manipulating local leaders is highly effective, for once a 'leader' has agreed to move, the resisters, even if they constitute the vast majority of the community, are placed in a highly insecure and vulnerable position (Claassens, 1984).

Further reinforcement of the act of 'voluntary' removal is provided by the state's deployment of several other tactics (Claassens, 1984; Morris, 1986; Morris and Brown, 1986). Most importantly, in those instances where community resistance is mobilized towards removal, the state simply prohibits as 'illegal' all meetings designed to discuss and plan an effective response to the removal threat (Platzky and Walker, 1985). Equally compelling is a strategy of creating slums through a failure to maintain or extend facilities such as roads, schools or health centres. This policy of 'deliberate neglect' conveniently allows the state subsequently to proclaim that settlement conditions are 'unhygienic' and that communities would benefit by voluntarily removing themselves to alternative sites (Morris, 1986; Morris and Brown, 1986; Cole, 1987; Platzky, 1987). Almost inevitably the progressive degeneration of settlement conditions influences a steady trickle of families to 'choose' to relocate. Commonly, however, this choice is speeded by the state cutting off essential services. Examples would include the closure of schools or clinics, the non-payment of pensions except at the area of resettlement, the cessation of transport services and the non-renewal of trading licences.

Beyond the purging of essential community services, further steps in the process of persuasion into voluntary removal have included the establishment of an encampment outside the threatened community with a removal squad of parked lorries, buses and bulldozers. Finally, if brute force is not applied, the most effective strategy is simply one of doing nothing, for there are limits to how long communities can survive without schools or pensions in a climate of uncertainty over their future. Accordingly, it is apparent that to speak of 'voluntary removals' of communities in South Africa is a contradiction in terms (Claassens, 1984). Quite clearly, as new relocation sites continue to be prepared it is evident that there has been no fundamental shift in South African policy, no abandonment of the policy of forced removals (Platzky and Walker, 1985; Morris, 1986; Platzky, 1986, 1987).

Under the several states of emergency declared in South Africa since 1985, the removal programme has surfaced once again high on the apartheid state's agenda (Platzky, 1987). Increasing application is being made of emergency regulations to expedite removals, crush resistance and render communities leaderless and in disarray. Of crucial significance was that the official call for 'suspension' of removals applied to only two of eight major categories of removals (Platzky, 1986). Among the unreprieved communities were the families of redundant, disabled and aged farm workers, communities affected by Bantustan consolidation proposals and urban squatters, the target of the state's new programme of 'orderly urbanization' which replaced the notorious system of pass laws and influx control (Hindson, 1985, 1987; Cobbett, 1986a; Mabin, 1987; Platzky, 1987). Most dramatically, during 1986 there occurred one of the most brutal forced removals of squatter communities in terms of the destruction of a series of satellite communities around Crossroads, Cape Town (Cole, 1987). The razing of the homes of between 60,000 and 70,000 people at Crossroads was undertaken by groups of vigilantes (*witdoeke*) covertly supported by South African police and defence forces (Cole, 1987; Platzky, 1987).

THE 'VULTURES' OF DISASTER

The 'place of refuge', Botshabelo – formerly Onverwacht – has only been in existence since 1979. Yet Botshabelo's population has burgeoned to a present (1987) total of some 500,000, making it the second largest township in South Africa after Soweto (Cobbett, 1986b). This dry, desolate area of the Orange Free State (see figure 18.1) has been a focal point for the resettlement of several forcibly removed communities and a stream of former farm workers, labour tenants and their families (Murray, 1981, 1983, 1984, 1987). The construction of up to 60 new toilets per day, with an increase to 100 per day, signifies the continuing march of removals and the significance of Botshabelo as a place of resettlement (Walt, 1986). The future of Botshabelo is currently the subject of much controversy and conflict with bruited proposals for the settlement's 'incorporation' into QwaQwa, the smallest and already most grotesquely overcrowded Bantustan, situated some 300 km distant.

The rural 'slum' of Botshabelo is a place of deprivation and abject despair (Murray, 1987). At this desolate location 'there are no tarred roads, fewer than 10 telephones, electricity for one-half per cent of residents, one tap for every 200 people and no water-borne sewage' (Walt, 1986). The resettled populations of Botshabelo exist in an environment devoid of trees, plants and grass, with scarce public transportation and no recreational facilities (Walt, 1986). Unemployment levels are known to be at least 40 per cent, with some observers suggesting that the true figure may be as high as 70 per cent of the work force (Goodspeed, 1987). The majority of Botshabelo's unfortunate residents perforce must eke out a precarious existence either dependent upon monies from long-distance commuting or by searching out a survival niche in the informal sector (Cobbett, 1986a, 1986b; Goodspeed, 1987; Murray, 1987).

In order to attract manufacturing capital to relocate to this economically eviscerated part of South African space, the state offers large packages of tax incentives and labour concessions. Industrialists are being lured to Botshabelo to take advantage of the large pools of labour trapped by removals and the stringencies of orderly urbanization (Murray, 1987). Recent surveys disclose findings of 50 existing factories, employing some 5,000 (mainly women) workers and capital originating largely through third world multinationals, most importantly from Taiwan and Israel (Rogerson, 1986; Cobbett, 1987). Nevertheless, conditions of industrial employment are described as 'appalling, with rampant poverty-in-employment, as wage-levels amount only to the equivalent of a hamburger-a-day, (Cobbett, 1987). The reality of work conditions is best captured by the observation made by one factory manager that 'about once every week to 10 days, one of the women on the production line faints or collapses from hunger while working' (Cobbett, 1987:103). Overall, Cobbett's survey reveals 'new levels in the exploitation of workers that leave the observer lost for words' (1987:95).

In the final analysis the saga of Botshabelo is that of the forced removal of thousands of people, uprooting their communities and smashing their essential social fabric. Beyond this experience, however, the state now seeks to invite industrial enterprises, both local and foreign, to take advantage of the misery it has created (Cobbett, 1987). For these 'vultures' of disaster, apartheid forced removals are simply good business.

REFERENCES

Baldwin, A. (1975) Mass Removals and Separate Development, *Journal of Southern African Studies*, 1:215–27.

Christopher, A. J. (1986) The Inheritance of Apartheid Planning in South Africa, *Land Use Policy*, 1:330–5.

Claassens, A. (1984) *The Myth of 'Voluntary Removals'*, Conference Paper 74, Second Carnegie Inquiry into Poverty and Development in Southern Africa, Cape Town.

Cobbett, W. (1986a) 'Orderly Urbanisation': Continuity and Change in Influx Control, *South African Labour Bulletin*, 11, 8:106–21.

Cobbett, W. (1986b) A Test Case for 'Planned Urbanisation', *Work in Progress*, 42:25–30.

Cobbett, W. (1987) Industrial Decentralisation and Exploitation: the Case of Bothshabelo, *South African Labour Bulletin*, 12, 3:95–109.

Cohen, R. (1986) *Endgame in South Africa?*, James Currey, London.

Cole, J. (1987) *Crossroads: The Politics of Reform and Repression 1976–1986*, Ravan, Johannesburg.

Freund, B. (1984) Forced Resettlement and the Political Economy of South Africa, *Review of African Political Economy*, 29:49–63.

Goodspeed, P. (1987) On South Africa's Garbage Heap, *Toronto Star*, 25 January.

Harries, P. (1987) 'A Forgotten Corner of the Transvaal': Reconstructing the History of a Relocated Community through Oral Testimony and Song, in Bozzoli, B. (ed.), *Class, Community and Conflict: South African Perspectives*, Ravan, Johannesburg:93–134.

Henderson, P. (1986) *Waaihoek*, Association for Rural Advancement, Pietermaritzburg.

Hindson, D. (1985) Orderly Urbanization and Influx Control, *Cahiers d'Etudes Africaines*, 99:401–32.

Hindson, D. (1987) Alternative Urbanisation Strategies in South Africa: a Critical Evaluation, *Third World Quarterly*, 9:583–600.

Mabin, A. (1987) The Land Clearances at Pilgrim's Rest, *Journal of Southern African Studies*, 13, 3:400–16.

Morris, A. (1986) Forced Removals Continue: old Brits Location under Threat, *South African Labour Bulletin*, 11, 8:46–52.

Morris, A. and Brown, M. (1986) New Strategies for Forced Removals, *Sash*, 29:24–7.

Murray, C. (1981) 'Ethnic Nationalism' and Structured Unemployment: Refugees in the Orange Free State, *Disasters*, 5, 2:132–41.

Murray, C. (1983) Struggle from the Margins: Rural Slums in the Orange Free State, in Cooper, F. (ed.), *Struggle for the City: Migrant Labor, Capital and the State in Urban Africa*, Sage, Beverly Hills, 275–315.

Murray, C. (1984) Land, Power and Class in the Thaba'Nchu District, Orange Free State, 1884–1983, *Review of African Political Economy*, 29:30–48.

Murray, C. (1987) Displaced Urbanization: South Africa's Rural Slums, *African Affairs*, 86:311–29.

Nash, M. (1980) *Black 'Uprooting' from White South Africa*, South African Council of Churches, Johannesburg.

Platzky, L. (1984) Relocation and Poverty, paper presented at the Second Carnegie Inquiry into Poverty and Development in Southern Africa, University of Cape Town, 13–19 April.

Platzky, L. (1986) Reprieves and Repression: Relocation in South Africa, in SARS (South African Research Service) (eds), *South African Review*, 3, Ravan, Johannesburg:381–97.

Platzky, L. (1987) Restructuring and Apartheid: Relocation during the State of Emergency, in SARS (South African Research Service) (eds), *South African Review*, 4, Ravan, Johannesburg:451–68.

Platzky, L. and Walker, C. (1983) Review of Relocation, in SARS (South African Research Service) (eds), *South African Review*, 1, Ravan, Johannesburg: 83–96.

Platzky, L. and Walker, C. (1985) *The Surplus People: Forced Removals in South Africa*, Ravan, Johannesburg.

Rogerson, C. M. (1986) Third World Multinationals and South Africa's Decentralization Programme, *South African Geographical Journal*, 68:132–43.

Rogerson, C. M. and Letsoalo, E. M. (1981) Rural Underdevelopment, Poverty and Apartheid: the Closer-Settlements of Lebowa, South Africa, *Tijdschrift voor Economische en Sociale Geografie*, 72:347–61.

Rogerson, C. M. and Letsoalo, E. M. (1985) Resettlement and Underdevelopment in the Black 'Homelands' of South Africa, in Clake, J. I., Khogali, M. and Kosinski L. A. (eds) *Population and Development Projects in Africa*, Cambridge University Press, Cambridge:176–93.

Surplus People Project (1983) *Forced Removals in South Africa*, 5 vols, University of Natal, Durban.

Tutu, D. (1980) Tearing People Apart, *South African Outlook*, 110, 1312:152–5, 158.

Walker, C. (1980) Weenen: Still a Place of Weeping, *South African Outlook*, 110, 1312:156–8.

Walt, E. (1986) City of Half-a-million People and ten Phones, *Weekly Mail* (Johannesburg), 12–18 September.

19

A Simulation Study of Population and Social Disturbance in Japan

Koichiro Takahashi

INTRODUCTION

The most severe natural disasters affecting population in Japan have been famines due to bad harvests. During the Edo era (roughly AD 1650–1850) the Japanese population remained almost unchanged at about 30 million, and even decreased somewhat 20 years after a decade of frequent bad harvests (Takahashi and Nemoto, 1977). This was the so-called 'little ice age', when unseasonably cool summers occurred often, bringing with them poor harvests and famine.

Japanese history is a series of 80-year cycles in social disturbance apparently triggered by changes in food production. To understand these phenomena and their influence on the Japanese population, per capita food consumption from the ninth century to the present has been calculated using a logistic equation that expresses the increase of population, introducing an estimated time series of yearly food production. Decreased per capita food production corresponds well with the occurrence of social upheaval.

FUNDAMENTAL ASSUMPTIONS FOR INCREASES IN POPULATION AND CHANGES IN FOOD STOCKS

Before 1860, Japan was virtually isolated from the rest of the world and the population was maintained by food produced within Japanese territory. In such a case, changes in population and food supplies can be expressed as follows:

$$\Delta N = \beta \, \frac{(K - N)}{K} \, N \tag{1}$$

where N is the population, ΔN the change in population, K the saturation population dependent on food supplies, β a constant expressing the rate of population increase when food supplies are sufficient. This is the logistic equation.

Saturation population K is given by

$$K = \frac{RW}{S} \tag{2}$$

where W is the food supply at the start of the fiscal food year, R the rate of food consumption in a year, S the food consumption per capita in a year.

Food consumption per capita depends on food supplies and it is assumed that

$$S = 1 + \alpha W/N \tag{3}$$

where α is a constant, and minimum food consumption per capita $= 1$. In other words, this equation expresses the food quality level.

The yearly change in the food supply ΔW is given by

$$\Delta W = P - SN \tag{4}$$

where P is annual food production.

If the time series of annual food production is known, the annual population, food supply and food quality are calculated using the above equations, assuming the proper initial conditions. For instance, if the annual food production is constant, these values are given by the following equations for a stationary state:

$$N = K = \frac{R - \alpha}{R} \, P \tag{5}$$

$$W = P/R \qquad (6)$$

$$S = 1 + \alpha/(R - \alpha) \qquad (7)$$

ESTIMATION OF PREVIOUS JAPANESE FOOD PRODUCTION

To apply the above calculation to the Japanese case, previous Japanese food production must first be estimated. The major Japanese staple food is rice, and food production is assumed to be represented by rice production. Annual production after 1873 is recorded in national statistics, but values before this period must be estimated by other methods.

During the Edo era, the population census was taken 22 times, so the population for that period is known. The appoximate population before this can be estimated from fragmentary historical and archaeological data. The population in the thirteenth century is estimated to be roughly 10 million and in the seventh century 5 million (see table 19.1).

In the first approximation, the population is dependent on food, and the approximate value of food production can be estimated from the population. The yearly production of food, however, varies with the annual weather, so food production decreases in years having cool or excessively dry summers. Historical records of famines, droughts and cool summers are available from the eighth century. Therefore, values of the ratio of food production to the normal value are estimated from these data. Here the normal value of rice production is the expected rice production if the summer weather is normal. Table 19.2 gives the ten-year mean rate for estimated food production. Historical yearly production can be estimated by multiplying the rate of food production by the smoothed value of normal food production estimated from the population.

Of course, there are many uncertainties in such estimations, and estimated values are never exact. There is no other way, however, to determine or observe the general characteristics of time variation of food production.

Table 19.1   Japanese Population, 670–1980

Era	Year	Population millions
Yamato	670	4.80
Nara	750	7.00
Early Heian	800	8.40
Kamakura	1250	10.00
Azuchi–Momoyama	1590	16.00
Edo	1721	29.07
	1726	29.55
	1732	29.92
	1744	29.15
	1750	28.92
	1756	29.06
	1762	28.92
	1768	29.25
	1774	28.99
	1780	29.01
	1786	28.09
	1792	27.89
	1798	28.47
	1804	28.62
	1822	29.60
	1828	30.20
	1834	30.06
	1864	29.91
Meiji	1872	34.81
	1880	36.65
	1890	39.90
	1900	43.85
	1910	49.18
Taisho	1920	55.47
Showa	1930	64.45
	1940	71.93
	1950	83.20
	1960	93.42
	1970	103.72
	1980	117.51

CALCULATION OF VARIATION IN JAPANESE POPULATION AND FOOD PER CAPITA

Calculation of the previous Japanese population and food available per capita will now be made, using the equations stated earlier,

Table 19.2 Mean value per decade of rice production in Japan, in relation to the normal (%)

Lower limit	Decade beginning									
Year	00	10	20	30	40	50	60	70	80	90
800	100	95	100	100	100	95	95	85	85	100
900	96	96	100	100	102	100	96	96	96	100
1000	100	96	95	96	100	105	100	96	92	92
1100	92	95	90	92	92	100	100	92	90	90
1200	96	96	88	88	92	92	92	100	105	100
1300	98	88	92	86	92	90	85	88	92	96
1400	90	86	86	88	96	91	88	88	92	88
1500	86	90	92	98	95	95	98	98	99	99
1600	95	94	93	92	91	90	93	92	90	88
1700	92	98	99	97	92	92	97	99	89	100
1800	100	99	96	85	100	96	94	99	97	97
1900	102	100	98	101	96	101	104	100	99	

from time series food production as estimated in table 19.2. For numerical calculation, the following values are assumed for the constants in the equation:

β (rate of
  population increase)   = 4.1 per cent per annum
R (ratio of food
  consumption to supplies)   = 80 per cent
α (coefficient for
  expressing food quality)   = 0.3

Calculations are made by different equations in increments of decades, because estimated annual values are approximate. Figure 19.1 gives observed and calculated populations, food per capita, mean ten-year values of the ratio of food production to the normal, and mean ten-year degrees of social upheaval.

Although social upheaval is difficult to define, it may be assumed that the length of historical description in historical chronologies indicates the degree of social unrest. Of course, editorial differences in the compilation of historical chronologies exist, but overall trends should not vary greatly. Note also that the length of histori-

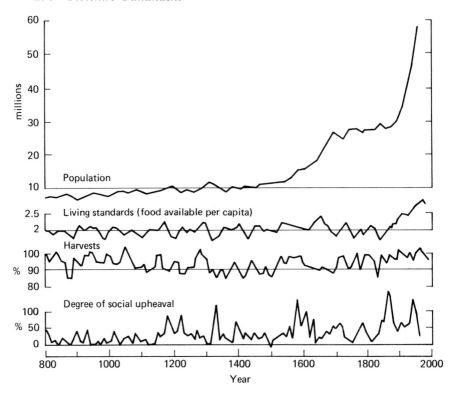

Figure 19.1 Estimated ten-year means of population, living standards, harvests and degree of social upheaval in Japan, 800–2000

cal description increases as time proceeds and discontinuities are observable in times of social revolution, due to the fact that data have been scattered and lost. The degree of Japanese social disturbances shown in figure 19.1 is based on data from three books on Japanese history by Inoue (1963), Inoue et al. (1977), and Yasuda (1979). The lengths of description over decades in these books are averaged by multiplying the proper weight based on the total length of the description and corrected for the increase of data over time and abrupt changes during social revolution.

INTERPRETATION OF RESULTS AND THE 80-YEAR CYCLIC
CHANGES IN SOCIAL DISTURBANCES

Calculations show that the Japanese population increased exponentially, accompanied by minor variations such as 80-year cycles, as shown in figure 19.1. This agrees roughly with the observed mode of the increase in Japanese population, which is to be expected, because the increase of population is calculated based on food production, which in turn is estimated from the observed population. However, minor variations in the population, such as the 80-year cycle, must be caused by other reasons, such as bad harvests due to abnormal weather, which itself is independent of observed population.

Figure 19.1 also shows that the Japanese population during the Edo era decreased somewhat with a 20-year time lag following a decade in which bad harvests predominated. This is found in changes in both calculated and observed population. Note that 80-year cyclic changes are observable in relation to social disturbances and calculated food per capita, and social upheaval when calculated food per capita decreased. This relationship is understandable in that insufficient food will itself give rise to social disturbances. The 80-year cycle is explained by the coupling effect of increased population and changes in food supplies.

Thus, the results of the simulation agree at least in first approximation with the observed increase in population and changes in social disturbance.

The curve in the figure shows that the recent level of food per capita is higher than in previous times, which is explained by the rapid increase in food quality, itself due to rapid progress in agricultural techniques and industry. The simulation suggests that, if the progress in science and technology slows, food per capita will decrease and social disturbance will rise again. The 80-year cycle of social disturbance suggests that the next social upheaval will peak in the early decades of the next century.

This simulation is based on rough assumptions and there is no definite reason that such conclusions will hold in the future; still, such an approach is useful at least in the qualitative study of changes in population and social phenomena, given the lack of any better approach at the present stage.

REFERENCES

Arakawa, H. (1955) *Kikohendo-ron (Theory of Climatic Change)*, Chijin Shokan.

Inoue, K. (1963) *Nihon no Rekishi (Japanese History)*, Iwanami Shoten.

Inoue, M. et al. (1977) *Nihonshi (History of Japan)*, Yamakawa Shuppan.

Kobe Marine Observatory (1941) *Nihon Kisho Shiryo (Chronology of Japanese Meteorological Phenomena)*, Central Meteorological Observatory.

Okajima, K. (1894) *Nihon Saiishi (Chronology of Japanese Natural Hazards)*, Nihon Kogyosha.

Sekiyama, N. (1948) *Kinsei Nihon Jinko no Rekishi (Historical Research on Modern Japanese Population)*, Ryugin-sha.

Takahashi, K. and Nemoto, J. (1977) Relationship Between Climatic Change, Rice Production and Population, in K. Takahashi and Yoshino M. M. (eds) *Climatic Change and Food Production*, University of Tokyo Press, Tokyo: 183–96.

Yasuda, M. (1979) *Nihon no Rekishi (Japanese History)*, Shakai Shiso-sha.

20
Conclusion

John I. Clarke

The theme of this volume is one of very great significance internationally, as all populations are affected to a greater or lesser extent by numerous types of disasters, yet many projections of population assume a continuation of present general trends. However, environments, societies, economies and polities all produce unexpected events which affect the distribution, composition, mobility and growth of populations, large and small, in diverse ways. Unfortunately, planning for disasters usually only occurs in wealthy countries – often not where they are most frequent or devastating.

Although disasters are commonplace, they lack definition. The term is used to describe a wide variety of phenomena, ranging from those determined by purely physical events, such as earthquakes and typhoons, to those which are of entirely human origin, like wars and industrial accidents. Between these two poles of causation there is a wide spectrum of disasters, as for example famines and floods, which are provoked by combinations of physical and human factors. In this volume we take a very broad connotation of the word 'disaster', and, unlike many authors, do not confine its meaning to so-called natural disasters or hazards (chapters 2–5). Hence we include studies of international and internal wars (chapters 15 and 16), the disastrous problem of Palestinian refugees in the Gaza Strip (chapter 17), apartheid forced removals in South Africa (chapter 18), and the effects of disasters upon social disturbance in Japan (chapter 19), as well as a number of other studies of disasters of mixed natural and human causation, such as the Sahel drought (chapters 7 and 10).

Generally, disasters of human causation tend to be more severe than those of entirely natural origin, precisely because they are ralated to population distribution. Indeed, the term 'disaster' is generally only meaningful in relation to populations. Remote natural hazards which occur in empty areas and do not impinge upon populations are rarely perceived as disasters. Obviously the density of population has a close relationship to the magnitude of a disaster. In absolute terms, therefore, disasters are more likely to be larger among the packed deltaic populations of Bengal, Bangladesh (chapter 6) and China than in the deserts of Mauritania, Libya and Saudi Arabia, and larger in the crowded streets of Mexico City (chapter 5), Managua (chapter 3) and Bhopal (chapter 14) than in Fruili (chapter 4) or Three Mile Island (chapter 13). Indeed, demographically it is questionable whether Three Mile Island justifies this terminology – by standards elsewhere it was more threat than reality. But when is a demographic event a disaster?

It is not only the density of population which is relevant, but its overall size. Large populations may be more affected than small populations in absolute terms, but less relatively. The loss of tens of millions in China or India, though appalling, at least does not have an eliminating effect. Many smaller populations, however, as for example the indigenous Caribs of the Caribbean islands, have been destroyed by a disaster even to the point of total extinction. The Tasmans of Australia are one recent example of the eliminating impact of conquering colonizers. Obviously, the relative significance of the impact of such disasters upon small island populations is much greater than that of larger demographic disasters among bigger populations. On the other hand, few disasters provoke total extinctions of population, at least from a genetic viewpoint, because the contact of peoples invariably leads to miscegenation and the emergence of 'mixed' populations.

Any consideration of disasters raises the question of scale, which varies not only demographically but also temporally and spatially. Temporally, disasters are interpreted as sudden events, but how sudden? Obviously, it depends upon the context. Sudden within a single lifetime is different from sudden within the course of human history. On the whole, disasters are unforeseen or unexpected, though there maybe a latent fear of their occurrence. For example, if one is considering diseases, the term 'disaster' would be more applicable to epidemics than to endemic diseases, which have been a persistent part of the lot of mankind. Nevertheless, there is a real difficulty in deciding upon the maximum duration of a disaster, and naturally much depends upon the demographic effects. Thus, at one end of the time-scale is the almost instantaneous earthquake, violent volcanic eruption or aircraft crash, and at the other some human-determined disasters like the Thirty Years War (1618–48) in central Europe, the Spanish Civil War (1936–9; chapter 16), the Taiping Revolution (1850–64) and China's 'Great Leap Forward' (1958–61; Chapter 10), which are much more prolonged and more demographically severe. Yet, often the more momentary disasters are perceived as being more disastrous, just because they are so sudden. Some of the longer-term events are only perceived as disasters with the wisdom of hindsight (chapter 12). On the other hand, such is the growing power of the media, the growing longevity of populations and the latent fear of the impact of disasters that there is now an acute awareness of the dangers of such disasters within many populations. Disasters are news. One other temporal aspect is that some populations are so habituated to disaster-prone environments, as for example in much of Bangladesh (chapter 6), the Sahel of west Africa (chapter 7) and the highlands of Ethiopia (chapter 8), that the frequency of disasters becomes almost part of the life-style to which they become accustomed, if not adapted. Disasters in marginal environments become 'the will of God'.

Spatially, the impact of disasters is also extremely varied. Some are isolated and localized; some are diffuse and dispersionary. Hence, some affect only the immediate population, while others spread through many populations. The location of an air crash or a volcanic eruption is generally small and discrete, whereas that of a drought, famine or disease may be continental or even greater. The impact of the intermittent Sahel droughts, the Black Death in the fourteenth century, the Great Plague in the seventeenth century and the influenza epidemic after the First World War are obvious examples. Such disasters transcend political boundaries, with extensive swathes of mortality, though spatial continuity may be broken by pockets of low incidence.

Other disasters are less spatially specific and more demographically selective: Jewish pogroms, Armenian massacres, the Spanish Inquisition and innumerable other ethnically, culturally, politically and religiously motivated onslaughts and genocides. Not all such attacks lead to high mortality; many result in exodus or expulsion, so common in the third world today. The plights of millions of refugees and displaced persons are tragedies of the political division of the earth's surface and its lack of coincidence with the complexity of human divisions. Many refugee movements are provoked by the complex combination of human and natural disasters common to poorer parts of the third world, which are now the main 'hot spots' of the world refugee movements.

It should also be remembered that the impacts of disasters are indirect as well as direct; in other words, disasters can break down communications networks and cause shortages and famines (chapter 9) which affect much larger areas and populations than those in the immediate vicinity of the event. Inevitably the extent of such indirect effects is greater wherever there is a tendency to social or political instability or where populations are living on the margins of existence. It should be no surprise, therefore, that the populations of the poorest countries (Clarke, 1985), the so-called least developed countries (LDCs) by UN definition, are most prone to disasters, natural, man-made and of mixed origin. Hence the tragedies of Afghanistan, Bangladesh, Chad, Ethiopia, Laos, Somalia and the Sudan.

It is one of the inherent difficulties of this type of study that disaster-prone populations in the past and present tend to be among the most problematic to analyze demographically. Administrative and statistical services often cannot cope in countries with limited infrastructures. The chaos of disasters and the ensuing instability deters demographic analysis, especially in countries where basic demographic data are rare, as for instance in Ethiopia or Afghanistan. Consequently, estimates of the casualties of wars, cyclones, famines and floods tend to be rounded and to vary considerably, until they gain the dubious or even spurious legitimacy of international authority, when they are published as estimates by the UN or the World Bank. Then their constant repetition, even when caution in their use is counselled, tends to give them an air of accuracy which may be far from deserved.

In fact, most disasters have escaped precise reporting of their demographic effects (Bouckaert and Lechat, 1987). Concern has naturally focused upon mortality, rather than fertility or mobility, and particular attention has been given to the magnitude of mortality crises (Richardson, 1960; Hollingsworth, 1979; Dupâquier, 1979) for which some simple indices have been devised relating numbers of deaths to the duration of the period of the disaster. In this way attempts have been made to quantify, within the limitations of the data, the relative mortality significance of major disasters like the Black Death (1348–50), the Mexican Crisis (1519–1608), the Lisbon Earthquake (1755) and the Irish Potato Famine (1845–52). Fortunately, progress in medicine, sanitation, hygiene, communications and other technological improvements have done much to alleviate the devastating effects of epidemics, famine and many other disasters over the short and long term. Inevitably, such progress is much more evident in the more developed countries than in the third world, although the international work of disaster relief and rehabilitation is growing rapidly. Unfortunately, there are always new disasters: the galloping spread of AIDS reflects to some extent the earlier lack of immunity of indigenous peoples to diseases introduced by European and other colonizers and traders, and there are growing fears about nuclear disasters and the 'greenhouse effect' of increasing pollution upon climates and sea levels during the twenty-first century.

example when environments become less habitable for physical and/or human reasons. So, in the late 1840s, people from the depressed western districts of Ireland suffering from the potato famine set sail for Britain and the Americas. In some cases, migrants have had no choice: among these are the Palestinians of the Gaza Strip (chapter 17) and Black South Africans forcibly removed in the cause of apartheid (chapter 18). For them the migration is a disaster in itself rather than safety-valve.

One often forgotten of disasters is that they may be extremely depressing upon population fertility, as seen in the case of the Chinese famine of 1958–61 (chapter 10). Wars have particularly drastic effects upon family life and age structures; the Spanish Civil War (chapter 16) exemplifies this, as do the so-called hollow classes (*classes creuses*) so characteristic of the French population pyramid, which were caused as much by wartime birth deficits as by mortality. Any age and sex-selective disaster is likely to have effects upon fertility not only immediately but on succeeding generations, because 'hollow classes' beget smaller reproductive age groups in the next generation, who also beget fewer children. And as disasters like wars are often succeeded by 'baby booms', it may be said that they contribute to fluctuating cohorts, which pose planning difficulties for governments faced with providing educational, health and other social facilities. China's cohort problem is enormous. On the other hand, wars in the twentieth century have become less age and sex-selective, involving increasing numbers of civilians, both directly and indirectly. A nuclear holocaust would have even less selectivity.

In short, although the immediate direct demographic effects of a disaster may appear to be definable, the long-term indirect effects may persist for centuries. Populations reflect their demographic heritage, not only their dynamics and composition, but also their distribution. The village patterns of Europe were greatly affected by the Black Death, as were those of Vietnam by the recent war, and as will be those of Ethiopia, Sudan and Bangladesh by the disasters of today.

Disasters cause all manner of ramifications in the population system, some light and localized, some catastrophic and continental. Any study of population trends should take into consideration their possible magnitude, frequency, duration, speed of onset, areal extent and demographic effects. They will always be with us. However, perhaps one should conclude by stressing that continuous and persistent phenomena tend to have had greater impact upon populations than disastrous events. Thus, phenomena like son preference, earlier marriage of women, lower longevity of men, higher male economic activity rates and differential mobility rates have had more consistent effects upon patterns of pupulation than more dramatic phenomena. Nevertheless, such phenomena should not be ignored in forecasts of future populations.

REFERENCES

Bouckaert, A. and Lechat, M. (1987) Consequences of Catastrophic Mortality Arising from Epidemics and Natural Disasters for Social Structures and Economic Systems, *Genus*, 43, 1–2: 19–43.

Clarke, J. I. (1985) Populations of the Poorest Countries, *Geography*, 70: 212–21.

Dupâquier, J. (1979) L' analyse statistique des crises de mortalité, in Charbonneau, H. and Larose, A., (eds), *Les Grandes Mortalités: Etude Méthodoligique des Crises Démographiques du Passè*, IUSSP, Liége: 83–112.

Hollingsworth, T. H. (1979) A Preliminary Suggestion for the Measurement of Mortality Crises, in Charbonneau, H. and Larose, A. (eds): 21–8.

Richardson, L. F. (1960) *Statistics of Deadly Quarrels*, Pittsburgh.

List of Contributors

AYNALEM ADUGNA is a lecturer in the Demographic Teaching and Training Centre in Addis Ababa University, Ethiopia. He has an M.A. from the University of Durham, and is researching for a Ph.D. at the London School of Hygiene and Tropical Medicine. His main work has been concerned with population redistribution in Ethiopia.

JÜRGEN BÄHR is Professor of Geography in the Geographical Institute of Christian-Albrechts-Universität of Kiel in the Federal Republic of Germany. He has published extensively in population geography, especially in relation to Latin America, and is currently a member of the IGU Commission on Population Geography.

JOHN I. CLARKE is Professor of Geography, Pro-Vice-Chancellor and Sub-Warden of the University of Durham, UK. From 1980 until 1988 he was Chairman of the IGU Commission on Population Geography. Most of his many publications are concerned with population geography, especially in relation to Africa and the Middle East.

PETER CURSON is Associate Professor of Human Geography in Macquarie University, New South Wales, Australia, and has been a member of the IGU Commission on Population Geography since 1984. Originating in Auckland, New Zealand, he has taught in Auckland, Tasmania and Macquarie, where his research has been mostly in historical epidemiology, especially disease diffusion.

AHMED SAID DAHLAN is Assistant Professor in the Islamic University of Gaza, Gaza Strip. A Palestinian, he undertook postgraduate work at the University of Durham, England, and wrote his Ph.D.

thesis on the population geography of Gaza.

K. MAUDOOD ELAHI is Professor of Geography and Dean of the Faculty of Social Sciences at Jahangirnagar University, Dhaka, Bangladesh. He was a full member of the IGU Commission on Population Geography during 1976–84 and was co-editor of its volume 'Population Redistribution and Development in South Asia'. He has been involved in sponsored research with various international organizations.

CHRISTOPHER R. DE FREITAS is a Senior Lecturer in Geography in the University of Auckland, New Zealand and Vice-President of the Meteorological Society of New Zealand. He has published widely, especially about human bioclimates, the impact of climates and climatic change upon populations, and catastrophe theory.

ROBERT GEIPEL is head of the Department of Geography, Technical University of Munich and Director of the Bavarian Institute for Research and Planning in Higher Education, Federal German Republic. Since 1976 he has studied the Friuli (Italy) earthquake and the reconstruction of the destroyed area, supervising 10 dissertations and MA-theses in sequence. His publications are in German, English and Italian, including *Disaster and Reconstruction*, George Allen & Unwin, London 1982.

HANS HECKLAU is Professor of Economic and Social Geography at Trier University in the Federal Republic of Germany, and Chairman of the Geographical Society of Trier. His fields of interest are population, medical, urban and agricultural geography of the Third World, and he has written several books about aspects of East Africa.

A. J. JOWETT is a lecturer in the Geography Department of Glasgow University, UK. His publications on China's population have appeared in China Quarterly, The Geographical Journal, Geography and GeoJournal. He has also contributed chapters to several books on China. In 1988 he spent five months undertaking demographic research in China.

S. L. KAYASTHA is Chairman, Advisory Committee for the National Atlas and Thematic Mapping Organization, Government of India, Calcutta, and Senior Fellow of Indian Council of Social Science

Research, New Delhi. He was formerly Professor and Head, Department of Geography, Banaras Hindu University, Varanasi, and has contributed over 175 research articles to national and international journals and books. His publications focus especially on environmental issues and population studies.

MARIA TERESA GUTIERREZ DE MACGREGOR is Director and Professor of the Institute of Geography of the National University of Mexico, Vice-President of the IGU, Honorary Corresponding Member of the Royal Geographical Society, and a Membre d'Honneur of the Société de Géographie. Her many publications are mainly concerned with population geography, especially in Mexico.

TAKESHI MIZUTANI is Head of the Disaster Analysis Laboratory in the National Research Centre for Disaster Prevention, Japan. He has recently published works on the impact of disasters upon urban populations in Japan.

PRITHVISH NAG is Deputy Director of the National Atlas and Thematic Mapping Organization, Government of India, Calcutta, and Chairman of the Commission on Population Cartography of the International Cartographic Association and a former member of the Commission on Population Geography of the IGU. His many publications all relate to population, mapping and the environment.

TAKAMASA NAKANO is a Professor Emeritus of Tokyo Metropolitan University, Japan, whose main research interest is in natural hazards, including disaster preparedness and loss mitigation.

STANISLAW OTOK is Professor and Head of the Department of Social Geography in the Faculty of Geography and Regional Studies of Warsaw University, Poland. His research interests are in social and political geography, and he has written extensively about the effects of war on the social situation in the world.

CHRIS PARK is Principal of Furness College and Lecturer in Geography at the University of Lancaster, England. A graduate of the New University of Ulster and the University of Exeter, he taught previously at St David's University College, Lampeter (University of Wales). He has published several books about environmental hazards and environmental management, including one about Chernobyl and another about acid rain.

MARIA CARMEN FAUS PUJOL is Associate Professor of Human Geography in the Department of Geography in the University of Zaragoza, Spain. She is a Catalan from Barcelona, who is a current member of the IGU Commission on Population Geography and has written extensively about the geography of Aragon and about Spanish rural areas.

CHRISTIAN M. ROGERSON is an Associate Professor and Reader in Human Geography at the University of the Witwatersrand, Johannesburg, South Africa. He is the author of over 90 publications in the fields of industrial geography, development and population studies of Southern Africa.

KOICHIRO TAKAHASHI is the former Director of the Japan Meteorological Agency and a Professor of Tsukuba University, as well as the present Chairman of the Japan Meteorological Agency's panel concerned with climatic change related problems. His main publications have been concerned with climatic change and its relationship to man.

A. TRILSBACH is temporary lecturer in the Department of Geography at the University of Durham. He has several years relevant research experience in the Sudan and has published widely. He is also Secretary of the Sudan Studies Society of the United Kingdom and editor of *Sudan Studies*.

Index